code
SWITCHING

how to talk so men will listen

Claire Damken Brown, Ph.D., and
Audrey Nelson, Ph.D.

ALPHA

A member of Penguin Group (USA) Inc.

ALPHA BOOKS

Published by the Penguin Group

Penguin Group (USA) Inc., 375 Hudson Street, New York, New York 10014, USA

Penguin Group (Canada), 90 Eglinton Avenue East, Suite 700, Toronto, Ontario M4P 2Y3, Canada (a division of Pearson Penguin Canada Inc.)

Penguin Books Ltd., 80 Strand, London WC2R 0RL, England

Penguin Ireland, 25 St. Stephen's Green, Dublin 2, Ireland (a division of Penguin Books Ltd.)

Penguin Group (Australia), 250 Camberwell Road, Camberwell, Victoria 3124, Australia (a division of Pearson Australia Group Pty. Ltd.)

Penguin Books India Pvt. Ltd., 11 Community Centre, Panchsheel Park, New Delhi—110 017, India

Penguin Group (NZ), 67 Apollo Drive, Rosedale, North Shore, Auckland 1311, New Zealand (a division of Pearson New Zealand Ltd.)

Penguin Books (South Africa) (Pty.) Ltd., 24 Sturdee Avenue, Rosebank, Johannesburg 2196, South Africa

Penguin Books Ltd., Registered Offices: 80 Strand, London WC2R 0RL, England

International Standard Book Number: 978-1-59257-926-6
Library of Congress Catalog Card Number: 2009923295

11   10   09   8   7   6   5   4   3   2   1

Interpretation of the printing code: The rightmost number of the first series of numbers is the year of the book's printing; the rightmost number of the second series of numbers is the number of the book's printing. For example, a printing code of 09-1 shows that the first printing occurred in 2009.

Printed in the United States of America

Note: This publication contains the opinions and ideas of its authors. It is intended to provide helpful and informative material on the subject matter covered. It is sold with the understanding that the authors and publisher are not engaged in rendering professional services in the book. If the reader requires personal assistance or advice, a competent professional should be consulted.

The authors and publisher specifically disclaim any responsibility for any liability, loss, or risk, personal or otherwise, which is incurred as a consequence, directly or indirectly, of the use and application of any of the contents of this book.

Trademarks: All terms mentioned in this book that are known to be or are suspected of being trademarks or service marks have been appropriately capitalized. Alpha Books and Penguin Group (USA) Inc. cannot attest to the accuracy of this information. Use of a term in this book should not be regarded as affecting the validity of any trademark or service mark.

Most Alpha books are available at special quantity discounts for bulk purchases for sales promotions, premiums, fund-raising, or educational use. Special books, or book excerpts, can also be created to fit specific needs.

n Street, New York, NY 10014.

To my husband, Larry; sis, Mary; and nieces and future business leaders:
Allison, Maggie, Samantha, Brittany, Stacey, Shanna, and Sadie (who is
one day old as of this writing)

—Claire

To Geoffrey Wade Simpson

—Audrey

Contents

Introduction

My female coworker keeps saying I never listen to her ... or something like that.

That's our twist on an old cliché. And sometimes it feels true—for both men and women in the workplace.

Did he hear me? Is he ignoring me? What do I need to do to get someone to notice me around here? Why doesn't he take me seriously?

Chances are, these questions or some variation thereof have run through your mind while you've been waiting to talk to a man at work.

We've heard it over and over, the same story across the nation. A woman throws an idea on the table, and no one reacts. She may as well have just cleared her throat. Ten minutes later, Bob offers the same idea and the room perks up; that's the best idea since the underwire bra.

To the woman's amazement (read: horror), the supervisor and coworkers began discussing the idea. So innovative! This new approach could save time and money. They commend Bob on his creativity, while she sits next to him in a haze, jaw dropped, thinking, "This is so surreal. I just said that."

Should she demand credit or let it go? What is she supposed to do now?

Well, for starters, read on. The authors of this book have 60 years of combined work experience with businesswomen who feel ignored, not part of the game, isolated, or unable to make an impact at work. Using their expertise in gender communication, office politics, and organizational rules of engagement, Audrey and Claire teach women how to prepare for these situations, take charge, and communicate effectively—how to go for it. Short of carrying around a bullhorn with you at work, their advice starts with understanding the gender differences and then using that knowledge to "code-switch."

Code Switching: How to Talk So Men Will Listen is a hands-on tool for everyday use at the office. It is a practical resource with how-to steps to help businesswomen conquer the communication nuances between men and women in the workplace. This book explores the gender impact on business talk. It teaches using true stories and case studies, while providing valuable code switching tips to help women gain and strengthen credibility, and make a greater impact on the job.

This is not a male-bashing book! (For that, see our male-bashing underground best-seller *Now Hear This! Get Your Own Damn Coffee!*) This is not about whether women are better than men or men are better than women. We're just different—genetically and socially.

We're also not saying that women have to act like men. That is a formula for failure because it's impossible, and it alienates everyone at the office. Plus, when you try that, you give up your femininity, and we're the first to admit that it's wonderful to be a woman. The workplace thrives with a balance between both the feminine and the masculine.

Bits and pieces of men's and women's communication styles benefit the workplace, make employees want to be there, and impact the bottom line. By gaining insight into men's and women's communication styles, we create an awareness of our communication choices. It's about consciously mixing it up using both the male and female communication styles to produce an overall androgynous, synergistic approach. This blend makes things happen. With knowledge of both styles of communication, you can intentionally switch between the two, based on your goal.

We've adopted the term *code switching*, used in the study of linguistics. It refers to having knowledge of two cultures or languages and readily swapping between them as you communicate.

code SWITCH *The ability to use your knowledge of two or more cultures or languages and switch between them, depending on the situation, to best communicate your message.*

To code-switch, you must have the flexibility and plasticity to move in and out of numerous everyday encounters. You don't use the same communication style in all encounters; you adjust to meet specific needs as they arise.

Knowing how men and women communicate and being able to switch between the two styles is crucial in the workplace—not to mention at home and beyond the office. Trying to understand men and women has become a lifetime challenge for most of us. We might be able to get away with a shrug and a *"Vive la différence!"* in some more casual personal relationships, but not at work, where coordination and synergy have a serious ripple effect.

The number of women entering the workforce has gradually increased over the past three or four decades. In entering the male business domain, women often were viewed as misfits and had to modify their ways to suit the masculine work culture. Today nearly as many women are working as men. According to the U.S. Department of Labor, 46 percent of the workforce are women. Of those working women (a whopping 68 million), 75 percent work full-time and 25 percent work part-time. The Department of Labor's statistics show that close to 60 percent of all U.S. women age 16 years and older have a job or are looking for one. For the first time, more women than men hold professional and managerial positions: 51 percent of the 48 million people in these positions are women—double the percentage of two decades ago. More women than men are graduating from college, and with higher GPAs. Medical and law schools are approximately 50/50 in enrollment. Every day on the job, we interact with people of the opposite sex. There's no getting around it.

We mean business! How do women unlock the door and get men to listen? Many businesses are concerned about inclusiveness. They conduct diversity training but ignore or don't emphasize educating their employees to be fluent in women's and men's communication styles. How many companies provide mentors for women employees that coach them on how to present ideas and make an impact on the men they work with (usually their bosses)?

Are men still the bosses? The October 2008 Catalyst Research Pyramid of women in U.S. companies indicates that women make up 2.4 percent of the Fortune 500 CEOs, and 6.7 percent of the top money makers and 15.4 percent of corporate officers in Fortune 500 companies. As much as things are changing, they're not changing fast enough when it comes to moving women up the corporate ladder. If a woman is talking at work, there's a high probability that a man is on the receiving end *and* making a career-impacting decision for her based on what she just said.

Our Promise

Code Switching: How to Talk So Men Will Listen focuses on day-to-day communication at work. Our goal is to make women more aware of their communication strategies. The primary focus is on how women can get through to men. We provide advice on how you can use your newly acquired skills to enhance your career. Look for code switching tips in each chapter. These are simple, doable suggestions that you can implement right away.

For additional reading, see the Resources appendix for a list of books and articles mentioned in our chapters.

Everything in the office—from problems to personal and companywide successes to satisfaction—boils down to communication. There's a direct link between our ability to communicate and our overall *success*, not just at work, but in life! Men and women come with a set of complex communication behaviors that create an undeniable challenge. And no operation manual exists. When careers and paychecks are on the line, effective communication between genders is critical, regardless of whether you work in the mailroom or the boardroom.

Listen up! Yes, we use the same English language—but in different ways. Men and women use different speech patterns. You already know this—just open your ears and eyes. Welcome to the world of guerilla gender talk. Put on your camouflage and pull out your ammunition, because you're going to need it! We'll be fighting our way through stereotypes and assumptions that limit women's impact in the workplace.

In this book, you'll learn how …

- The power of choosing your words can either pull the rug out from underneath your credibility or close the deal.
- Men and women manage conversation differently, and "chit-chat" 10 minutes before getting the meeting started has value.

- Men use "report" talk and women use "rapport" talk.

- Men use e-mail to emphasize who's in control, while women use it to connect and build relationships.

- Humor is used as a power play to build territory or exclude others (mostly women).

- What you don't say means the most.

- Unspoken messages rule in the critical first few seconds of an initial meeting.

- We judge a book by its cover, and that includes how you dress.

- The only way to get to the top is with a mentor.

- You can use tricks to effectively shut down sex talk and stop harassment in its tracks.

- Women are often seen but not heard.

- Being in the front of the room and on stage is an opportunity to get noticed.

If you've ever wondered what your coworkers at the water cooler are thinking about you, if you've ever worried that you lack credibility in important business interactions, and if you've ever felt concerned about whether others understand what you're *really* trying to convey at the staff meeting, *Code Switching: How to Talk So Men Will Listen* will set your mind at ease and pave the way to new and improved communication!

Acknowledgments

Twenty-five years ago, we met at a women's conference in Denver. We both chose different career paths—Claire in the corporate world, and Audrey in the entrepreneurial arena. We share common grounds of a Ph.D. focused on gender communication and a desire to improve the work world for women.

We are professionally grateful for the support and guidance of our agent, Linda Konner, and the confidence displayed by Tom Stevens at Alpha Books, who told us our proposal was one of the best! Thanks, Tom. A "thank you" goes to Lynn Northrup, Megan Douglass, Krista Hansing, and other Alpha staff who helped make this book happen.

We acknowledge all the women who have shared their stories from the corporate trenches. We recognize all the frustrated men who wish a woman had a barcode on her forehead to better understand her. *Code Switching: How to Talk So Men Will Listen* is a response to their need. We thank the men and women who selflessly opened doors and supported us along the way.

Aimee Heckel read every word of this book and provided a Gen X perspective. Without her input, it would be only a Baby Boomer view.

—Claire and Audrey

Thanks to the members of my gal pal group who offered encouragement and a slap on the back when needed. This family of friends includes Michelle Haines, Anne Herrald, Herta Hess Kahn, Cindy Knutson, Maureen Mckee, and Laura Webster. Some of their stories are included in this book.

As always, my greatest motivation to pursue my goals is Alexandra and Armand. My children are a constant reminder that, despite sex role conditioning, you can step outside the gender box to achieve excellence in both interpersonal and academic pursuits.

—Audrey

A special shout-out to my colleague Clorinda Lucero for her research and Gen X insights. A tip of the hat to my family—that batch of brothers, wives, sister, husbands, nieces, nephews, and in-laws—for encouragement, great stories that make me laugh and cry, and a steady push up the hill. An enthusiastic hug to Imogene for sharing the post–World War II view of a self-made woman entrepreneur. And to my husband and all-round awesome dude, Larry, a hardy high five for his willingness to share the male perspective, from hot rods to bad-ass bosses.

—Claire

1

From the Playground
to the Boardroom

Boys will be boys and girls will be girls, or so the saying goes. And maybe it's on to something. Parents can often see their sons in Dr. Seuss characters, Thing One and Thing Two, racing from room to room, creating havoc by tearing apart everything in sight. Then there's the idea that girls are "sugar and spice and everything nice," wearing T-shirts proclaiming "Princess" and "Angel."

So what does it mean when we say that boys will be boys? Can girls be as rambunctious and defiant as boys? What happens when they move into the boardroom as adults? We need a manual to navigate the gender differences—what they are, why they exist, and what that means when men and women try to (gasp!) communicate.

Lucky you. You are holding that manual. Buckle up. We're about to journey into the complex psychosocial, biological, hormonal, and genetic issues that underlie every child's behavior. To break it down, these are the stops on that road map:

1. How children begin orienting themselves to the world from the moment of birth

2. When and how boys' and girls' methods of communication begin to differentiate

3. How these different communication styles eventually impact what men and women do as adults

4. How environmental influences, brain functioning, genetics, and hormones contribute to these differences

The Power of Social Engineering

We can't escape it: from the cradle to the grave, we are bombarded with messages of what it means to be a girl or a boy. One of the first questions people ask when a baby is born is answered with "It's a boy" or "It's a girl."

Once a baby is defined by its sex, he or she immediately receives messages that translate into gender-related expectations. Social engineering began the instant the nurse wrapped you in a pink or blue blanket, and it relentlessly continues throughout our lives. We can't escape the messages from our parents, our peers, the media, educators—everyone.

You might even argue that "sex typing" begins even *before* the baby is born. The importance of separating boys from girls has led to guessing games. Throughout the ages, folklore has tried to predict the gender even before doctors could. If a pregnant woman is carrying high, has intense morning sickness, and grows large throughout her body, it must be a girl. If she's carrying low and her weight gain is primarily in her belly, then it must be a boy.

Another in utero experience is "prebirth talk." Yep, we begin communicating differently to babies before they're born. Dr. Kara Smith, a language education professor at the University of Windsor in Canada, examined how people spoke to babies before and after the sex-identifying ultrasound. She found that before the ultrasound, people use gender-neutral language, such as "Hi you, I can feel you moving around in there." Before the ultrasound, in the fifth month of pregnancy, some women say they think of the baby not as a certain sex, but as an androgynous being. One woman in Dr. Smith's study compared it to a "plant." No genitals, no gender—just growing and developing like a plant. Before learning the sex, people call the baby "it" or "little one"—a nameless, colorless being with no label.

Then comes the gender announcement. Knowing the sex after the ultrasound changes everything, sparking the process of forming the baby's personality. According to Dr. Smith's findings, mothers start talking to boys with a lower-pitched voice and to girls with higher tones. Boys receive pats on the stomach; girls get soothing and soft rubs. Mothers feel less of a need to be gentle if it's a boy. Even before birth, ingrained methods are used for categorizing and handling males and females. Parental socialization has already begun, and the baby isn't even born yet.

Dr. Smith was shocked by the findings. If even the most conscious and critical mothers don't escape this endemic, gender-socializing process and seem bound—through generations of indoctrination—to pass it on, what hope do we have as a society to escape the stereotypes? Is there any point in studying gender roles and trying to change them if our fetuses aren't getting the message?

The term "code switching" refers to having knowledge of both the male and female cultures or languages and readily swapping between them as you communicate.

code SWITCH *The ability to use your knowledge of two or more cultures or languages and switch between them, depending on the situation, in order to best communicate your message.*

Knowledge of how boys and girls are impacted by both environmental influences as well as their DNA is the starting point. Trying to understand men and women has become a lifetime challenge for most of us and begins with how it all gets started.

It's about consciously mixing it up in parenting children using both the male and female communication styles to produce an overall androgynous, synergistic approach—a blend that makes things happen and allows children to get outside the restricting gender box.

code SWITCH *Watch how you talk to the tummy.*

The Emergence of Manhood

Now we're at the hospital, and the baby begins to receive more gender-specific messages. Now it's the delivery room nurse's turn. Nurses use different pitches and tones with boys and girls. They are more apt to pick up a baby girl if she is crying than a boy. Feminist Gloria Steinem put it like this: "It is almost as though they are already trying to toughen the boys." Big boys don't cry, and apparently little boys shouldn't, either.

Now venture to the greeting card aisle to get a card for the new parents. Dr. Lynda Willer, a communications professor at Purdue University, examined 300 "Welcome, baby" cards from major greeting card companies. There she found definitive messages about what it means to have a baby boy or a baby girl. Amid the pink and blue, sugar and spice, and snakes and snails, the greeting card industry apparently perpetuates the social construction of gender.

Consider the impact these cards have on sex identities. The greeting card industry is worth more than $7 billion a year, and, more important, women purchase 90 percent of greeting cards. Cards have vast communication potential, particularly for women and gender issues. Yet sex differences are often taken for granted.

Audrey has her own gender lab at home. Alexandra is a 22-year-old college senior and Armand is a 19-year-old college freshman. Having them around is a constant reminder that sex-role socialization is alive and (too) well. When Armand was only 4, they were shopping together at the store. Audrey reached for dark purple (not lavender, mind you) socks to match his plaid jumpsuit. He jumped in, shaking his head.

"No, that's a girl's color. I won't wear those socks!" he said defiantly.

Here, Audrey had been hypervigilant not to promote gender stereotypes for clothes, toys, and colors, and the kid had learned it anyway. How far have things come since her son was a purple-protester? Just recently, Alexandra joined a co-ed crew team at school. They practiced on the Seattle waterways in the early mornings. At the first practice, the male coach decided to start off the season with this line: "We have girls on the team to make the boat look pretty."

No child leaves childhood without being told that some toy or activity is for boys or for girls. Even if parents are careful not to use such labels, other adults in a child's life probably aren't.

Try this for a code switch. Practice conscious sex role parenting. Parents should be conscious of their sex role expectations before the birth of their child. What color are you painting the nursery? Set up the baby shower to have gender-neutral colors for clothing. What kind of plans do you envision for your son or daughter? Remember, children will pick up on the script.

The Risky Business of Femininity

When Maureen Dowd, a columnist for *The New York Times*, was 21, her mother gave her the book *365 Ways to Cook a Hamburger*, by Doyne and Dorothy Nickerson. At 25, it was *How to Catch and Hold a Man*, by Yvonne Antelle. Dowd quotes some of the more revealing secrets, such as these: "Keep thinking of yourself as a soft mysterious cat …. Men are fascinated by bright shiny objects, by lots of curls, lots of hair on the head … by bows, ribbons, ruffles and bright colors …. Sarcasm is dangerous. Avoid it altogether."

To Dowd, these gifts felt like training manuals. Her mother's intention was to prepare her for the inevitable—marriage—and to help her succeed at it. That was almost 25 years ago. I know what you're thinking. That kind of message is outdated and doesn't exist today.

Not so fast.

Dr. Laura Schlessinger's 2005 book, *The Proper Care and Feeding of Husbands*, would have been a natural addition to Dowd's mother's selections. This book reads like a throw-back to the 1960s and the "Fascinating Womanhood" movement. During this campaign, women received instruction booklets and a suitcase (pink, of course) with all kinds of props to entice and keep their men happy. It included tactics such as lessons on how to make him think

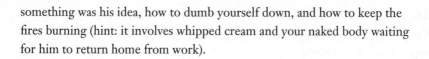

something was his idea, how to dumb yourself down, and how to keep the fires burning (hint: it involves whipped cream and your naked body waiting for him to return home from work).

Forty years later, Dr. Laura offers up similar prescriptions. She claims men have simple needs, like food and sex. Satisfy those simple needs, and you are on your way to a happy relationship. Or so she says.

How the Media Shapes Our Views

We are bombarded by daily messages from the media, parents, teachers, bosses, and coworkers on what it means to be a boy or girl. No one is immune to these messages.

You can't overlook the influence of mass media. The average American child watches six hours of television every day, not to mention video games and the Internet. By age 6, our kids have already watched an average of 5,000 hours of television. By age 18, the number soars to 19,000 hours.

How important is television and other media in shaping our views about men and women?

First, we have to consider the extent of the media in American life. The statistics are staggering. In 1950, only 9 percent of households had a television, according to the Television Bureau of Advertising. Today 98 percent of homes have TVs and two thirds have more than one television. More than 70 percent have cable, which suggests that people also watch a lot of movies at home.

Try this. Turn on your TV with a discriminating eye. Don't watch only the programming. Also notice what the commercials are saying about women and men. What gender themes are prevalent? Is it only our imagination that all we see are babes in bras and lingerie, women acting helpless and still cleaning the toilet bowl?

Diana Ivy and Phil Backlund, communication professors at Texas A&M in Corpus Christi and authors of *GenderSpeak*, summarize the following gender stereotypes in advertising:

1. Fewer women depictions than men

2. Women in sleepwear, underwear, and lingerie more often than in professional clothing

3. Young girls portrayed as passive and in need of help

4. Women appearing in more ads for personal hygiene products

5. An abundance of women serving men and boys

6. Women more often depicted in family- and home-oriented roles than in business roles

7. Women portrayed as decorative, nonfunctioning entities

8. Women depicted as being obsessed with physical attractiveness

9. Few women depicted actively engaged in sports

10. Fewer depictions of older women and minority women

Generally, older men are perceived as handsome and distinguished. Older women are seen as past their prime and not particularly attractive.

Advertising has apparently decided that the benefit of crudely impressing men trumps the disadvantages of dishonoring women. How many times do fathers across America sit down with their sons for the ritual of an afternoon watching football? Now they both get to share the stereotypical images of women! And don't forget, they are also sharing the ultimate image of masculinity played out in football.

Alas, media gender stereotyping is an equal opportunity field. Men also get their fair share. Children's TV shows typically show men as the aggressor and engaged in exciting adventures. And the rewards are predictable: luxury cars, beautiful women, mansions in the suburbs, and vacations in the Caribbean.

Take a look at prime-time television. It reveals men as independent, aggressive, and in charge. Donald Trump's "You're fired!"—the signature line from the TV show *The Apprentice*—comes to mind. Beyond cartoons, TV for all ages depicts men more as independent, powerful, capable males in high-status positions. Once again, the media reinforces stereotypical roles of men as in control, aggressive, unafraid, and, more important, in no way feminine.

SWITCH IT UP!

An ABC documentary on sex differences interviewed parents and questioned them about their toy selections. One exasperated woman said, "I watched my twin boys pull out a Barbie and begin sword-fighting with her! My daughter grabbed her and said, 'Oh, Barbie you are so beautiful, but you need more makeup!'" In a disappointed tone, the mother added, "And I don't even wear makeup!"

In 2004, California Gov. Schwarzenegger reminded us of that when he spoke to a crowd of political supporters at a mall in Ontario, California. During this political debate, he resorted to the tough rhetoric of his acting days and proclaimed that there's no room for "girlie-men": "The legislators cannot have the guts to come out there in front of you and say, 'I don't want to represent you. I want to represent those special interests; the unions, the trial lawyers' … I call them girlie-men. They should go back to the table and they should finish the budget. I want you to go to the polls. You are the terminators, yes!"

Consider television shows that are supposed to be gender neutral, like *Sesame Street*. Almost all the main characters are male: Ernie, Burt, Oscar, Big Bird, and Kermit. How about popular toys that are gender neutral, like puzzles, puppets, board games, and Uno? Audrey thinks if a retailer positions the toy in the "girl's aisle," the boys don't want it, and vice versa. Same goes if one of these toys is shown in a commercial or movie being used by children of the other sex. That's instant gender classification. The media continue to further gender stereotypes and gathers even more power from the numerous hours children spend being raised by the tube.

Just Give Jack a Doll and Jill a Truck

Examples abound of parents attempting to crush gender stereotypes by exposing their children to all toys, especially ones designated for the other sex. Audrey visited a friend who has a Ph.D. in engineering from the Massachusetts Institute of Technology; many women engineers struggle with the male-dominated environment. She bought her first-born daughter the largest toy fire truck she have ever seen. Her daughter never played with the darn truck.

code SWITCH *Parents should be hypervigilant with outside influences (such as teachers and coaches) and the messages they send to their children. Model gender behaviors that cross traditional boundaries. Dad, cook a meal. Mom, work on the car. Children do what they see, not what you say.*

Allowing your daughter to play with dolls will not prevent her from becoming a surgeon or a lawyer, and playing with toy guns will not prevent your son from becoming an elementary school teacher or a nurse. Instead, share with your child your objections to the toy (the real danger of guns) and expand the role of the toy, such as, "What will Barbie do after she is married?"

Every society forms certain expectations for each gender. Men go off to fight in wars, women keep the home fires burning; men bring home the bacon, women fry it up. Of course, these expectations have evolved over time and reflect our particular cultural biases, and some of them certainly have been changing.

Such forces for change notwithstanding, in our society, traditional masculine attributes include assertiveness, ambition, and independence. Sensitivity to others' feelings, the ability to express emotions, warmth, and passivity are considered feminine. Take, for example, how coy behavior evolves among boys and girls. Girls continue to enact this kind of social peek-a-boo, even at the ages of 4 and 5. They'll turn around and hug their mother's leg and either make eye contact and smile or, for safety's sake, ask Mom to pick them up and hold them when encountering an unfamiliar adult.

SWITCH IT UP!

Girls' sensitivity to other people's feelings could be because women have had more practice at some interpersonal communication skills. Psychologist Daniel Goleman wrote in his best-seller *Working with Emotional Intelligence,* "In cultures like the United States, girls have been raised to be more attuned to feelings and nuances than are boys." This may be what we have historically called "women's intuition." Simply put, girls are rewarded for taking care of people and relationships.

The result: a focus and attention on how others are feeling. Take this one step further. You might argue that being rewarded for taking care of others also develops a critical interpersonal skill: empathy. Because women are so plugged into people's feelings and their own, have they developed the ability to be more empathic than men?

Big Boys Don't Cry and Take It Like a Man

On the other hand, boys are rewarded for keeping their feelings "in check." You've heard the sayings "Big boys don't cry" and "Take it like a man." Before you can truly empathize with another, you must be in touch with and aware of your own emotions.

A review of the social psychology research argues that men have just as much latent ability for empathy as women; men just have less motivation to be empathetic. Boys get the message that showing feelings is a sign of weakness and contradicts the masculine code. Boys are encouraged to keep feelings in check, and women are rewarded for expressing their feelings.

William Ickes, one of the primary researchers on empathy, makes the argument that men have less motivation to appear sensitive, and possibly more to be machismo. So when we hear women complain that men are insensitive, it may have more to do with the image the guys are portraying than with their actual ability to be empathetic.

Then there is the level of self-disclosure among men and women. Both men and women say they'd rather talk to a woman about personal things, and the main reason appears to be a shared perception that women are more empathic listeners. In short, the level of disclosure of intimate and personal details are highest among women, and women are the primary recipients of these messages from both men and women.

Almost any level of personal talk is nonexistent among men. Sure, there are the "safe" topics, such as frustration at work, disappointment in the final score of a baseball game, or a poor financial investment. But it's not the kind of intimate detail shared among women.

During professional seminars, we've seen women who are complete strangers make deep confessions to each other in group exercises. It just seems that part of a woman's job description is to take care of people and relationships, both at home and at work. This starts the circle: empathetic listening leads to the perception that women have a receptive ear, which attracts more people to talk to women than men.

One of the most compelling arguments that sex differences are learned comes from anthropologists. In exploring the cultural landscape, anthropologists have discovered variations in the definition of masculinity and femininity. Margaret Mead was one of the first to argue that sex differences were not simply biological, but rather were learned, when she said in her classic book *Sex and Temperament*, "I have suggested that certain human traits have been socially specialized as the appropriate attitudes and behavior of only one sex, while the other human traits have been specialized for the opposite sex."

Mead compared other cultures to that of the United States. *Sex and Temperament* examines three cultures in New Guinea that define masculinity and femininity differently. The first two presented more similarities between men and women. Women and men were not "opposite" sexes. For example, the Arapesh culture was gentle, passive, and emotionally warm. Men and women shared child rearing and were perceived as equals. In contrast, the third culture, the Mundugamor, was a tribe of headhunters and cannibals. Both men and women were aggressive and violent. Women demonstrated little maternal behaviors, had little regard for pregnancy and nursing, and were always eager to return to war. In short, these tribes saw gender differences as nonexistent.

Mead's work stirs up debate, sparking additional questions about the origins of gender behaviors. Are they purely influenced by the environment, or could they be hard-wired? The answer is a combination of both. No one can definitively prove whether *nature or nurture* has more influence. That leads us to some of the more intriguing recent research on this tug-of-war.

The Influence of Evolution

We have reason to suspect that evolution has had a strong hand in producing gender differences. In 1860, when told of Charles Darwin's theories of evolution, the wife of the Bishop of Worcester, England, exclaimed: "Descended from monkeys? My dear, let us hope it isn't true! But if it is true, let us hope that it doesn't become widely known!"

Today thousands of scientists can present a multitude of examples of how human behavior echoes that of other animals. Don't underestimate the power of evolution. Go to the zoo and take a look at the animals. Remind you of some of the people you know? Ethnologists, sociobiologists, behavioral ecologists, and geneticists are just a few of the scientists who grapple with the unanswered questions involved with evolution and gender differences, but one thing seems certain: you can't ignore the influence of evolution.

Men Don't Ask for Directions

On the former ABC television series *Commander in Chief*, a woman is president of the United States. On one episode, a member of her staff joked that if Moses had been a woman, she would have stopped and asked for directions. Ah, yes. Then it wouldn't have taken him 40 days and 40 nights to get to the Promised Land.

Are men generally better at reading maps than women? Some evidence suggests that men score higher than women in tests involving spatial skills. Men can also see better in 3-D. Their greater aptitude in spatial relationships makes them more adept at reading maps. In contrast, many women rely more on landmarks.

Consider an example. A couple has been driving for 90 minutes in a circle, yet he won't stop and ask for directions. And all she can remember is that the destination was "somewhere near a Starbucks, just past a green house and one of those big trees." If only there weren't 25 Starbucks in town. Sound familiar?

It's a similar scene in the world of rats. In their research, psychologist David Barash and psychiatrist Judith Eve Lipton found that male rats possess a mental map and female rats employ objects for points of reference. In other words, the next time you hear your wife say, "I remember that oak tree by the white fence" to find her way, it may be her biological and evolutionary roots talking.

This also might explain why more boys like to play video and computer games, and are the primary market for them. Research indicates that boys are more visually and spatially oriented than girls. The toy industry could double its profits if it could get girls interested in the spatial experience of video games. Madison Avenue gave it a try by developing Barbie video games, but they never took off. Retailers continue to try to counter the designations of toys by using gender-neutral advertising and gender-blending messages. Yet no one has been able to penetrate the video game market and neutralize the biological predispositions of boys.

At Audrey's house no Barbie dolls were allowed. Another richer and more appropriate choice were the American Girl dolls. This line of dolls, which is now the fastest growing doll collection in the United States, includes a historical background and book detailing each doll's cultural heritage. If we bring Barbie to a life-size model employing her miniature dimensions, she is an anorexic with a C cup. With girls and women suffering from 90 percent of eating disorders like anorexia and bulimia, is this the role model of the ideal body image? Remember when Mattel got in trouble for Barbie having a voice box that said, "Girls can't do math"? And think about it. Do we have an MBA from Harvard Barbie?

As for boys, do we really need to encourage the use of guns as toys? Call your local police department. They will counsel you to avoid having boys play with guns because of the danger of mistaken identity as a real gun. Toy guns today look so much like the real thing. Read the headlines about young boys and men shot by police because they thought the toy was a real gun. Finally, should guns be a part of our everyday life and handling conflicts?

code SWITCH *Aim for more gender-neutral toys. Include gender-neutral choices, such as Legos, Monopoly, Uno, and Go Fish.*

Are women genetically doomed to do poorly in math and science? Another body of research shows that expectations heavily influence performance, particularly on tests. At the same time, little evidence shows that students who score at the top of standardized tests are likely to have more successful careers in the sciences.

The suggestion that the status quo for women in science and engineering may be "natural," inevitable, and unrelated to social factors should be challenged. After all, gender differences are a result of many systems interfacing: neurological, hormonal, evolutionary, and social.

The Hormonal Connection

Although women's hormones have been the brunt of many jokes (and excuses), men also experience hormonal changes throughout life. Male testosterone levels drop when men are in happy marriages. Men also experience a decrease in testosterone as they age.

Modern research reveals that only a small number of women, about 4 to 6 percent, experience a mood swing related to menstruation. We know that we can't attribute all gender differences to hormones; however, a link does exist between some communication behaviors and hormone levels.

Women tend to be the "talkers"—to each other, to men, to the dog, to anyone who will listen (or not). Research suggests that this chattiness stems from influence that sex hormones have on subtle cognitive functioning.

Hormones affect verbal fluency. And the levels of estrogen and testosterone fluctuate during different parts of a woman's menstrual cycle. This hormonal variance impacts the "speaking" part of the brain, resulting in increased activity. This might explain why women have the "gift of gab."

The Mystery of Testosterone and Estrogen

Testosterone and estrogen add even more mystery to this gender differences riddle. Take, for example, congenital adrenal hyperplasia, an "accident" of nature. While a girl infant is still in the womb, small amounts of testosterone from the adrenal glands flood her brain. After she is born, these girls are typically more like boys in their toy choices, have more interest in mechanical things, and prefer to play with boys instead of girls. This provides clear proof that testosterone before birth dramatically affects a person's behavior.

Testosterone may be calling other surprising shots as well, according to psychologist Hara Estroff Marano. She claims that women have the ability for a "top-down, big-picture take," whereas men tend to focus on detail. The reason: hormonal levels of testosterone. Male and female minds are drawn to different perspectives of the world around them, impacting their relationships and communication.

Testosterone may also influence eye contact. Simon Baron-Cohen, a Cambridge professor of psychology and psychiatry, presented a controversial thesis asserting that women are wired for empathy and men for building systems. Baron-Cohen's study found that the more testosterone a child is exposed to in the womb, the less able that child is to make eye contact at age 1.

The results bowled the authors over. As Baron-Cohen said, "Who would have thought that a behavior like eye contact, which is intrinsically social, could be shaped by a biological factor?" And that's not all. The study also found that the testosterone level during fetal development impacted language skills. The higher the prenatal testosterone level, the smaller a child's vocabulary at 18 months, and again at 24 months.

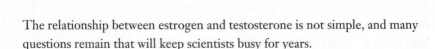

The relationship between estrogen and testosterone is not simple, and many questions remain that will keep scientists busy for years.

Are Men and Women Wired Differently?

Combined with evolution and hormones is the configuration of the brain. Gender differences may be all in our heads, literally. Boys are born with bigger brains. But girls' brains are more densely packed with neurons. The isthmus—a bridge that unites the two sides of the brain—is 10 percent thicker in women than men.

The 1999 ABC documentary *The Battle of the Sexes* suggests that the female brain is better connected, which is why girls find it easier to absorb information simultaneously. This may be why it seems that women can multitask better than men. We watch women juggle taking care of the kids, putting the finishing touches on a project at work, making the grocery-shopping list, and calling the washing machine repair person. This ability to multitask and divide tasks could be because women naturally have more connections than men between the right and left brains.

Male and female brains are "wired" differently, says neurologist Dr. Christiane Northrup. According to her research, men primarily use their left hemisphere, the seat of analytic and goal-oriented behavior that "gets to the point." You can hear this when men talk. Sayings like "What's the bottom line?" stem from the male culture. Women, in contrast, use other areas of the brain when they communicate. Because the right hemisphere has richer connections with the body, women can better read people and access their own emotions. A woman's brain is relational, which could explain why women tend to be more relational. It might also explain why women prefer to talk about people and relationships instead of the "bottom line."

Brain hemisphere research has interesting implications for communication differences between the sexes. You've heard people say that women are right-brained and men are left-brained. The right brain handles emotions, and the left is all about language. This might be why women tend to find it easier to talk about emotions, express their feelings, and pull the full picture together, and why men are less connected to emotions.

Audrey's American Singing Canaries give insight into the male and female brains. Captain Marvel, the male, has a loud piercing song that rings throughout the house. Snow White, the female, has no song, just a simple chirp. The difference here is the song itself. Generally, the males are the musicians; their song is used for courting.

In fact, Audrey's previous female canary died after producing too many eggs in response to Captain Marvel's captivating repertoire of songs. Because male songbirds sing and their mates do not, the males use their brains differently. A male has a "music box" near the front of his brain. Located in this compact nucleus, the neurons expand into a space up to six times greater than that of females. It is so apparent that scientists can visibly see it when they do a simple dissection of the brain.

Bigger Is Not Better

As we mentioned earlier, male and female brains differ in size. Researchers have found that the male brain is about 15 percent larger than the female brain. For a brain that weighs an average of 2.5 pounds, this means a difference of about 3 ounces. Some scientists make the logical assumption that men need bigger brains to move their bigger bodies. Yet the part of the brain that controls muscle movement is not super-sized, and it doesn't account for the overall difference.

In our culture, we hear it everywhere: bigger is better. The resulting implication is obvious. Women have smaller brains, so they must be dumber than men. For the last 20 years or so, this has baffled scientists, leading them to make all kinds of interpretations. One argument is that women don't *need* larger brains; it's a quantity-versus-quality issue. Instead, women have a brain more densely packed with neurons, making it more efficient.

The bottom line is this: we don't know how—or whether—brain size and density affect gender communication, behavior, and intelligence. Some people say to just forget it; the difference is irrelevant and best left alone. Others, like Pulitzer Prize–winning science writer Deborah Blum, say we should acknowledge that the difference is there—better to explore it, figure it out, and explain it rationally than to "wish it away."

Saying "No" to Genetic Impulses

Looking at the factors that shape gender differences helps us understand why men and women do the things they do. It's also important to note that men and women are alike in many areas.

Scientists have tackled many questions, but many more remain unanswered. And despite it all—hormonal, genetic, neurological, and social—we still have the power of choice over our communication behaviors. As conscious, thinking beings, we have the ability to say "no" to our biological tendencies and genetic impulses. Biology is not destiny. As Betty Friedan proclaimed in her historic book *The Feminine Mystique,* "In the end, a woman, as a man, has the power to choose, and to make her own heaven or hell."

2

Women in the Social Maintenance Department

During a gender communication seminar, one woman raised her hand.

"Do men feel?" she asked.

The audience burst out laughing. The question was obviously a joke, but the underlying message was not. Of course men have emotions. But what the woman meant was, "Why don't men express their feelings?"

Well, they do. Men just express their feelings differently. First of all, they have more control over their facial expressions, where most feelings are communicated. They have emotional control reflected by a neutral expression or by masking facial expressions. Women are what experts call high-expressers and externalizers, whereas men are low-expressers and internalizers.

Feelings: His and Hers

Society conditions women to think they are the emotional gender. Women are taught a separate set of rules that allow a wider range of self-expression. Women aren't as good at hiding their facial expressions; you can often read them like a book (helpful when women say they're "fine" but feel the opposite). With men, it's more of a guessing game.

Self-expression isn't purely learned. The different brains are also at work. According to Morgan Road in her book *The Female Brain*, "The areas of the brain that track emotion are larger and more sensitive in the female brain."

Men notice subtle signs of sadness in a face only 40 percent of the time, whereas women pick up on the signs 90 percent of the time, Road says.

Imagine how life would be if we lost our ability to express our emotions. A man in the same gender communication seminar said, "Work would be less messy if people could just leave their feelings and emotions on the sidewalk before they came into work." Which is true? An emotionless workplace would be free of fear, boredom, frustration, and hurt feelings. But this pain-free existence would have a trade-off. We'd also forfeit happiness, joy, enthusiasm, and pride—major motivators and rewards.

In this book we're not saying that the way men do it is right and women should model that behavior. We do not want women to become men; rather as women we should embrace our attributes and incorporate communication behaviors that meet the need of the immediate context. As women, we do not want to throw the baby out with the bath water. The goal is to incorporate both women's and men's talents and skills.

code SWITCH *Embrace your ability as a high-expresser and externalizer. An emotionless workplace is a dull workplace. The office would not be ignited by passion and joy. People would become bored. The office atmosphere would be over-run with monotony. When you are expressive, people also know where you stand. This, in turn, increases their comfort level and feeling of familiarity. We are always suspect of the people we can't seem to get to know. They won't let us in, so what are they hiding?*

What's Sanctioned for Men and Women?

Why don't many men show their emotions?

In his book *What Men Don't Tell Women about Business: Opening Up the Heavily Guarded Alpha Male Playbook*, Christopher Flett claims men don't often exhibit emotion "because we are taught that it is weak to do so. Men don't cry! Or if we do, we'll rarely admit to it. The truth is we do get emotional; we just don't show it. Our fathers pull us aside and tell us to be two-faced: a private face you have outside of the public eye, and a public face that shows no weakness."

One of the Ten Commandments of masculinity is "Thou shall not feel." This kind of mind-heart disconnect begins when boys are in the early years of elementary school. You'll see kindergarten and first-grade boys bringing stuffed animals from home to comfort them amid their fear of the social demands of school. They'll even hold hands and put their arms around other boys and girls to show affection and express joy. By second grade, male indoctrination begins. Boys are sissies if they show fear, pain, or—heaven forbid—the most taboo expression of all: crying.

For girls, that shift never really happens. Girls have the license to continue a full range of emotional expressions—that is, except for one: anger. Girls get angry, of course, but it is taboo for them to express it. It is not feminine to get angry or express anger. This is a commandment that has caused women a world of grief into their adult lives. Ironically, anger is one of the few acceptable emotions sanctioned for boys to publicly express.

Take the story of Brit, for example. The woman came to work one morning with red, swollen eyes and slouched shoulders. She had obviously been crying. A coworker asked her what was wrong, and she began to cry again. Her boyfriend hadn't returned her calls in a week, and she was supposed to fly across country to visit him that weekend.

"Someone needs to invent a new word for how I'm feeling," she said, between tears. "It's like I'm sad, but I'm also mad. Maybe I'm 'smad.'"

Her coworker stepped in: "Are you sure you're not just plain mad? That's really horrible what he did."

Brit's tears stopped, and she swallowed hard.

"You know what? You're right. I am mad. I'm really, really freaking furious. I'm not sad at all," she said. "I just didn't realize it."

Here's a different scene from one Boulder, Colorado, office. Paul comes out of the meeting, furious. He throws his keys across his desk and kicks his chair. The room seems to stop. Coworkers sit up, attentive and silent, until he leaves the room. Paul is known for his occasional tantrums, but no one ever talks about them. They're considered an extension of his passion and commitment for his job. Plus, even though everyone likes him, they don't want to mess with Paul.

In her book, *You Don't Say,* Audrey cites an example of display rules for boys.

When her son Armand was 10 years old, she popped by his elementary school midday during recess to give him an antibiotic for his ear infection. He wasn't expecting her. First, she bumped into his pals and asked if they knew where he was. Right then, he walked around the corner and was surprised to see her—so surprised and happy, in fact, that he jumped up into her arms and wrapped his legs around her.

Then Audrey noticed his friends' reactions. They looked at each other, rolling their eyes and poking each other in disapproval of this public display of affection.

"Gosh, Armand," one of the boys said. "Get a hold of yourself."

Emma works in the same office. She has never kicked her chair. When she gets mad, she speaks assertively and bluntly—not with malice, just matter-of-fact. She has never cried at work, and her coworkers joke that she has no soul. They don't like her, and they show it. They think she's "hormonal," out of control. She must hate her job.

Although Paul is the one acting out and he could be labeled hormonal and the "drama queen," Emma still gets the label. By being blunt and assertive she is labeled hormonal.

The Expressive Trap

Emotions can be broken down into joy, surprise, anger, disgust, sadness, and fear. Unspoken rules dictate a muted level of expression of these emotions at work. A sort of "monotonic rule" is enforced. Express yourself after work and at home.

Many people think professionalism requires them to mask their feelings in the workplace. This might sound constraining, but it's usually in everyone's best interest. This can be difficult for women. And if men break these rules, it makes headlines; they're often admonished.

Tom Cruise made headlines in May 2005 when he appeared on *Oprah* and enthusiastically disclosed his love for Katie Holmes. He got so emotionally worked up that he repeatedly dropped onto one knee and punched the air, shouted, and leaped onto Oprah's sofa, jumping up and down. People called him crazy, emotionally unstable. They said he must be using drugs. His mismanaged emotional display even spawned a new term. When someone "jumps the couch," that now means he has lost control.

At work, free-flowing self-expression rarely contributes to credibility. This is especially a problem for women, who are generally more expressive and aware of their feeling than men. Their expression can undermine them. The problem might be the interpretation of women's expressive behaviors.

Still, women can use their self-expression to their benefit. The more in touch you are with your own feelings, the better you are at reading other people. And the awareness of feelings connects with a wide range of other important traits, playing an essential role in effective communication.

Building a Relationship That Impacts the Bottom Line

The metaphor is "walking in someone else's shoes." Empathy is the ability to acknowledge how someone else is feeling and to share in their emotion. Scientific data (and popular notion) says women are the empathy masters. They adopt other people's feelings more often than men do.

Don't confuse sympathy with empathy. Sympathy is simple: an emotional reaction. It's feeling sorry for someone else and showing pity. When you commiserate, you are sympathetic.

Empathy is a highly developed and complicated skill. It involves multiple levels of ability. You must first be able to read someone's feelings. Then you must feel that feeling yourself, and then express it. Empathy often requires some prerequisites. For example, the more similar we are to someone, the easier it is for us to empathize with them. If a person is close in age, race, upbringing, religious beliefs, socioeconomic status, or experience, empathy comes easier.

On the other hand, you don't need similarities for sympathy. Feeling sorry for someone doesn't require much depth. You can feel sympathy for someone without empathizing with them.

Making Sense of People

In an attempt to make some sense of human behavior, Harvard professors Neil Rosenthal and Judith Hall developed a test called the Profile of Non-verbal Sensitivity. They tested men and women from third grade to college, showing them video clips with the sound omitted. The clips showed people's facial expressions after they were told various things, like they just won the lottery or their pet died. The results were profound. Women performed better than men 80 percent of the time at guessing the correct emotion.

Other tests have had similar results. One study by psychologist Shirley Weitz concluded that women have a sharp ability to interpret nonverbal clues. Weitz claimed women have a "female monitoring mechanism" that's especially attuned to male characteristics and needs. Women adjust their behaviors to fit the needs of men, especially "dominant" men.

So where does this ability come from? How did it evolve? And why do women have this edge?

What's Behind Women's Intuition?

Women are a socially subordinate group, and this power-down position has forced women to acquire certain nonverbal (and verbal) skills. Historically, you can see this kind of adaptation in other societies and cultures, and even within different subcultures in the United States.

Women had to learn to become reliant on nonverbal behavior, both sending and receiving it. Women needed to pay attention to the moods, likes, dislikes, emotions, and reactions of the dominant group—that is, men—almost as a survival instinct, hence the concepts of "women's intuition" and "womanly wiles." Daniel Goleman calls it the "politics of empathy" in his book *Working with Emotional Intelligence.* Those with little power have the "expectation that they sense the feelings of those who hold power," says Goleman.

During the civil rights movement, Martin Luther King Jr. expressed surprise at what little insight white people had into the feelings of black people. Black people, he said, had to be much more sensitized to how white people felt—if only to survive in a racist society.

The same goes for women. To the degree that women have been oppressed in society, they have had to become more empathetic than men. It's been generations of practice, and now women have developed an acute sensitivity to nonverbal cues and reading others' emotional states. Women are now expected to have a heightened sensitivity and emotional awareness.

For centuries, women were called witches and burned at the stake for possessing these so-called supernatural powers. It couldn't be natural to be able to predict what others would do, spot liars, and uncover the truth.

In the book *Why Men Don't Listen and Women Can't Read Maps,* Barbara and Allan Pease conducted an experiment that highlighted women's ability to read the body language signals of babies. The women were asked to watch 10-second video clips of crying babies, but with no sound—only the visual cues. Most of the women (who were mothers) could detect a wide range of emotions, from pain to hunger to exhaustion to gas.

When the fathers took the same test, the results were "pitiful," the report said. Fewer than 10 percent of the men could identify more than two emotions. And even then, they were guessing, the study said.

To see if age made a difference, the study then tested grandparents. Most grandmothers scored in the 50 to 70 percent range of the mothers' high scores, while many of the grandfathers couldn't even identify their own grandchild!

She Has the Information, Now Does She Know What to Do with It?

The ability to decode nonverbal cues is ultimately valuable and essential for effective communication. So women must ask themselves, how can we use these skills to enhance our effectiveness instead of letting them divert us? Women must not focus on others for a definition of what is "normal" or acceptable behavior; they must define it for themselves. This ability can be a gift. Use it as such.

Women, practice this mantra: trust your inner knowledge, your intuition, that gut feeling. It might be more than just a hunch.

If you don't trust someone when making a deal, go with that feeling. Question and investigate. You could save your organization from a bad deal. Women need to know that their ability to pick up on the subtle, low-level cues is historically developed. Women are often questioned when they object to something based on a "feeling." Remember, feelings are not credible in a man's world. Instead, suggest further investigation or a closer look, without disclosing that you're using your "intuitive" radar.

Take this story, for example. Amy is a reasonable girlfriend, level-headed and not the jealous type. One day, she stops by the art gallery where her boyfriend works to find a woman named Deb in the lobby. People regularly hang out at the shop, so at first, it doesn't resonate on Amy's radar. Deb works nearby and says she's interested in the art. But after a few minutes of chatting with Deb—just small talk, nothing specific—an uneasy feeling drifts over Amy.

That night she tells her boyfriend to be cautious of Deb.

"I just get a weird vibe from her. I can't explain it, but something's sketchy," Amy says.

He becomes defensive. Deb is funny and polite, plus she is the shop's neighbor. She hasn't done anything wrong, and he thinks Amy is being irrational. Still, she insists. Even though it makes no sense to him, he agrees to keep his distance.

The next time Amy hears about Deb is three months later. She had been having an affair with the shop's owner, and she is now trying to destroy the business and blackmail him with private photos. Everyone is shocked—except Amy. Somehow, intuitively, she had known Deb was a threat.

Emotional Intelligence

It's 8 A.M. Monday. The staff is gathered in the conference room, catching up on the weekend and attempting to warm up to the idea of another week at work. The boss, a woman, walks in and reads the group's mood. Who has had a good weekend, and who looks like the dog's dinner? Who is laughing easily, and who seems distant? Who appears pensive? Now they sit down to begin business.

She knows from her "read" of the group that she should gently ask questions to one member and that she can lean hard on another. The meeting goes smoothly because she has set the stage and made adjustments according to the needs of the individuals. Chalk up another successful Monday staff meeting to women's nonverbal fluency. This is just another example of the social maintenance women do at the office. Unfortunately, this is rarely valued and often goes unnoticed.

code SWITCH *Follow the female monitoring mechanism. You have the ability to read the environment. Now make adjustments accordingly. Your teammate looks discouraged, so you can check it out. You notice coalitions; now figure how you can use them constructively. Transform your ability to figure out the inside scoop into a benefit to your boss. Use your skills at reading the politics of the group to benefit your organization.*

Author Daniel Goleman gave birth to the Emotional Intelligence movement that has Fortune 50 companies taking notice and getting on board. Historically, the American management world has been characteristically male: task and goal oriented with little attention to people skills. We suffered. So did the bottom line. Companies could not retain employees. Other countries were more successful at gaining employee loyalty. The ripple effect goes on.

With the influx of women into the workplace during the last four decades, you could hypothesize that the rules of work are changing. A feminization of the workplace has occurred. We've undergone a shift in our thinking about how we achieve and define success. We are beginning to value people and judge our managers by how they handle their employees. And in the spotlight are personal qualities, such as empathy and adaptability.

What Women Bring to the Table

As corporate communication trainers and consultants for the last 35 years, we remember the day not that long ago when men bad-mouthed any training that had to do with so-called "soft skills" or emotional intelligence training. Often they told us directly that they thought it was a waste of time.

"Why do I need to get along with people? I am the lead on this project and the most knowledgeable," one engineer claimed. "Why are we spending company money and my time on this touchy-feely stuff? What a waste."

True, he was a bright engineer. But he had zero people skills. No one wanted to be around this guy. As a result, he alienated his entire team.

How It Impacts the Bottom Line

These soft skills are not a passing fad. Strong evidence shows that these skills benefit a business. Organizations such as FedEx, L'Oreal, and Volvo boast improved bottom lines after training employees and implementing soft-skill principles.

The Power of the Three S's: Social Cognition, Synchrony, and Self-Presentation

Several aspects of interpersonal awareness contribute to a high emotional intelligence, in which we believe women excel: social cognition, synchrony, and self-presentation.

> ## SWITCH IT UP!
>
> Even the U.S. Air Force, a traditionally male bastion, testifies to bottom-line profits and savings from emotional intelligence. The U.S. Air Force used the EQ-I emotional intelligence test to select recruiters (the Air Force's front-line human resources personnel) and found that the most successful recruiters scored significantly higher in the areas of assertive-ness, empathy, happiness, and emotional self-awareness. The Air Force also found that by using emotional intelligence to select recruiters, it in-creased its ability to predict successful recruiters by nearly three-fold. The immediate gain was a savings of $3 million annually. These gains resulted in the Government Accounting Office submitting a report to Congress, which led to a request that the Secretary of Defense order all branches of the armed forces to adopt this procedure in recruitment and selection.

Social Cognition: Women's Social Savvy

Social cognition is social savvy. You can see this in women who accurately read the political currents of an organization. Such a woman is adept at decoding social signals. She mobilizes social cognition to navigate the inter-personal world. She makes sense of banter that may offend one person but be playful to another. She catches a team member rolling his eyes in mutual agreement across the room with another team member; she realizes the two are a coalition disapproving the idea. Nothing gets past her.

Synchrony: How She Finds Solutions to Social Dilemmas

Jean was Tom's lead on a project. They had a meeting with key players from the organization purchasing their product. Although Tom was doing his best in pitching the project and its selling points, he missed the subtle (and some not-so-subtle) cues being exchanged among the members. Jean caught the shifts of posture, the rolling eyes, and some eyes looking away, which she interpreted as a no-go on the deal. Tom kept pressing on, with no adjustment in his presentation. He was essentially clueless to the cues.

When the meeting was done, Tom asked Jean, "How do you think it went?"

She said, "I think we've got problems."

He was totally surprised: "What do you mean?"

"Well, I saw some negative reactions," she explained, "and I don't think they're completely on board. I think you'd better give them a follow-up call and meet with the members who were showing the most push-back. I can tell you who they are. Focus on them; they're not sold. As is, I don't think we can close the deal."

A follow-up call from Tom revealed that Jean was right on. When he asked for feedback on his presentation, sure enough, they had concerns.

Tom missed the opportunity to make adjustments on the spot. If he could have read the cues like Jean and seen that he was out of sync with the group, he could have made immediate changes and addressed the concerns without needing to make an extra phone call.

When we conduct corporate training and present some difficult—and some-times controversial—ideas, we see folks squirm. It's time to take notice of what's underneath the squirm. Get at what is driving the bus, why it's difficult for them to accept the ideas you're pushing.

Women have long been experts at the nonverbal dance of synchrony with other people. Women can sense immediately when synchrony is off. Remem-ber, women are the masters of taking in all the nonverbal signals that guide us through smooth interactions. Women often do damage control for men who step on someone's toes. Most women employ synchronicity in daily interac-tions with grace and ease. Women have the natural ability, so they operate out of awareness and spontaneity.

Synchrony is largely learned. Consider the lack of synchrony, the social and psychological disorder of dyssemia. Initial dyssemia research has been con-ducted on children who are often viewed as school rejects. They stand too close, laugh too loudly, stare too long, and make different facial expressions than their peers.

As adults, they show similar out-of-sync behavior. They are often considered immature and socially awkward, and they struggle with relationships. About 85 percent of adults with dyssemia struggle with the deficit because they failed to learn and read nonverbal cues as a child, and they don't know how to respond to them. This is usually because they haven't had a lot of social interaction with peers, or their family did not display a typical range of emotions.

The goal of most therapy for dyssemia is to teach what most of us take for granted—the nonverbal ingredients of synchrony such as gestures, eye contact, personal space, posture, and vocal cues, like tone and pitch. Note that significantly more boys than girls have dyssemia, as well as related disorders such as autism and Asperger syndrome.

Self-Presentation: Animated Energy and Charisma

Daniel Goleman states that charisma is one of the most important aspects of self-presentation. In communication, a person's charisma quotient is directly correlated with the ability to persuade and the perception of being credible. Charisma is like an energetic spark—something intangible and hard to pinpoint—that magnetizes you to someone.

Charisma comes from the Greek word *Charis*, the name for the Graces, the three sisters, goddesses and daughters of the king of gods, Zeus. (Surprise: they are all women.) The Graces are Brightfulness, Joyfulness, and Bloom, a trio of grace and beauty.

Leadership coach Martha Lasley writes about this and the importance of developing personal charisma on her website. She says charisma is, therefore, often considered a gift from the gods, an elusive quality for a chosen few.

When you hear the word *charisma*, whom do you think of? Politicians like Barack Obama or Sarah Palin? Martin Luther King Jr.? Margaret Thatcher? Which public figures know how to "play" an audience? Like physical attraction, charisma is a subjective quality. We cannot walk into a room and announce to an audience, "Hello, I'm Audrey. I have charisma." It's like beauty. People don't always agree on who has it, but they're often very opinionated on who doesn't.

Charisma is a key point in credibility, and you can't persuade people if they don't think you're credible. Credibility is a combination of perceived qualities that make listeners predisposed to believe you. And key characteristics of credible speakers include charisma and dynamism.

Furthermore, "one reason babies are so attractive is they don't hide their emotions," Lasley writes. Like most women, what babies feel can be seen on their faces and felt by others around them.

"As we grow older, some of us can maintain this magnetism. But more often than not, we become conditioned to hide our feelings," says Lasley. That's especially true of men. In fact, there is sometimes a homophobic reaction to men who are overly exuberant and animated, the very energy of charisma. We associate a dynamic style as somewhat feminine.

code SWITCH *Harness that animated energy and charisma. Because you exhibit animation, you are a charm magnet. Pull people in with your charisma. Get them on board with your ideas and mission. Now you have opened the door to persuasion. You can get them to do anything. Express yourself. Don't be ruled by the outdated masked man. Charisma moves people. Move them where you want them to go!*

Balancing Expression with Gaps in Self-Control

Audrey remembers one seminar with a very distracting participant. Although about 100 people were in attendance, one woman was very distracting in her nonverbal reactions to almost everything Audrey said. She looked disgusted, rolled her eyes, and then laughed joyfully, offering an ongoing commentary to every point Audrey made. Audrey had to force herself to ignore the woman; her signs of approval or disgust were distracting her from her presentation (not to mention interfering with the people sitting around her).

Finally, the woman became so overcome with something Audrey said that she got up and left the room for a break. She had a problem balancing and managing her expression. She needed to practice more self-control, a topic we explore further in Chapter 13.

Is There a Place for the Office Mom?

Because women are good at reading and handling people's emotions, they often perform the social maintenance role at work. This often turns some women into a sort of Office Mom. You know this character. When someone has been treated poorly, they run to Mom to complain and have their hand held. She plays a powerful and influential role in the office. Men often consult with her when they notice that someone's work performance is off. She has become a source for insider information.

For women, playing Office Mom has some power.

Women managers' ability to *read* emotions leads to higher performance and satisfaction ratings by their subordinates. Communication expert Kristin Byron's research revealed that, within organizations, "the expression and perception of emotions plays a critical role in providing information, sense-making, forming relationships and forging group identity." Her research tested the hypothesis that there is an expectation that women fare better than men in these roles. Along those lines, women are also often expected to reflect a concern for others and be kind and nurturing. Byron calls that "communal characteristics."

The theory states, in part, that women who fail to manifest these communal characteristics, such as being sensitive and caring, are seen as less favorable. The same expectation simply does not exist for men. The ability to read nonverbal expressions of others is arguably a communal characteristic. So the better women can do that, the more favorable others might see them.

Tell Mom Everything

Office Moms are the recipients of high levels of self-disclosure (which can span sharing emotions to personal stories to nasty office gossip). Decades of evidence reveals that both men and women would rather tell something personal to a woman than a man. Teenage boys and girls are more likely to disclose something touchy to mothers or a female friend than fathers or a male friend. This self-disclosure plays a critical role in communication and relationship development. It boosts connection and familiarity with others.

Work can be stressful. Talking about it can be good for mental health and can relieve stress. Especially when the information is troubling, keeping it inside can escalate stress levels and result in immune breakdowns (have you ever observed a stressed team where everyone is sick all the time?), ulcers, and high blood pressure. Bottling upsetting thoughts inside is a major distraction and keeps you from doing your best work. We hear people say all the time, "I feel better just telling someone." Hello, confession. Telling the Office Mom can make you feel better.

It's also how we build *trust*. I tell you a little something about me, and you respond in kind. We go back and forth, until we have established a sense of knowing each other. And we do business based on who we think we can trust. Trust closes deals and impacts the bottom line.

There's an unspoken rule that every office needs an Office Mom. It doesn't necessarily have to be a woman manager. However, we do expect her to play the role at least part-time. An office can also have a couple Office Moms. Who's your Office Mom?

Annie has worked her way up the office totem pole by listening to others' complaints and diffusing tension. Sure, she's a hard worker, but she gets more attention through her social interactions than for the work she produces. When there are rumors about changes in the company or lay-offs, her co-workers buzz around her desk, expecting her to know the latest news.

And she does. When her boss had to can one of the products, he told her first and asked her to spread the word on a sort of grass-roots level before he organized a meeting about it. He used Annie to pad the bad news and absorb some of the negative emotion because he knew she had good relationships with her coworkers. They trusted her and knew she would take their concerns to the people in charge, as an unofficial mediator. After all, she had previously talked more than a few of them off the ledge of quitting. Annie says sometimes she feels like she should add the word *Babysitter* to her job title. A colleague shared a new title employees gave her role as both office manager and Office Mom: the *Empress of Everything*.

Use this code switch to your advantage. Remember, every office needs a mom. Every high-functioning office needs an Office Mom. She is there to soothe the hurt, bandage the wounded, and stitch up the broken relationships. She also wields a lot of power. She knows the inner workings that can potentially undermine her team or propel it to success.

The Other Side of the Story

People feel comfortable telling you things. Both men and women line up outside your office door to share some hurt feeling that happened at the water cooler or an injustice served up by the boss. The line has become so long that you are finding it hard to get your work done. This does not go unnoticed by your boss. He calls you in and tells you to back off playing armchair psychologist. He may also not see the value in this "work" and role you play in the big picture of office politics. Now your performance is on the line, and you are exhausted listening to everyone's problems. That's one risk of playing Office Mom.

Women's Work

Officially or not, a part of a woman's job description is social maintenance. She is expected to take care of people and relationships. Someone has to do it. And where would we be without this critical care? We spend the biggest chunk of our day at work. We need women who can attend to feelings, read the mood of the boss and coworkers, and provide an arena for employees to work through their negative feelings. All in a day's work for her. Where there are people, social maintenance is required for the success of day-to-day operations.

3

Getting Down to Business

Jack says, "She just goes on and on, when all I want is a 'yes' or 'no' answer! Can you get this report to me by Friday? Yes or no? Instead, I get her life story."

Just look at a man listening to a woman who is rambling on. He enters the trance, kind of like a dog staring at a fan. He looks dazed and confused. His eyes seem to beg, "Why is she telling me all of this needless information? Just tell me 'yes' or 'no,' woman!"

During one seminar, a man used that old saying, "You ask a woman what time is it, and she tells you how to build a clock!" Do we have a gender gabber dilemma here?

Give Me the Bottom Line

Sayings such as "Get to the point" and "What is the bottom line?" are borne out of male culture. Women are more process oriented. They want to share their stories and provide the details that they think make the stories rich. Women want to go on more than men want to hear. Simple as that.

When Beth's grown son, Nathan, calls home to ask a simple question, such as what time they're meeting for dinner, he always asks for Dad.

"No offense, but if I get Mom on the phone, I'll get sucked into the 'mom zone,'" he jokes. "No one can escape the 'mom zone' in less than an hour."

> **SWITCH IT UP!**
>
> If you tend to be a ramblin' kind of woman, we recommend speaking in *pyramid style*. When a man asks a question, begin your answer with a one-word or one-sentence explanation. Imagine this as the top of the pyramid, the smallest part. Good. You've given him what he wants: direct and to the point. Now, if you must elaborate, shorten your descriptive explanation by half. Finish with silence. If he wants you to go on, he will ask for it. But most of the time, you won't hear him begging for more. He's too busy doing the internal happy dance that you cut to the chase. If he doesn't request more info, you're done. Turns out, he does not want to hear the history of everything you know about the topic. It may feel unfinished to you, but he is satisfied.

Jill complains that Jack is a man of few words. He is blunt and direct, and often comes off as harsh and insensitive. His defense: something along the lines of "You asked me how you handled that client, and I told you" or "I've seen you do better. Why do I have to 'sugarcoat' everything?"

The complaints go on. You've been there!

If you really want his feedback, you're going to get it. Can't stand the heat? Then don't ask. Distance yourself, and don't take it personally. This is more about Jack's communication style and less about Jill. But don't miss what he is saying, just because you're wounded. He may be giving you valuable advice or feedback. Remember, social maintenance is not his primary concern. His mission is to tell it like it is.

Same Language, Different Styles: Lots of Confusion

Women and men may be using the same language, but just different styles of it. That's why it's important to get a grip on why a woman says the things that she does, the way that she does. What drives the way she speaks? What are the motivations?

Answering these questions helps us understand women's verbal styles. Then we can move beyond confusion to true connection with the opposite sex. There is no right or wrong style. Different is good. Men and women both bring unique communication styles to the table.

Of course, that doesn't stop the differences from occasionally driving both men and women crazy.

Take Charge Versus Take Care

So what's going on? Why do women talk that way? Well, for starters, women's communication is their primary way to establish and maintain relationships. Women talk to share themselves and to learn about others. It's deeper than just transferring information; it's opening up, and inviting in. As Judith Wood, professor of communication studies at the University of North Carolina, claims, "For women, talk *is* [her emphasis] the essence of relationship." Her speech is characterized by connection, bonding, understanding, and support.

Women are "other" oriented in their speech. They focus on what other people are communicating, including everyone, soliciting opinions, and making sure the quiet member of the team is pulled into the discussion. In the office, women-talk is often an attempt to support and understand coworkers' feelings. Communication professors Debora Borisoff and Lisa Merrill suggest this:

> For women, communication is social, a way to create bonds. Men are raised to see talking as a way to exchange information. If she is chatting with her coworkers, she must be gossiping. If he is talking with his coworkers, he must be discussing his latest deal.

> Hold up. What is gossip, anyway?

> Well, it revolves around people and relationships. No wonder women get pegged as the gossipers; isn't that the center of their universe? Who is getting along? Who will be gone for two weeks because they are getting married? Who was chosen for the promotion?

code `SWITCH` *Women, next time he thinks you're gossiping to coworkers, let him catch you talking about closing the biggest deal in your career.*

Women are also much more personal than men in their speaking style. Women share anecdotes and stories about things that happened to them, giving their speech an intimate tone. Part of this style of speech serves to develop feelings of closeness and connection.

Your Right to Be Heard

According to *Cosmopolitan*, it's just a "girl thing." Women "like to blab ... about everything," the magazine says. You'll rarely hear men talking about cellulite, Pilates, footless tights, breastfeeding, or what size they are. Among women, there are no sacred topics immune to discussion.

He Is Direct and She Beats Around the Bush

We know that guys tend to speak bluntly. They mouth off without thinking sometimes. How many times have we wished we could censor that guy in the Monday staff meeting, after a woman colleague asks for feedback on her proposal? Ouch! Painful. He doesn't hold back. He just lets her have it. Now other coworkers are scrambling for ways to help her save face. That guy just slammed her in front of the team!

You may have heard the term "that guy." You don't want to be That Guy— not at the company party, not at a restaurant, and not at work. "That guy" refers to the man (everyone knows one) who is so blunt and detached from others' feelings—and the sometimes not-so-subtle flashing nonverbal "stop" signs—that he becomes an unspoken joke. He's awkward and steps over the line. People don't listen to him, much less respect him. Being called "that guy" is a pretty nasty insult.

Remember that old saying about children, "Better to be seen and not heard"? Over the ages, women have received the same message.

In fact, some grown women talk like children. Linguists like Robin Lakoff claim that women and children share similar linguistic patterns and speech styles. Yikes.

Walk around your office listening to women talk. Does she sound soft spoken, self-effacing, and compliant? Women have internalized this socially imposed stereotype. In many cases, women are reluctant to speak out and express themselves in public.

We see this with women at gender-communication seminars. They are paying to be there, and even after we call on them, they still ask our permission to speak.

It sounds a little something like this:

- I was wondering if I could ask you …
- May I ask you one thing?
- Could I ask a question?
- I would like to ask …
- Would it be all right if I ask you …?

Others use apologetic sentence intros, as if the opinion that follows needs justification or a disclaimer:

- No offense, but …
- Not to sound mean, but …
- I'm not trying to stir up problems, but …

You rarely hear a man start a sentence by disclaiming or asking permission.

In our experience—and that's about 60 combined years of seminars for Fortune 50 companies and government agencies (to properly disclaim!)—not only do men rarely ask permission to speak, but they are also quick to interrupt the seminar leader, even when we're right about to make a point.

It's not uncommon for a deep voice to blurt out midpresentation, "Hey, that doesn't make sense" or "Wait a minute, that's not true."

Women need to realize that they have a right to be heard. Your company pays you for your opinion, so speak up. Remember, the United States was built on the freedom of speech. It is a gift we are lucky to have and a shame to waste.

No two ways about it: men are direct in their communication.

When asked why they're direct and what are the advantages of being direct, men usually cite two factors:

- No games, no 20 questions. You ask and men tell you straight up. This eliminates confusion, and you get a "real answer."

- It saves time. In our fast-paced culture where everything is done at warp speed, we value this, especially in the business world.

Now for the downside. On the receiving end, women perceive and interpret this as uncaring and insensitive. Women often walk away from a board meeting feeling like they have just been hit with an emotional baseball bat.

A man once said, "A woman at work told me I needed to go to charm school after I provided the evaluation and feedback she asked for. What a trap. She asked for it, but she couldn't take it! What's a guy to do?"

What Women Talk About

Women talk about everything and anything. You name it. Women will reveal their insecurities, their latest diet, the trials of their uterus, their dreams— the list goes on. Any topic is fair game. Two women strangers sitting next to each other on a two-hour plane ride will arrive at their destination knowing how many children each has, their marital troubles, any school dilemmas, and what kind of birth control they each use.

Another popular chick topic is the blues. Women talk freely about their troubles—personnel or personal. They're not afraid to discuss fears or self-doubts. "Get me out of here," men scream. "Geez, I don't want to hear it."

Chick topics are the same ingredients as "chick flicks." Why do you think *Sex and the City* was so popular among women and loathed among men? When the movie came out, men all but hid under couches to avoid it. But it was like home for women, where they could laugh at Miranda's overgrown bikini line ("Jesus, honey? Wax much?") and empathize over Carrie's broken heart. And the movie's biggest problem: when Miranda didn't tell Carrie something. Alas! That's *so* not okay among girlfriends.

No male version of *Sex and the City* exists, and moreover, there's no demand for one. Men tend to talk about "safe" topics: sports, finances, and work. Can you imagine two men discussing their qualms with Viagra? Yeah, right. The level of disclosure is higher among women than men.

In one of our training programs, one woman said she talked to her sister on the phone for an hour, and when she was done, her husband exclaimed, "You just talked to your sister about nothing for an hour!" Those "nothing" topics? Her aging parents, the trials of raising teenagers, and at what house they would spend the holidays. Not her husband's favorite topics. Not to mention an hour-long phone call. But for women, this is the stuff of life.

Psychologist and corporate consultant Dr. Judith Tingley once described the differences in women and men's conversation topics. It stemmed from a sailing lesson she took with four men and a male instructor. In Tingley's words: "The majority of the conversation centered on business and money. ... There was no discussion of people, feelings, or relationships. No one mentioned a wife, a child, a brother or sister, a mother or father. The conversation was almost totally about each individual man and what he had done or seen or been, relative to sports, business, or money. Men are private about anything having to do with relationships, feelings, and emotions. They usually only disclose to significant others the private aspects of their lives."

You'll Never Guess What Happened to Me Today

In *Nice Girls Don't Get the Corner Office 101*, Lois Frankel says women need to practice beginning their sentences with declarative "I" statements, such as "I think," "I feel," "I believe," "I intend," and "I need." Women often feel the need to almost *trick* the listener into listening to them. Instead of tricking the listener, women need to use the more assertive "I," taking ownership and putting opinions on the table. No behind-the-scenes strategy.

Do Women Talk Like Little Girls?

This brings us to another common linguistic pattern that women and children share: they tend to use "attention beginnings" to bait the listener. For example: "You're not going to believe this," "D'ya know what?" and "I had a crazy thing happen on the way to work today." These intros sound like teasers on television news programs: "Stay tuned, because you don't want to miss the next report!"

It seems like women need to coax the listener's attention. A woman simply cannot get the floor and gain the listening ear unless she entices the listener.

Women and men are two different speech communities. From the college classroom to the corporate world, women typically use forms of speech that you rarely hear from men, such as "qualifiers," embedded with disclaimers.

Disclaimers are apologies and excuses that women offer before they make a point. Women use this to distance themselves from the claim they are about to make rather than take ownership for it. After all, if a woman is wrong or someone doesn't like it, hey, she warned you first—don't hold it against her. Disclaimers are a form of protection, as well as an apology for speaking.

A classic qualifier sounds something like this: "Um, I don't know if this is a good idea (disclaimer), but I thought we could … (hypothetical, not a direct request)" or "This probably sounds stupid (disclaimer), but I thought one way we could handle this … (once again, just a suggestion)." Starting a sentence like this pads it with unnecessary verbiage.

This is a strategy to make an idea more acceptable to the listener, but in the process women, pull the rug out from underneath their own credibility. As soon as others hear the words "This might be stupid …," they disengage. If you think it's stupid, don't waste our time with it. They write off the idea— and the speaker. They don't listen.

Many men agree: women can't just say something; they need to say something before they say it.

When women qualify their statements, they do sound less categorical, making them less likely to offend the listener. Qualifiers have their place. Use qualifiers when you want to convey politeness, connection, or thoughtfulness. However, a word of warning: if you use qualifiers too much, they become your crutch. And when you need to take a strong stance, this crutch will get in the way. Listeners will view you as too soft. You don't sound authoritative, and you have diminished your credibility.

We once had a woman in a seminar ask why men sound like they know it all. She went on to say that men talk with such authority and certainty that no one would think to question them.

This is taking charge. A man like this is assertive and acts confident, even when he's uncertain. He has learned the lesson that you must fake it until you make it. And his image is on the line. For men, these verbal efforts at control start when they're young boys.

The Tag Question Game

When women speak tentatively, they open Pandora's Box of problems. We hear women say all the time, "Why can't I get anybody to do anything around here?" or "Nobody takes me seriously."

Well, now we know why. Women set themselves up for rejection and open the door for people to refuse their requests. This is another reflection of women's socialization into subordinate roles and low self-esteem.

Tentative speech goes beyond qualifiers and disclaimers. It also uses *tag questions*. A tag question is an unnecessary question added at the end of a sentence. It also comes with a musical feature. At the end of the last word, the pitch goes up a few notes. The speech can sound flimsy.

"I need this report by Friday, okay?" (The pitch goes up, as if to imply that the listener has the option to say, "No.")

Compare this to men's primary use of declarative sentences. Their last-word pitch goes down.

"I need the report by Friday." (Pitch going down, signaling finality—no ifs, ands, or buts.)

If you want to get it done and the listener has no choice, lose the tag question.

Of course, like qualifiers, the tag question does have a place when your speech is strong but you want to interject a sense of collaboration—for example, "I think we need to stick to our original timetable. What do you think we need to do to achieve that goal?"

►SWITCH IT UP!◄

A woman who owns and runs a multimillion-dollar international recreation equipment company was sharing that people often give her feedback that she "sure is strong." But it doesn't feel like a solid compliment. Instead, the tone implies that she's stepping out of the gender box and presents her in an authoritative manner. She said, "It is almost as if it's not good for me to be strong."

Meetings Start with Chit Chat and Men Go Nuts

Women engage in communication as a primary way to establish and maintain relationships. Women's speech tends to display identifiable features that foster connections, support, closeness, and understanding. Women express concern, sympathy, and empathy in their speech. This is a daily ritual for women both at work and at home. We commonly hear women say, "Oh, no. What happened next?" or "Gosh, that had to be difficult for you." As discussed in Chapter 2, part of a woman's job description is social maintenance. Women take care of people and relationships, and their speech reflects this.

A frustrated man cornered Audrey after a meeting and asked, "Why do women need to spend the first 10 minutes of a meeting talking with everyone about how their son did in his game this weekend, who their daughter chose to go to prom with, and how someone's sick mother is doing? Our meeting is supposed to start at 8 A.M. But it never does. The women need to check in with everyone about how they are doing."

This is social maintenance, or what some people call chit-chat. Chit-chat does perform a function. It establishes relationships, serves as the warm-up before getting to the task, and can create an atmosphere of trust. So it may seem like a waste of time, but it does serve a critical role in building relationships and increasing the likelihood of a smooth meeting.

Word Choice: Proceed with Caution

Ann was seething. She had asked Greg, a freelance photographer, to take 13 photos for her monthly women's magazine. She was on deadline, and he had turned in only nine.

She sent him an e-mail asking about the four missing photos.

"What missing photos?" he responded. "I shot and turned in everything you asked me to."

Ann went back over her content plan. She was sure she had asked him to shoot those four pictures. She went back through her e-mail outbox and found the original e-mails she had sent him. Sure enough, she was right: four "photo requests."

She forwarded them to him again with the original time and date stamp, feeling a little smug and highly frustrated. Greg instantly wrote back, confused.

"Ann, those are photo *requests*, not *assignments*. I thought they were optional because they were just suggestions."

Oops. *A simple word change*, with consideration for how men hear words and interpret instructions, would have prevented this mix-up. Next time, Ann would call them "photo assignments," to be clear.

And it should be noted that Greg scrambled and shot the four photos anyway—as soon as he realized they weren't optional. He made deadline, and the magazine was published without a hitch—or empty page.

Nothing can erode your credibility quicker than poor word choice. Women sometimes use cute or folksy language, much to their detriment. Poor word choice often turns into bad grammar, improper syntax, or a loop-de-loop language nightmare. What did she just say? The way a woman arranges her words syntactically determines whether she will be taken seriously.

Women need to be sensitive to their overuse of adjectives and adverbs. These can make speech sound trivial. Adverbs of intensity, like *terribly, lovely, adorable*, and *awfully* can diminish impact. Adjectives that distinguish but contribute no importance can confuse people. Who cares if the lobby reception color scheme is *taupe?* This is calling attention to something that is not important at work. Now, this could be valuable when she is picking the wall color for the entrance of her home.

Sometimes women are just a little too loose with their adjectives, adverbs, and nonstandard speech. Pat Schroeder was famous for telling a male colleague on her first day on Capital Hill, "I have a brain and a uterus, and I use them both." She had a bad habit of referring to programs she disapproved of as "icky" and punctuating thoughts with exclamations such as "golly," "doggonit," and, our favorite, "yippy-skippy."

Here are a few words that we wish would disappear from women's speech (more evident in Gen X and Y women): the use of *like*, "you are the *bomb*," and "you are a *rock star.*" Save it for the girlfriend lunch, not the corporate board meeting.

Why Women Struggle with Requests

Asking someone to do something for you requires assertiveness. Remember, women tend to focus on others. They do for others. If you ask a woman to get something or do something for *someone else*, no problem. If you ask a woman for something for *her,* she may become uncomfortable.

In contrast, most men employ more *imperatives:* "I need this now!" This is a command.

The strategy of compound requests works like this. The more words a woman uses, the more she softens the request. It is a *polite* form of speech. So the request becomes, "Will you do this now?"

code `SWITCH` *Develop a self-awareness of how you phrase your requests. If you routinely employ indirect compound forms of speech, you will not be able to elicit cooperation from your coworkers.*

It feels like we are extracting teeth sometimes trying to get information from women. Well, let's reverse this situation to get at why women use this strategy. What do we call a woman who is direct? (Rhetorical question.) (*Hint:* It rhymes with "code switch.")

So this is the "darned if you do, and darned if you don't" syndrome. Our advice: take the "darn" that will get you somewhere. Speak up.

▶ SWITCH IT UP! ◀

A man in one of our seminars shared how manipulative he thought women were in their speech. Because men usually have a direct style of communication, they feel that being indirect is a way to trick them. They almost feel that it is a bit deceitful. He said he was uncomfortable with that style. He cited an example that felt like a trap.

A female coworker on his team had a problem with his approach on a design issue. She approached him with "Are you going to do it like that?" He responded with "Yes." He was puzzled because she did not continue, but walked away. He caught up with her later and asked her directly if she had a problem with his design. She seemed uncomfortable and reluctantly replied, "Yes." Then he had to pull it out of her. "Well, could you share your concerns with me? I need to know before I take it to Corporate."

He seemed exhausted just recounting the story. The bottom line is that the team decided to adopt her adaptation of his design, and it saved the company thousands.

Different Rules for Standard and Nonstandard Speech

Women use more standard forms of speech. If they venture into the non-standard territory, they can get into trouble. During a seminar, Audrey used the saying "Ain't no way." Sure enough, when she read her evaluations, several participants suggested that she drop the nonstandard speech and said that it actually dinged her credibility.

"She added nothing to her presentation by using slang."

"Doesn't she know how to speak correctly?"

Sometimes it's good to not leave the gender box, because it isn't always worth it.

Profanity Is Taboo

The issue of profanity is an interesting one. Profanity is generally not accept-able in any business context. However, men often use it, and it is perceived as a representation of their vigor, passion, and commitment. When a woman uses a "hell" or "damn," she gets her hand slapped. A double standard oper-ates here.

We are reminded of a communication professor, Dr. Janice Rushing, who taught a course on communication and social change. Janice looked younger than most of her students. She was petite and unassuming, and had a low-key demeanor. During one of our sections on the 1960s protests, Rushing was reading excerpts from fiery speeches that were full of profanity. At the end of the class, she shared that several of the students admonished her for "not talk-ing like a lady." They understood that she was reciting from speeches directly, but that was still a violation of the sex role code. Simply repeating the words was enough of a violation.

We're not suggesting that you begin talking like a dock-worker. Be cautious if you use profanity, and be selective in what contexts you do so (don't choose the board of directors' meeting). Choose to use it rarely, and when you do, it will carry a wallop.

Silence Is Golden

Maybe it just seems that women talk more because men expect women to be silent. When silence is your yardstick, any woman who talks at all seems to be talking too much. The truth is, men get the floor more often, and when they get it, they hang on to it! We live with a myth of a loquacious woman, with the ideal of the silent one. We want her to be quiet, unpretentious, and basically more involved in listening than speaking. Just the act of speaking up is assertive in nature.

code `SWITCH` *Women, be the first to speak. This is a bold act and commands attention. You also have the opportunity to set the tone of the interaction and meeting. People will be more likely to sit up and take notice.*

Remember "Please" and "Thank You"

Women's speech is hyperpolite. They use "please" and "thank you" more often than men. A man would say, "Close the door." A woman would say, "Please close the door."

To make the request even more palatable and beg for the listener's cooperation, a woman will lengthen it: "Would you please close the door?" or "I feel a draft in here. Would you please close the door so we can warm up?" She uses a lot of explanation for a simple request. So once again, we have the well-behaved woman ingratiating herself with others. It almost borders on begging.

Here is an opportunity for a code switch. Women, try only occasionally using a "please" or "thank you." Don't use it every time you make a request.

Talk the Talk

Language is a powerful tool. It shapes our world and our thoughts about ourselves and others. We need to avoid language that makes us seem unfriendly or inappropriate. We reveal a lot about ourselves by what we say and how we say it. We know that our speaking style influences perceptions of power. Tentative speech makes women seem polite, approachable, and warm, but not necessarily credible. Such speech may contain hedges, qualifiers, tag questions, intensifiers, fillers, adjectives, and adverbs for emphasis. Tentativeness can also be conveyed via pauses and hesitations, which may show a lack of clarity, a deficiency of knowledge, and the need to cogitate, or be deferential.

On the other hand, assertive speech is simple, direct, fluent, and specific. You're not playing 20 questions. Assertive speakers talk more, use direct (rather than tag) questions, and feel free to offer their opinion. This style makes a speaker seem powerful, competent, and, consequently, more persuasive.

So let's go back to the board meeting: his feeling confusion and her not being taken seriously. We have choices.

4

Is Anyone Listening?

Can you tell when the boss is listening to you? Or when you get tuned out? Listening plays a major role in communicating successfully. Yet we often don't devote any time to understanding the hows and whys of listening. We just let it happen to us instead of taking control of the listening process and making it work to strengthen us.

Why is it so important to women that we feel the other person is listening to us? Why do men state something once and walk away—they're done? Women seem to be looking for a particular response from men to indicate not only that they're listening, but also that they have absorbed, understood, and accepted the message. But conversation doesn't always pan out that way.

Listening is something that you can actively control, model yourself, and help teach to others so they can be better listeners themselves. Listening is not just one of our five senses, to be taken for granted and pushed to the back of your mind. Listening is a skill—and a tool for success.

Do I Have Your Ear?

Nod, nod, uh huh. Listening is good and, uh, it's good. Totally.

Stop. Now. Listen up.

You're faking it, and we know it. Listening is easier to fake than, say, some other kinds of indiscriminate activities, and it's easier to admit, too. It's also easier to remedy.

There's always an excuse to not truly listen. At an early morning staff meeting? I need my coffee. At a 1 P.M. budget meeting? It's right after lunch—I'm digesting. On a conference call? Keep it on mute so I can continue doing my "real work." But don't forget to periodically unmute, murmur "I agree," mute again, and keep on working on your computer (*not* surfing the web for new shoes, I swear). The others know you're still there, and you chime in occasionally. That's listening right? Nope.

> Jennie worked for a large sales company that had weekly mandatory conference calls that lasted hours. She worked from home, so she would "listen" on speaker phone, but on mute, while watching TV, doing the dishes ... anything but fully paying attention. One day during a conference call, Jennie had a call on the other line and flipped over to answer it. As she flipped back to her work call, her friend knocked on her door with good news. After jumping around in excitement, the friends took tequila shots and were laughing and complaining about how nasty the shots were when Jennie noticed the conference call was eerily silent. Then her boss came through: "Are you done with your tequila, or are you going to share with the rest of us?" Jennie had forgotten to put the phone on mute when she had clicked back. She didn't lose her job, but she did learn a lesson: faking it can be as hard to swallow as cheap liquor.

Men and women have learned to be successful at faking their listening. But can women learn to succeed in actually getting the men at the office to listen to them?

Put Down That Report and Listen to Me!

Sandra sighed under her breath, "Why doesn't Bob listen to me?" Sandra needs to know she's not the only woman who's had those thoughts about men's listening skills.

By the way, Bob has great listening skills. He's listening right now, a lot. He's in his office, where he keeps two CNN channels playing, wears his Bluetooth in one ear waiting for a call, and talks with a client on his landline. During football season, he listens only while watching TV—multiple games, at that. He flies between channels with his remote control like he's switching gears in his imagined Indy racecar along the straightaway. Bob needs to use his existing listening skills and empathy ("Bummer, the quarterback tore his hamstring and he'll be out the rest of the season; that's gotta be rough") and apply them in listening to Sandra.

Many of us learned what constitutes a good listener by sitting in front of our TVs watching *Romper Room*, *Captain Kangaroo*, *Mister Rogers' Neighborhood*, *Teletubbies*, and *Sesame Street*. The message was something about sitting still, being quiet, looking at the person talking, and nodding to show you understood. This demonstrates respect and hasn't changed that much. Yet Sandra can learn additional ways to focus what she says so Bob will hear it.

Are Men Really Lousy Listeners?

In Audrey's research, she asked more than 1,000 people to identify the strengths and weaknesses of men's and women's communication. Women's top complaint about men was that men are lousy listeners. Men agreed. And they added that sometimes men "don't even make an effort to pretend they're listening," "fail to read nonverbal communications," and "don't show emotion."

Covering pretty much all of these bases is a story from one training session. A woman commented that her husband had the habit of muting her. When she started talking while he was watching one of his favorite TV programs, he would point the remote at her, act like he was pushing a button, and say "Mute!" In Audrey's study, women also complained that men take things literally and at face value, focus on the words and not the feelings, and try to respond or fix things before hearing the entire issue.

Before you get all smug, ladies, there's more. Women tend to read too deeply into things and provide too much empathy, according to women's critique of their own listening skills.

Sometimes women go beyond taking things at face value and overanalyze a statement or movement. Was he tearing up because of something she said, or was there a speck of dirt on his contact lens causing him to shed a tear?

Men tend to be self-oriented in how they apply their listening skills. This does not mean they're egotistical (and we're not simply being politically correct here). Men simply tend to be good at representing themselves in what they say, do, and need. When they're listening to your words, their focus is on how those words impact them.

Women are considered other-oriented; their listening focus is often on how they can help the other person. The end result: men often miss out on valuable nonverbal cues that accompany the message. And women may wrongly assume that men understood there was more to their message than mere words.

code SWITCH *Be specific with your message and your needs. Don't make him use his mind-reading skills to divine the full meaning of your message.*

Screening Your Messages

What's keeping you or him from listening? Put away the distractions. We each have our own screens that we tend to use to automatically filter or rearrange data that we're hearing. We each have a screen door, so to speak.

Think of yourself standing inside the house looking out the front door. The screen is keeping out the bugs. Your view may be slightly blurred due to the screen. Someone is standing on the front stoop talking to you. You're seeing and hearing this person through your screen door. The messages you're receiving are as accurate as allowed through that screen.

What is your screen door that keeps some information or bugs out while letting in other information? Just as your assistant may be screening your calls and allowing in only callers or messages that meet your listed criteria, you screen the information that you will allow into your brain. Your screening criteria may be based on your past experiences and what you've learned through school, parents, newspapers, magazines, TV, friends, music, sports, or religious affiliations.

Screening factors may include your views on the following:

➡ **Age**—"They're too young to have any real information." "They're too old to get promoted."

➡ **Education**—"He wouldn't know; he went to night school." "Those Ph.D.'s think they know everything."

➡ **Weight**—"He's too skinny to play football." "She's too fat to be sitting at the receptionist desk. What will our clients think?"

➡ **Gender**—"Women don't belong as brokers on Wall Street." "Men make terrible nurses."

➡ **Accent**—"There's no point listening when I can't understand you." "He's British; what he said sounds smart, so it must be."

➡ **Language**—"Why can't they speak English?"

➡ **Race**—"Asian Americans make great accountants."

➡ **Writing skills**—"The engineers may know software, but they can't write a complete sentence." "Artists can barely count to 10."

➡ **Wealth**—"These rich people are totally out of touch with the everyday workers." "Poor people don't understand how to budget."

➡ **Supervision**—"I never listen to anything the boss says." "He's one of them."

➡ **Employees**—"You've got to watch over those employees like a hawk; otherwise, nothing gets done."

These are just some of the screens we use to limit or revise the messages we hear and send. We often screen out what or who we choose to listen to—sometimes before the speaker even opens his mouth. If we're not screening out the whole message, we may be deciding what information we will allow in or how to rearrange the message so it confirms what we already know.

code SWITCH *Think about your top three screening factors for your incoming and outgoing messages. How might they impact your ability to listen to others and to respond appropriately?*

The Split Ear Phenomena

Audrey describes women's listening skills as the "split ear phenomena." Women listen with both ears, each aimed in a different direction. During her years of horseback riding and training, Audrey learned that when faced by an angry young colt, a mare points one ear forward and one ear backward. The ear pointed forward focuses on the misbehaving colt. The ear pointed backward aims at the remaining herd.

This is the same way Audrey describes women's listening. Each ear may be paying attention to different levels of surrounding activities. On one level, a woman is focused on the words being said, just as a man does when he listens. But on a second level, she's reading between the lines, interpreting the nonverbal messages in the social and emotional arenas. Women *collect* more information; they *hear* more by listening and paying attention to *all* the information being broadcast across the channels. Men tend to focus solely on the *verbal* channel or message. When a woman is listening to you, you're getting two for one. She's hearing your words *and* your nonverbal messages (vocal sounds, facial expressions, plus body movement). With men, it's usually a single-price ticket for words only.

Listening Is a Full Contact Sport

Here's the problem: women expect men to listen more like, well, women. Women invest a lot of time and energy in listening, showing empathy, and picking up on the nonverbal cues. One male manager described it this way: "It's like she [his business partner] can read my mind." It's not mind reading. Women listen with their eyes *and* ears. They look more at the person and, therefore, get more information. A woman physically turns to look at and orients her body to face the speaker. She's using her eyes to get more information through visual cues. Men generally don't do this. They orient themselves shoulder to shoulder and don't look at the speaker. Some men never make eye contact with the speaker and miss out on a lot of information in the person's facial expressions.

Women have learned to listen with their whole body, not just their ears, and to use that information to understand and build relationships.

Men generally have learned to listen to get the facts, be direct, spit it out, not show emotions, make quick judgments, and fix the problem. A man hears what he thinks is enough information and interrupts with a solution. Problem solved. Let's move along.

A woman wants someone to listen to the issues (preferably a few times), mull them over, and hear her voice as she contemplates the situation. She's generally not looking for a solution; the emotional processing of talking it through *is* the solution. She just wants him to listen and hear her concerns and empathize a bit. Then she can move on.

Decide what you're looking for before the upcoming conversation, and then tell him. You can help him listen and focus on what you need. Do you want action, acknowledgement, or information? If it's action, say, "Bob, I need you to take the next step on this." If it's acknowledgement, try saying, "I'd like you to listen to this and not act on it." Or say, "I'm still thinking this through and would like to try it out on you." If you're looking for information, say, "I need your input" or "You're good at this. I'd appreciate some background information." Invite him to listen. Ask, "What do you think?"

Be a Better Listener

Men and women know how to listen. They just do it differently. And men want women to listen like (imagine this) women. Men and women both agree that women are good listeners. Men have many great things to say about how women listen.

Back to Audrey's research. Men said that they liked how women can observe subtle nuances. "Women are usually more thoughtful and sensitive to other people's communication," men said. So listen like a woman. But men want women to *speak* more like men so men can *listen* like men. If Sue didn't spend time giving every excruciating detail of who said what, who did what, and "go on and on, not saying much of anything," Fred could get in there, get the facts, fix the problem, and get back to the game. But alas, it cannot be.

Sure it can! Fred and Sue just need to learn more about listening techniques and their own expectations.

Paraphrasing, Reflective Listening, and Active Listening

Once men and women understand the differences in their listening behaviors, they can choose to make a few changes around the office. They can practice assertive, active, and empathic listening to show they are hearing the message.

When we listen to each other we are looking for the meaning and the feeling of what someone is saying. To show we understand the meaning, paraphrase what the speaker just said. To show we understand emotions, reflect back to them how you interpret what feelings you hear. Effective paraphrasing and reflective listening help men and women understand each other better. Women who want to be heard and understood would love to talk with a man who responds with feedback and empathy that shows he's listening. However, we don't believe most men take listening classes to learn this.

We think women can use their knowledge of the listening process to be brief and precise—what men would like to hear. For both men and women, active listening techniques help move the discussion from a win/lose, power-oriented mindset to a win/win situation.

Those who have taken a general workshop on communication skills have heard of active listening, paraphrasing, and reflective listening. As a review, paraphrasing refers to restating in your own words what the speaker just said. This shows that you were listening and heard the speaker's meaning. If the speaker feels that the paraphrase is not accurate, the speaker can state the issue again. The listener then again restates or paraphrases the speaker's comments. For example, a coworker says, "I can't stand my supervisor. He thinks he's the only one with the right answer." A paraphrased reply might be, "So what you're saying is that you don't like your supervisor because he's a know-it-all." It's not a quick-fix answer, but an acknowledgement that you heard and understood the speaker.

Reflective listening is another way to actively listen. This technique shows that you understand the speaker's feelings and can reflect them back. A reflective listening response could start with, "What I hear is …" or "Sounds like …" and then address the emotion you're hearing. So using the previous example, a reflective response would be, "Sounds like you're upset with the way your boss acts." This response shows that you heard the initial comments and understood the feelings behind them. Paraphrasing and reflective listening are great skills for men and women to use.

Do you have a woman in the office who everyone goes to when they need to talk? Why do they seek her out? Usually because they know she'll empathize with them and listen in a caring manner. She could be an expert at listening in a way both men and women expect women to listen. She probably does this:

- Stops what she's doing

- Turns and orients herself toward the speaker

- Doesn't interrupt

- Establishes eye contact

- Focuses her sole attention on the speaker and the speaker's issues

- Asks open-ended questions (like *who, what, when, where, why,* and *how*) to learn more

- Asks questions to clarify points that are being made

- Nods her head to indicate that she's listening (not necessarily agreeing)

- Hears the speaker's feelings and emotions

- Comments by reflecting the feelings she's hearing

- Paraphrases statements to indicate that she heard and understood

- Jots down a few notes to keep track of key points

- Schedules a time when she can talk (like a lunch break) so it doesn't distract her from work

All of these are examples of active listening skills. She's probably *not* doing these:

- Answering the phone

- Typing on her computer

- Deciding whether the speaker is even worth listening to before he opens his mouth
- Looking at her watch or getting distracted in some other way
- Telling the person what to do
- Telling the person that his feelings are absolutely wrong
- Interrupting
- Stopping the conversation (without rescheduling)
- Doing her filing (nails or otherwise)
- Running off to a meeting
- Indicating disbelief
- Looking away, breaking eye contact

Most women already practice active listening, whether talking to men or women.

When talking with men, women could benefit by making briefer statements and staying on track. If the listener needs more information, he will ask for more details. Think of it like using talking points or bullets on a slide. Eliminate the description. Be brief and cut to the chase. Focus on sharing the facts and not all the background information.

Is a Good Listener Better Than a Good Lover?

Tough question? One 49-year-old woman named Robin—a student in one of Claire's college-level diversity classes—said, for her, a good listener can (and did) turn her legs into mush and have her stomach doing flip-flops.

Claire was discussing gender communication workplace issues when Robin raised her hand and began her tale. She told the class that he wasn't particularly good looking. But he wasn't bad looking, either. She wasn't attracted to his appearance.

Robin sat in on a conversation with the young Mr. X and another woman. The woman left. Then Mr. X and Robin spent the next hour talking in the hotel lobby. When they parted ways, she says she felt this weakness in her legs as she stood up and began to walk away. As she got in the elevator, she noticed her palms were sweating. What's going on? She thought she was having her first hot flash. In her mind, she started reviewing their conversation. He didn't physically touch her. He sat across from her, leaned in on the table, nodded a few times, and intently looked at her eyes as she spoke. Robin realized he never interrupted her, something she was accustomed to by the men who surrounded her daily at work. Her senses could feel the difference in his listening style before her brain could label it. What a wonderful feeling it was to be able to talk, express herself, and not have someone cut her short or shut her down.

When she ran into Mr. X the next day, she could feel her palms beginning to sweat again and the heat flushing up her neck and into her cheeks. For an in-control woman, this out-of-control feeling was not acceptable.

She never saw him again after that meeting. Over the next few years, in the darkest hours of the night, Robin often thought of how she felt that day with him.

Would Robin tell us a good listener is better than a good lover? We don't think so. She would say that a good listener is a fabulous aphrodisiac. Take note of those good listeners. This young man was decent, but no doubt other "good listeners" use their skills to take advantage of women in desperate need of a piece of ear.

Once you experience being with a good listener, you realize what you may be doing to others by *not* being a good listener yourself. When you talk with your employees, do you leave a wake of hurt feelings in your path?

code SWITCH *Pay attention to your listening behaviors and the listening responses of those you're talking with.*

Excellent Listening Is the Path to the Executive Suite

How does a good game-show host become a great game-show host? Bob Barker, longtime host of the TV show *The Price Is Right*, would often comment that it was his ability to focus and really listen to his contestants that made him successful. The same thing goes for being a good manager. Choosing if, when, and how you'll listen to your employees makes a big difference with their respect and response to you as their boss. Women are good listeners. But don't overdo it. Don't spend all your time listening to others. Yes, show empathy and understanding. But also respect yourself, your needs, and your time.

At a 2008 human resources association meeting in Denver, the presenter, attorney and mediator Stephanie West Allen, talked about how to be more purposeful in our behaviors: taking charge of our brain, breaking habits, and shaping new behaviors. Her example reflected the brain-based consulting she does with attorneys to help them essentially listen more and talk less.

Allen taught us about the "golden moment of choice," when there's a stop in the conversation between the attorney and client. A flash of self-awareness or recognition occurs during that instant when an attorney knows he can either continue listening to the client or start talking.

His brain is subtly luring him back to his habit of talking. The reason is that the brain has very deep synapses for the existing talking behavior that take less energy to use than those for a new behavior. Each time you choose to not jump in and talk, and instead to listen, you are developing new synapses. These make it easier the next time to ignore the old habit and choose to listen. Watch for your golden moments of choice. Choose to listen.

Monica's New Year's resolution for 2008 was to listen more. As a talkative and opinionated woman, this was no easy task. So she made a ritual out of it. She kept a journal of interesting things she heard throughout her day and while interviewing people on the job as a journalist. This was counter to her nature because, as a writer, she was so used to journals full of her own words. But she held her pen.

Soon she found that she always seemed to hear the perfect thing for the exact moment she was in. All she needed to do was listen—actively, consciously, and intentionally—and she found the answers all around her. By listening to others, Monica said she learned more about herself than she could have ever learned alone. After all, she already knew everything that she was going to say!

Effective listening takes time and effort. If you don't have the time now to do a good job listening, ask to schedule time when you can meet and listen to each other. No more faking it! Listen up!

5

The Mechanics of Gender Communication

"It's like going into an auto shop and talking with a mechanic. It's a different culture. Those men talk different and they dress different. I don't know what they're saying or going to do. I have to ask my boyfriend to translate," stated a young woman in one of our seminars. Instantly all the other women nodded their heads. They knew exactly what she was talking about.

I don't know what women fear most, going to get the oil changed or talking over a business idea with a male colleague. Each has the potential for unexpected surprises that can freak you out and cost you more than planned. Understanding some of the language and the major car parts and functions would certainly help you talk about car needs. We're not talking about getting a degree in auto mechanics, but code switching can help you feel confident about getting your point across and being heard when talking with men. Likewise, by understanding and anticipating men's talk patterns, women can prepare themselves to succeed in the business world.

Know Your Communication Patterns

Talk patterns have been examined over the years in terms of who talks, who interrupts, and who talks the longest. Our focus is on men's and women's talking styles and understanding where and when women benefit from code switching and using a man's style of talking.

Wouldn't it be great if we came equipped with blinkers we could use to signal when we want to talk? At a business meeting we could visibly let people know we had something to say. Since we don't, the next best thing is to learn how conversation works and flows. Folks take turns when they speak with each other. Taking turns can take different forms:

- **Actual turn taking**—One stops talking and the other responds by starting to talk.

- **Interruptions**—One breaks in and starts talking, causing the other to stop before finishing her sentence or train of thought.

Interruptions are disruptive, taking control of the discussion away from the speaker. Overlapping or talking "on top" is another form of turn taking. Someone starts talking while the other person is still speaking: they're both talking at the same time. For women this can open up a Pandora's Box because they tend to make comments like "uh huh" or "um-hmm" while the other person is talking. She's just politely showing agreement, not looking to take over the conversation. But hearing her comments, he thinks it's okay subsequently to interrupt her.

When men interrupt, they usually aim to take the floor or take charge of the conversation. These nonsupportive interruptions are all about power and require the woman to step up to the plate and get the floor back. By understanding how and when interruptions may occur, women may be able to take steps to lessen interruptions and/or help them regain control if interrupted.

The Politics of Turn Taking

What are the consequences of blurting out a comment or question and interrupting the speaker? Those being interrupted often feel that the listeners aren't really listening, but instead are planning how, when, and with what they can interrupt the speaker. If a woman intrusively interrupts a man, there may be a stronger sanction (the "bitch" label). This is the paradox of acquiescence and power. Some women were taught to speak when spoken to or defer to men in speaking. Women tend not to interrupt out of politeness. But guess what? If a woman chooses to be *too* polite, she may not get heard. Conversely, if she goes to the other side by interrupting and speaking up, she risks getting labeled a bitch. Politeness has its usefulness and value. Women support others with compliments and friendship, but they also need to know when to jump in and take the floor. This doesn't require moving to the opposite extreme and being rude. There are ways to speak assertively, which we discuss throughout this book. Here our focus is on women keeping the floor and managing interruptions. Women simply need to use their patterns of relationship to be supportive *and* use their skills to take charge.

Close-Up on Polite Behavior and Interruption

We've said that women tend to interrupt less than men, out of an effort to be polite and let the other person finish before responding. These talking patterns aim at maintaining the relationship between people—the woman's role. Women's job description is social maintenance (see Chapter 2). Men, on the other hand, tend to interrupt to take control of the conversation, according to linguistics professor Janet Holmes, but without the intention of causing disrespect or offending others. Men want to get to the bottom line. They want to hear the end result and take action—the man's role (Mr. Fix-it). Finish your thoughts and sentences before permitting him to respond or play Mr. Fix-it.

Let's go back to how people view interruption. The speaker may view the intrusion as disrespectful, as harassing, or as an effort to discredit her (or him). Those who witness the interruption also may view the interrupter as rude or disrespectful. Marianne LaFrance, a Yale psychology professor, determined that "the interrupter was rated significantly more indifferent, irrational, strong, argumentative, assertive, rude, dominant, competitive, overbearing, and concerned with self than the interruptee." There's the tightrope again. We can't always be Miss Congeniality, hoping everyone will still like us after we speak up. LaFrance also found differences in perceptions of the interrupter: women interrupting men were perceived more negatively—as rude, irritable, and self-centered—than women interrupting other women, or men interrupting women or men. Has that ever happened to you? You're in a meeting, sitting at the big wooden conference table. You interrupt the man speaking and you get a disapproving glance from the others, as if they're saying, "Who are you to interrupt him?" The message: women, don't interrupt a man.

Interestingly, Holmes noted that women displayed different types of polite behavior than men. This polite behavior included cooperativeness in which women show support for other women by completing each other's sentences. On the other hand, many men seem annoyed when a woman completes their sentences.

Are interruptions used as power plays, an attempt to take over the conversation, or an effort to change the topic? Or is the behavior supportive, like an overlap, confirming that the listener understands and supports the speaker's view?

Turbocharged Turns

Interruptions have been described as disruptive and disrespectful attempts to dominate the discussion and grasp power by taking charge of the topic. Displays of power while interrupting are what we refer to as "turbocharged turns." Where's all that power coming from? Higher status, higher job level, assigned authority, or just personal thoughts that someone has more power or is better than others can influence how and when one interrupts others or lets themselves be interrupted.

Beware of Power Ploys from Power Brokers

Men interrupt for different reasons than do women. In *Gendered Lives*, Julia Wood says, "Research indicates that men are more likely to interrupt to control conversation by challenging other speakers or wrestling the talk stage from them, whereas women interrupt to indicate interest and respond to others." She offers another explanation for interrupting and perceptions of interruptions. Wood says that, as part of a man's banter, it's more accepted among men to interrupt each other in their everyday way of talking. Going back to that polite thing among women, many women interpret the interruption and topic change as inappropriate and borderline rude behavior.

code SWITCH *Don't take it personally when he interrupts. It's part of the way he talks with his buds. But be ready to direct the discussion back to you and your topic.*

Those with greater power, status, or authority (the boss) have been shown to interrupt others more frequently than those with less power or status. Someone with a higher status expects *not* to be interrupted by those with lesser status. Social linguist Peter Kunsmann concludes that power and status are major differences in interruptions by men and women. Men, generally viewed as having higher status and power than women, have a higher rate of interrupting others. Kunsmann thought that women tended not to interrupt as much especially when talking with men due to their frequently being viewed as lower status and acting more passively than men.

Interruptions can be viewed as power plays. LaFrance found that interrupters were viewed as more confrontational and disrespectful than the interruptees. She noted that when you interrupt someone you're saying that his or her view doesn't matter or it has less value than yours.

> ➤ SWITCH IT UP! ◀
>
> Claire has been known to use interruptions to disrupt power plays and to purposely make her move to take over the conversation. Here's how it plays out. He's talking. Claire jumps in; he keeps talking. Now both people are overlapping and dueling for airtime. To his surprise, Claire keeps talking. She sees the worried look in his eyes as she keeps talking, and he sees she's not giving in. He stops talking and Claire continues. She now has the floor for the time being and has made her point: she can play with the big boys. (Note: use this technique sparingly, otherwise people may start avoiding you!)

Bosses and Men Who Interrupt the Little Guy

Think about your boss—or better yet, your boss's boss. In meetings, that big shot isn't expecting the underlings to interrupt. If they do try it, the boss makes an effort to get the floor back and continue talking, to maintain power. How did the boss learn to interrupt? It was probably from Mom and

Dad. On the home front, fathers showed their power by interrupting their kids more than moms did. Both parents interrupted their daughters more frequently than their sons, as noted by communication experts, Deborah Borisoff and Lisa Merrill. The act of Dad's interruptions showing his power at home is similar to the boss showing power and status through interrupting others in the workplace. Those interruptions indicate and remind us the boss is the one in control.

In the medical field, gender differences are alive and well in the doctor's office. Female doctors are interrupted more frequently than male doctors in doctor-patient discussions. Sociology professor Candace West found that not status alone, but status *and* gender explained the number of patients interrupting doctors and doctors interrupting patients. Patients' interruptions of female doctors seemed to weaken the doctors' clout. They interrupted female doctors more often than the doctors interrupted them. However, patients interrupted male doctors less than the male doctors interrupted them. In this case, the male doctors seemed to use their interruptions to confirm their power or influence. Female doctors were interrupted much more by patients from all economic groups than male doctors. Male doctors interrupted their patients more often than female doctors. Is this an argument for women selecting a female physician?

The job interview is no different. Dutch researcher Iris Bogaers, at the University of Amsterdam, looked at interruptions during job interviews. Results showed a status and gender interaction. Applicants interrupted their female interviewers more than the reverse; however, they interrupted the male interviewers less than the reverse. Women, regardless of their roles as interviewers or applicants, were interrupted more than men. Both men and women interviewers disruptively interrupted the women applicants more than the men applicants. What does all this mean? Women, prepare to be interrupted during the job interview ... by both men and women.

Yield: Men and Women Talking

Men tend to take more turns and speak longer per turn in both general conversations and even in online chat rooms. Men get the floor more often and keep it longer. Men select the topic more often. When men are paired with women, men tend to control the topic of discussion by employing a disruptive or curt interruption style indicated by Judy Pearson in *Gender and Communication*. She describes that when men are paired with men, they tend to employ less disruptive methods to control the discussion topics. In business settings, the men, not the women, dominate interactions.

Media at Work

Women guests on TV shows are often overshadowed by the male TV hosts who tend to speak more and control the topics. Check it out the next time you're channel surfing—look at *Dr. Phil, The Tonight Show, Anderson Cooper 360*, or the anchors on your local news channel. Who usually gets the final word on NBC's *Today* show—Meredith Vieira or Matt Lauer?

Analysis of TV shows revealed that male characters used more *disruptive* interruptions than the females, and female characters used more *cooperative* interruptions than males. Hey, it's only TV, right? Wrong. To a great extent, TV, radio, newspapers, and the media in general reflect cultural norms. Some behaviors may be dramatizations and exaggerations—and, yes, these TV programs mentioned were scripted—but business consultant M. June Allard noted that to a great extent the media reflects and confirms the culture. Therefore, what we see on TV simply illustrates how our culture expects women and men to act toward each other.

People are watching more TV; they are inundated by the media's messages. Nielsen Media reported that, for the TV season from September 2004 to September 2005, the average person watched 4 hours and 32 minutes of TV per day, the highest amount of viewing by individuals in 15 years. Setting an all-time high was TV viewing by the average household: 8 hours and 11 minutes per day. That's a lot of time watching how men and women interact. How we see and hear women and men talk and behave on TV and in movies, and how we see them reported in newspapers and in other media influences what we think is appropriate behavior for men and women. We see it played out from discussions at the water cooler to the company awards night at the banquet table.

Avoid Verbal Car Accidents

Take charge and manage the conversation. Now you know what to expect when talking with men. Our current conclusions are not that much different than those of 20-plus years ago. (Yikes! I feel like I'm in a time warp!) In her 1985 book, Pearson came to many of the same conclusions we're discussing here. Pearson said men interrupt more than women, those with more power or status (often men) do most of the talking, and more men than women overlap the other sex. Males talk to win which makes women appear less interested in the win. We've come a long way, baby. Or have we?

Anyone at the office can use power to manipulate, take over, or redirect the conversation if that's his plan. Smacking into people in your bumper car was always fun as a kid (and, we confess, as adults). When talking with others, we encourage driving *with* traffic instead of *against* it in the workplace. It's like going the wrong way down a one-way street. We encourage all to go in the same direction.

What can you do when you're interrupted? You can ignore the person and keep talking. You can yell at him, "Hey, shut up! I'm talkin' here." You can even throw your shoe at him. However, we don't advocate responding to rude behavior with rude behavior or violence. What can you do to support your own power in owning the conversation?

Follow these steps when you find yourself being interrupted:

1. Establish control by making brief eye contact with the interrupter. Don't look too long, because then it seems like you're asking permission.

2. Make a statement that draws attention back to you and your conversation. Use the interrupter's name, if you know it. ("Steve, I wasn't quite finished.")

3. Make eye contact with the group.

4. Finish your statements or thought.

A facilitator or the person being interrupted might use these phrases to direct attention back to herself or the speaker.

➡ "Just a second …"

➡ "I'm not quite done yet …"

➡ "Hold on, I'll be with you in a moment …"

➡ "Let's hold questions until I'm (she's) finished."

➡ "I'll take comments and questions in a moment."

➡ "Hold that thought …"

➡ "Just a moment, while I (she) finish(es) …"

Take Control

Sitting at the conference table with several coworkers, Rob has just interrupted Rachel's input on the sales project. Rachel makes direct eye contact for a nanosecond with Rob.

Rachel's options:

➡ "Rob, just a second …." She turns her gaze to the coworkers and completes her discussion. (She doesn't need his permission to get the floor back that she had in the first place.)

➡ "Rob, I'm not quite done yet."

➡ "Rob, hold on, I'll be with you in a minute."

Here are some other suggestions for taking control:

➡ Lean toward the interrupter, make eye contact, and then continue talking.

➡ Speak louder than the interrupter, to draw focus back to you.

➡ If you're seated, you could stand up, drawing focus back on you, and continue talking.

Remain quiet (no sense everyone talking at once). When the interrupter is done speaking, then comment, "I will continue now without interruptions." Or, "Thanks, John, for that insight. I'll finish my thoughts now."

Are these too aggressive for a "nice girl"? A man wouldn't think twice about using them. What's worse? Being shut down in front of others at the meeting or not being able to show your expertise? Get the floor back and finish your thoughts.

Directing Traffic: Everyone Gets a Turn

If you're the facilitator (or any other woman at the table), monitor who talks and how long, to ensure that all present get an opportunity to state their views without being interrupted. When you act on behalf of others, you can be bolder. You have a responsibility. Even if you are not the appointed leader, as facilitator you can still take over and stop the bully from interrupting. For example, when Sam interrupts, you can say, "Just a moment, Sam," then turn to Martha, "Martha, were you done with what you were saying?"

You can remind the group that we must follow codes of conduct at meetings and that the interruptions at the meeting are not acceptable. Even the local comedy club announces the rules of engagement: hecklers will not be tolerated. The same goes for meetings: interruptions will not be tolerated.

Sitting at the conference table with several coworkers, Rob has just interrupted Rachel. Joan says, "Rob," as she looks intently at Rob. "Hold that thought ...." Looking at the coworkers, Joan continues, "until Rachel's done." Joan ends by looking directly at Rachel. Rachel nods and continues her comments. Joan has shown Rob and the others that there are certain rules that will be followed at this meeting, and that interrupting Rachel or any other person at the table is not acceptable behavior. It reinforces Rachel's power of owning the floor until she's done talking.

Just Listen to Yourself

Now it's up to you. Become self-conscious: start by being aware of your own conversation. Do you interact differently with men than you do with women? Monitor your own interruptions: who, where, and why you interrupt or overlap others' talk. Pay attention to the conversations around you, whether you're at the Monday morning staff meeting or your cafeteria. (Yes, we are giving you permission to eavesdrop on others. Remember, you have a purpose.)

Grab Some Talk Time

You've worked hard. You deserve to be heard. Men interrupt and take the floor and your power away from you. Speak firmly and let people know you're in charge. You're at the wheel. Your credibility is at stake. This is your chance to share your expertise. Arm yourself and smack down interruptions. Know what to say when that interruption happens. Develop the buddy system. Get a buddy and ask her to be your backup at the meeting. Grab back your power.

Light the Way

Whether you're at a meeting or in your cubicle, manage the conversation. When someone is interrupted, step in and remind the group that you want to hear this person out. Your efforts at monitoring the conversation will make you the office champion. Scrutinize your own interruptions, bite your tongue (not too hard), and let the other person finish. Everyone loves a good listener. Start practicing. Go on, try it.

6

A Talent for a Technical Age

Remember the days before e-mail? How about voice mail? And how did you ever coordinate plans and find your way around without a cell phone? It's hard to imagine life before we were tethered to technology. But there's no getting around it: face-to-face communication is being replaced by technical forms of communication to a great extent, and this impacts how men and women communicate.

Similar to sex differences in linguistic patterns, women and men use e-mail, the Internet, texting, and other technology to communicate in different ways. For example, there is a lot of confusion in the style and interpretation of e-mail between men and women. If women want men to look at their e-mail and respond favorably, a closer look at these differences is crucial. The length, format, and style of the e-mail can be a make-it-or-break-it with men. And whatever you do, don't use emoticons when sending e-mail to a man. We are hard pressed to think of an e-mail we've received from a male colleague, coworker, or vendor that had emoticons. And both of us receive e-mails daily from women clients and coworkers that employ emoticons. (We'll revisit emoticons a little later in the chapter.)

Another major concern is women's familiarity with various technologies and their presence in the technical world. The Society of Women Engineers is a group we have been involved with for three decades. We know from their resources and research that women comprise a minority, approximately 20 percent, of Computer Science graduates and engineers. The major players of technology were founded and are led by men like Bill Gates and Steve Jobs. Who is the female equivalent?

A perfect illustration of this point is Ellen Spertus, who was described in a 2008 *New York Times* article called "What Has Driven Women out of Computer Science?" A graduate student at M.I.T., Spertus "wondered why the computer camp she had attended as a girl had a boy-girl ratio of six to one. And why were only 20 percent of computer science undergraduates at M.I.T. female?" In 1991 she authored a 124-page paper, "Why Are There So Few Female Computer Scientists?", that identified several cultural biases that inhibited young girls and women from selecting computer careers. According to the National Science Foundation, computer science has changed since then. Unfortunately, we have fewer women entering the field now. Also, many men prefer and rely more on e-mail and technology. Men will often admit in our seminars that e-mail has become a godsend. If you want to get through and talk to men so they will listen, you have to know what works.

The Fight for Face Time

From a gender communication standpoint, we have many factors to consider in our wired world. But first, consider a brief comparison between face-to-face and technological communication.

E-mail and voice mail are efficient, but face-to-face contact is still essential to true communication. According to Albert Mehrabian, a University of California Psychology professor, approximately 55 percent of communication occurs through body movement, such as facial expressions, posture, position, gestures, and eye contact. About 38 percent comes from vocal cues (pitch, tone, quality of voice, pauses, rate of speech, and sarcasm). Only 7 percent is words alone.

Now imagine what that means for e-mail and voice mail. Potential communication problems between the sexes expound. They can be the evil twins that undermine our best attempts at communication.

At least voice mail provides vocal cues that add meaning to the words. Still, the hazard of misinterpretation compounds because of the lack of visual cues, not to mention the inability to ask follow-up questions, as in a phone conversation.

Audrey had an assistant who would save voice mails for her to hear instead of simply transcribing them so she could "get the full flavor of the message." That is, she wanted Audrey to "hear" the frustration, disappointment, or satisfaction a client was relaying. Simply writing the message did not capture the essence of the message; there was more to the message than a summary of words.

Then along came e-mail. With e-mail, we lack the 55 percent body movements and 38 percent vocal cues to help us interpret the communication successfully. In many ways, e-mail is a double-edged sword. On one hand, it's efficient, it's great for record-keeping, and it can save you time—but we lose that critical face time that provides so much more information and helps us avoid miscommunication.

Hence the birth of emoticons. These symbols are technology's best attempt at conveying facial expressions. To lighten the tone of a sentence, you might see a :)—a smile—or ;)—a wink. Emoticons live and flourish in the texting universe, and their very absence can indicate a lack of emotion—and, in that, a lack of information. When Aimee got a new cell phone and didn't yet know how to make emoticons, her coworkers kept responding, "What's wrong?" She insisted everything was cool; she hadn't said anything negative and couldn't figure out why everyone kept asking her that. Finally, she realized the lack of her ubiquitous (auto-text) smiley face at the end of her work texts was like wiping away the ever-present female smile or giggle. So she began using a double exclamation mark in place of the emoti-smile until she figured out her phone better. The concerned texts back stopped instantly. In the business setting women tend to use emoticons more often than men to add some sense of feeling to their e-mails or soften their messages, and this may be to their detriment. We're suggesting that women pay attention to when and to whom they send them, especially at work. A smiley face emoticon in an e-mail to the boss may be interpreted as not taking your job seriously.

Physical presence has no substitute. Meaning is lost in voice mail and more profoundly in simple written words.

code SWITCH *Make time for face time. Nothing replaces the dynamic and personal nature of face-to-face interactions. Be aware that more people are working in a virtual environment every day and may never have the opportunity to meet face-to-face. Do the next best thing and pick up the phone and talk to your e-mail buddy.*

High Touch Versus High Tech

One of the most striking observations we have made about corporate America is how e-mail evolved into a good reason not to interact with people. Women generally crave that high touch, and nothing can substitute for person-to-person interaction. Face-to-face communication is essential in female culture because women prefer the connection and bonding. Building and maintaining relationships is imperative in the female culture; when she cannot be face-to-face she will resort to using her cell phone or sending an e-mail. For men, eliminating the "human" factor makes it easier for him.

One male client joyfully announced that, thanks to e-mail, he did not "have to deal so much with people and all the mess that comes with it." Now instead of walking 2 feet to the next cubicle to talk with someone face-to-face, he could send that person an e-mail. Another corporate middle manager expressed it this way: "Sometimes you just don't want to hassle with all the garbage of feelings, emotions that people bring to the communication. When you e-mail them, it eliminates all that stuff and just makes it simple and easy. Then you don't get stuck in how much you don't really like that person or their ideas. You just get them the message with no strings attached!"

According to "Defending the Caveman" by Rob Becker, the longest running solo play in Broadway history, back in the caveman times, men were hunters and women were gatherers. Because of that, we've evolved with different sets of instincts to ensure survival.

Now in the Internet times, the Internet serves as an extension of those instincts. Men use it as a tool to hunt. I'm looking for a cherry 1972 Nova. I go on the Internet, I look through eBay, and there it is. Women, as gatherers, use the Internet to gather information. They use it to stay in touch with their friends. They keep community together.

In her book *Get Them to See It Your Way, Right Away*, Ruth Sherman warns that both business executives and politicians have turned to e-mail as a convenient way to communicate. She goes on to suggest that they should not overly depend on e-mail and advises executives that face-to-face communication is best. Talking by telephone is the next preferred way to communicate.

She makes an excellent point, because e-mail is void of all the nonverbal elements that reveal feelings and emotions. With e-mail we are left on our own to decipher the message. E-mails become a guessing game. What did the sender really mean by that? And, unfortunately, it is human nature that we think the worst.

Missing the Sound of Your Voice

When we go back to our percentages about the meaning of a message. With voice mail, we at least get the 38 percent. Contrast that with e-mail, where we get only 7 percent of the words. With voice mail at least we get the vocal cues, which can reveal attitude, intensity of the message, and provide us with more meaning.

Add to this more word shortcuts and acronyms. TTYL stands in for "talk to you later." 411 is information. CYE is "check your e-mail." @TEOTD stands for "at the end of the day." NP means "no problem." These quickies are not just for teenagers anymore. They have leaked into the workforce and continue to grow more acceptable. Thx 2 texts, our words and communication are getting shorter—and, in that, cheapened. LOL has taken the place of real laughter, which experts say has actual physical benefits. How many times do people truly "laugh out loud" when they write LOL? Nonverbal messages are not only being lost, they're also being distorted. We are missing the nonverbal component of our message—the live laughing or smiling in this case—which some would argue in communication is the most important part of the message.

Neal Conan, host of NPR's *Talk of the Nation*, conducted an interview with Lee Rainie, director of the Pew Internet and American Life Project, about e-mail and Internet use. Rainie revealed some trends in sex differences. He said men use e-mail and the Internet mostly for business or to check sports scores, get political information, download software, listen to music, use a webcam, take a class, and get stock quotes. Women are more likely to use it to look for health information, use websites to get support for personal problems, and connect with friends and family.

Compare these trends to sex differences in speech—that is, you can see similarities with how women and men speak and how they use the web. We shouldn't be surprised that linguistic patterns carry over to technology. Men use the Internet as a gateway and women use it for community. Women keep social networking sites, such as MySpace and Facebook, alive.

Are Chat Rooms for Chit-Chat?

In her article *Gender and Power in On-line Communication,* Susan Herring provided examples of male bantering (sarcasm and insults, similar to bantering in men's speech) and female-style messages (expressing appreciation, support, and a qualified assertion). Even online, men and women tend to follow their same communication patterns: women building relationships and men expressing competitiveness.

Consider this example of a man posting to a discussion group about a history project for an organization's one hundredth anniversary:

First man: Hey, do we include the tyranny of our government?

Second man: Well, everyone might get their underwear in a bundle.

First man: No one will. They all wear supermans, not boxers.

Second man: Yeah, right, twerp.

First man: Now we need to dig up some history, jerk-off.

Women posting to the same discussion group (responding to another woman's message):

First woman: Aileen, I just wanted to let you know that I have really enjoyed all your posts on Women Herstory. They have been extremely informative, and I've learned a lot about the women's movement and its impact on things like flex time. Thank you! Erika

Second woman: DITTO!!!! They are wonderful!

Third woman: Did anyone else catch the first part of a Century of Women? I really enjoyed it. Roberta

Likewise, compare how men and women use the public bulletin board of MySpace. A look at one woman's friends shows the following:

Red (a woman): A survey about herself

Hollie: A survey about herself

Lee (a woman): A survey about herself

Lee (yes, again): A different personal survey

Richard: An advertisement for his video business

Anthony: An article about his career as a UFC fighter

The women seem to be using the social networking site to share personal info about themselves, deepen relationships, and open up connections. The men are using it for information and fact sharing.

Audrey knew a male manager who disclosed the impact an e-mail he sent had on a long-time female employee. He said he was going fast and forgot to start with "Dear" and simply wrote two sentences about the due date and logistics of a project. Later in the day, he encountered this woman and she asked him if he was mad at her. He was perplexed because his intent was to be goal oriented and get the business done, not to "sugarcoat" his request. For her, she wanted only one word: "Dear." Or a "thanks." That would have taken care of the "relational" dimension of the e-mail that she needed.

We experience a distinct style difference in our e-mail correspondence with men and women. Men's e-mails, like their conversations, tend to be short, abbreviated, and to the point. A few of our favorite e-mails sent by men are one or two words: *yup, Roger that, okay, done, no, yes,* and *ditto.*

Often men's e-mails do not begin with "dear" or sign off with a "sincerely" or "best regards," which are more pervasive in women's e-mails. Women's e-mails often contain an acknowledgement of appreciation, a "thank you" or "please."

Another gender aspect of e-mails reveals women as more process oriented, whereas men are more goal oriented. Men are even more to-the-point in e-mail than in speech! While both are focused on the same end result, each will express status differently: she describing the process and he describing in a direct manner the end result or goal. A female attorney shared an illustration of this difference in describing a woman's and man's e-mail about the same case.

Her format: The process

I spoke with the SIU investigator to let him know that Mr. Insured has "lawyered up," and the EUOs have been postponed. He told me that he received a certified letter "purported" to be from Mr. Insured, asking for copies of reports. He forwarded the letter to Ms. Client to forward to us for handling.

After I spoke with Mr. Investigator, I was wandering through Parties and realized that Mr. Independent Adjuster was the person I was supposed to contact, not Mr. Investigator. I advised Mr. Independent Adjuster of the "lawyering up" and Mr. Insured's request for postponement of 30 days. Mr. Independent Adjuster may be in the hospital in 30 days. He has a suspected aorta aneurysm and will be having open heart surgery. He will keep us advised.

Court reporter has been advised of postponement.

His format: The goal

Mission accomplished.

It Can Cut Both Ways

The upside of e-mail is that it can eliminate emotional "garbage" and stay focused on difficult issues. E-mail can be advantageous when difficult, emotionally charged issues are on the table. Ideally, we wish people could handle all conflicts in person. But the reality is that many do not possess the skills and know-how to do this. Enter e-mail, which provides a safe distance and ability to "think before speaking." (Now if we can just get people to reflect on their e-mail before they press Send!)

Conflict is an excellent example. Conflict-related e-mails work best when they're unemotional and businesslike. One can certainly remain calmer and more civil via e-mail than in person. However, the flip side is that women may have more of an inclination to avoid painful but necessary topics and discussions. So e-mail can be like walking a tight rope. On one hand, it is an aid to remain unemotional; on the other, it can be an avoidance mechanism.

Audrey was involved in negotiations between two divisions of an organization. As the negotiations began to break down, the e-mail sign-offs started to become shorter and less cordial. So "I look forward to working with you" morphed into "Best."

How significant is the e-mail sign off? For women, it's very important. Not so much for men. The sign-off above your signature line with your name and contact information reveals a lot about status and hierarchies. This is where writers express themselves and how they see themselves.

Let's contrast it to common female sign-offs: "thinking about you," "let's chat soon," and "warmest regards." Occasionally, a woman may be a *XOXO offender.* She has known her female coworker for years, and although they are at work, she still feels compelled to send hugs and kisses.

Our local newspaper published suggestions for variations of "yours truly": "If you are taking suggestions for e-mail closings, let me offer the simple 'As sincerely as possible,' which covers all the eventualities." Audrey likes to use "My best" or "My best always."

Technology has continued to lead people to say things they wouldn't be brave (or rude) enough to say face-to-face—especially when their identity can be easily shielded. It's easy to hide behind an odd or deceptive e-mail name. Take the reader comments sections of blogs or video websites. Here you can find snide and insensitive comments about the people in articles, the journalists who wrote them, those who filmed the video, or the community in general.

Below one article about a bicyclist who was hit and nearly killed by a car, several readers commented on "stupid bikers, they think they are in charge of the road." Those same readers would never have said that to the bloody and injured man lying in Intensive Care on his deathbed.

Online as the Great Power Equalizer

The Internet is the new frontier that leads to gender equality, with women as the socially and economically less powerful gender. The Internet can empower women to find "community" in pursuit of their own interests.

Historically, women were slow to warm up to the Internet. Throughout much of the 1990s, women seemed not interested in investing time and effort to learn how to use the Internet. According to the *New York Times* article, "What has Driven Women out of Computer Science" it was clearly a guy thing. However, the increasing popularization of the Internet, coupled with its commercialization and business use, has made it a necessary and required tool.

Gender-Blind Opportunity

A study conducted by Anne Rickert and Anya Sacharow revealed that 50 percent of web users are female. The web offers an opportunity to be *gender blind*. User names and e-mail addresses can be gender-less words.

Unfortunately, our culture makes snap judgments about people based on their appearance and gender. There is no dress rehearsal for first impressions, and they have a staying power. Once formed, they are hard to change.

In his best-selling book *Blink: The Power of Thinking without Thinking*, Malcolm Gladwell talks more about gender and first impressions. He claims that "decisions made very quickly can be every bit as good as decisions made cautiously and deliberately." However, sometimes our instincts can betray us. The web and e-mail let us be gender- (and color-) blind for that critical moment, which often dictates whether we give a person a chance. So you could argue that the web and e-mail neutralize the playing field.

Instincts are powerful. Gladwell offers an illustration of a woman shielded from the bias of a traditionally male arena of orchestra musicians. Abbie Conant was one of 33 musicians applying for a trombone position with the Munich Orchestra. Because one of the applicants was the son of a current member of the orchestra, they decided to do a "blind" judging in which they put all the contestants behind a screen. Decisions were made by ear alone.

The trombone is traditionally considered a masculine instrument, and when the panel of judges selected Conant, they were shocked to find out she was a woman. They were expecting Herr Conant. This was Frau Conant!

The Internet offers opportunities for gender-blind judgments, sort of like the screen did for Abbie Conant in her audition. Plus, social networking and easy-to-modify websites give people a chance to delay their first impression, by finely crafting what information we choose to make public, selecting only the best photos (and Photoshopping them, while we're at it), and creating our own sort of personal marketing campaign. And we can change it at any time in a matter of minutes.

Is There a Place for Geekgirl?

Hey, girls need modems, too. Girls do math, and they do computers. Watch out, boys, blogs and websites seem to be where a girl struts her stuff. "Cyber-pioneers" of today "are digitally effusive teenage girls," according to Stephanie Rosenbloom, writer for *The New York Times*. She claims that research demonstrates that young Internet users and most writers of material like blogs and websites are not marginal geeky misfits. Move over, geeky male. You have not lived up to your reputation. Many boys and young men don't have the time and patience for blogging, creating their own websites, and any other content-creating activity. Girls are much more into putting something up and getting responses. Blogging is a form of connecting around a cause or issue which is appealing to girls and women.

Computers are a source of power, influence, and money. Women need to realize that they cannot afford to be marginalized or excluded from this medium. Women cannot afford to be information poor and disenfranchised in a technical world.

> ### SWITCH IT UP!
>
> Audrey had a client who asked if she would participate in a preconference blog. Audrey was the keynote speaker, and the client thought this would build enthusiasm and get people motivated for the conference. Indeed, not only did people become motivated about attending, but they told their friends. Consequently, registration for the conference had to be closed because of a record number of registrations. The client claimed it was a first! Historically, they had struggled to get their numbers and make the conference cost effective.

U.S. President Obama is said to be addicted to his BlackBerry—proof that people in power positions have and use this power toy. Their success often depends on it.

Are Women Addicted to Facebook?

Facebook and MySpace have become substitutes for family and other personal relationships, especially for Gen X and Y women ages 18 to 24. Facebook has 20 million users, surpassing MySpace (according to most recent survey research, which was probably obsolete before it was released!). These networking sites are transforming how we communicate. Because women place a high premium on their relationships with others, Facebook and MySpace become a seductive substitute for real friendships. Women get hooked into acquiring friends.

The concern for women at the office is two-fold. Because women tend to reveal more personal information about themselves and post it, they can jeopardize their professional image. What you do outside the office can follow you back to work, courtesy of Facebook! Stories abound of people researching coworkers for more information and the personal scoop by consulting MySpace and Facebook. Provocative pictures with detailed descriptions of your vacation in Cancun should not be the prime-time talk of the office. And absolutely no revealing photos taken with cell phone cameras that could end up as the new rage, which is grabbing headlines and appearing in courtrooms, sexting.

The second concern involves job hunting. More employers are pulling up MySpace and Facebook listings as a part of the background check on prospective employees. You did what in college? Do you really want your prospective employer to know about all the hell-raising you did at the sorority house? While privacy settings should be used to keep your Facebook locked down, you can avoid embarrassing situations by not posting material that you don't want your boss and coworkers to see. Remember many of your so called "friends" are people you have never had face-to-face contact with and how can you trust them not to forward your comments on your Facebook page about the boss from hell to your boss. This happens all the time.

Cyber Femmes Unite

Now we are about 20 years into the use of the Internet. In the early days, women's participation on the Internet was low, around 15 to 30 percent. It was a man's world.

A shift began around 2000: the feminization of the Internet. Wired women were cropping up everywhere, especially where it counts: the pocketbook. Online shopping became a mecca for women. Women make most of a family's financial decisions, and this carried over to her online shopping power. Female shoppers flex a lot more monetary muscle on the Internet. Case in point: Overstock.com's base is two thirds women.

The Internet has become domesticated. It is no longer the world held exclusively by male computer scientists and academics. Now it is politically correct to talk about bridging the digital divide with access and participation of women.

For women, *cyberspace* is really another word for *community*. Women can maintain connections and develop relationships, romantic and business. Women use the Internet with a greater emphasis than men to deepen connections. Men value the Internet for the breadth of experience it allows, and women value it for the human connection—ironic, since the Internet itself is not actually human or a face-to-face connection.

Women, Get Digital or Be Left Behind

An imperative for all working women who want to talk so men will listen is that they become less intimidated by technology. Men respond and expect a woman to be able to do a spreadsheet not by hand, but on the computer. He will not give her the time of day if she is still relying on antiquated systems such as hard copies, overhead slides, and other outdated techniques. Making a presentation for the board? Have a slick PowerPoint presentation. Additionally, he is impressed and it scores credibility points when they are on a business trip together and she whips out her GPS so they can find headquarters in a busy city. Men often view technology as another form of "toys." So a way to play with men and get them to listen is share the same toys.

Men still rule in cyberspace and computer use. Technology leaders like Bill Gates and Steve Jobs have staked their claim in the high-tech world. The majority of computer science majors are male. Men generally are still the first to vigorously seek out and try new programs and the latest technologies. This provides a power advantage and sure gets the attention of the boss. Here is an opportunity for a code switch.

code SWITCH *Become familiar with the latest tech toy or computer program that will benefit the office. Take a class or consult with a tech expert on the most recent advances that could streamline operations at work.*

Who knows what is around the digital corner? It changes monthly—maybe quicker. Move over, male cyber kings, because more women are climbing aboard the information highway. And if we don't, we will be left behind.

7

It's What You *Don't* Say That Means a Lot

You cannot *not* communicate. You're always sending some kind of message. From the moment you step in to the 8 A.M. Monday morning meeting, your team is watching you: your walk, your expression, your eyes. When the boss walks in with a strident pace and pensive look, we know we're in for it. Must be time for a budget cut.

Because we're communicating even when we don't realize it, it's crucial to become conscious of your behavior—to transform subconscious behavior into intentional and strategic choices. And then, when you're aware of the effects of your behavior, you can learn to code-switch. But first, how do you know when your boss doesn't like your work on the project? Is your first clue the rolling eyes, the quick glances away from you, or the snoring during your presentation? How can you translate these unspoken messages?

Learning the Right Messages

Do you worry about what messages you send to your coworkers by the smile or stoic look on your face? We learn as infants the power of nonverbal messages. We help meet our needs, whether we're hungry or wet, by crying. We learn how to convey a message with more than words. Are you still playing some form of peek-a-boo or crying game with the office hotshot? In your office, how does the message "Here I am" or a cry for attention move you from the realm of the invisible to the visible? How do these messages and behaviors get translated in the workplace? Silent messages speak loudly.

Read Between the Gender Lines

Nonverbal communication is everything except the written and spoken word. Communication professor Julia Wood described nonverbal communication as the sound and tone of your voice, body movements, and your surroundings, including the personal space around you. What we don't say plays a critical part in the overall communication process and how we determine meaning. It provides additional clues to help understand the spoken message.

Only 7 percent of communication comes from spoken words in face-to-face communication when there's a conflict between the verbal and nonverbal messages, or when verbal communication isn't clear, according to Albert Mehrabian, a psychology professor at the University of California, Los Angeles. Thirty-eight percent comes from the vocal cues or how the words are said. And the majority of the communication—55 percent—comes from facial expressions and body movement.

Of course, different types of conversations take place. Still, Mehrabian's stats indicate that a whopping 93 percent of communication comes from nonverbal behavior. In other words, what you *aren't* saying says the most.

Try a simple test. What do you trust when you're in a situation in which the verbal and nonverbal messages contradict each other? We've all experienced this: Your coworker has a tear-stained face. You ask her if everything's okay. She says "Yes," but her voice is shaky. Do you believe that everything's fine and go on your way?

Or your jealous boss tells you, "Great job"—but in between clenched teeth while wearing a frown. She avoids you in the hallways and "forgets" to invite you to career-building meetings with the CEO. Are her nonverbal messages telling you she's thrilled? We tend to undervalue the critical influence and significance of nonverbal behaviors because they happen quickly, usually at a low level of consciousness. People tend to believe the nonverbal message over the verbal words that they hear.

The Champs at Sending Double Messages

Much research in the field of communication has shown that women seem to excel at sending double messages. Consider a woman who wants to show that she's angry and fired up, but she's smiling. What's up with that? She can't be *that* angry if she's smiling, right? (Women, feel free to insert your rhetorical laughter here.)

The smile here is probably intended to soften the harsh words. But instead, the woman is just undermining her message. She's sabotaging her own efforts by sending mixed signals. Women need to make sure their verbal and nonverbal behaviors match.

During the 2008 U.S. presidential race, Gov. Sarah Palin followed up talk about a serious issue with a wink and broad grin at the audience. Some people weren't quite certain of her message. Was she talking about a serious health-care issue or posing for a cheesecake pin-up calendar? Was there some inside joke or reference to a dirty secret (wink, wink)? "Gotcha"? Many people had no clue how to decipher her conflicting verbal and nonverbal messages, and this surely damaged her credibility. Even if there was no secret meaning to the wink, it was distracting from the potential power of her intended message. Certainly one could argue that men, too, may give a wink when talking to a large crowd. U.S. President George W. Bush would sometimes wink. However, it was more of a flirtatious wink indicating humor; it was usually not contradicting his verbal message.

We often hear verbal messages from management that have different nonverbal meanings. From the importance of company values ("Of course we have them") to managers' nervous discussions about downsizing ("Of course we're not"), nonverbal messages come through louder than the verbal ones. First you hear "Don't worry," and the next week you're cleaning out your desk and heading for the door.

You've heard the expressions "It's not what you say, but what you *do* that's important" and "It's not what you say, but how you say it." Actions speak louder than words. These clichés ring true.

Ah, here's another one: seeing is believing. And it is. Seeing managers' non-verbal behaviors played out gives new—and often different—meaning to their verbal messages.

code **SWITCH** *Congruency is key. Make sure your nonverbal message matches your verbal message. Don't talk about the importance of upholding company policy and values, and then fall into the punch bowl at the sales awards banquet.*

On or Off the Record?

These subtle nonverbal behaviors are considered off the record; their meanings are generally not easy to qualify or substantiate. On the other hand, you might say that the spoken word is on the record. It's readily recorded—she said this, he said that. Nonverbal behaviors appear less concrete. For example, it's hard to "prove" that smile when she was expressing her anger at the team, or his heavy sighs and darting eyes when you entered the conference room. Was he tired from working late last night, or was he telling you you're not worth his time? Such behaviors may be off the record, but they do leave an impression.

Nonverbal behavior influences many work-related decisions. From who gets to do a presentation (who looks and sounds the best—sounds like a radio announcer and not a gravel truck?), to who gets hired (her go-getter attitude: arriving early, staying late, showing lots of energy, raising a hand and volunteering for more work), to who gets the sale (she's passionate about her work), we are constantly influenced by nonverbal behaviors.

Now let's look at nonverbal communication between men and women. This adds another layer of mystery. We're talking about touch, the use of personal space, body movement and facial expressions, and vocal cues (for example, this includes pitch, speaking rhythm, loudness of voice, or inflection).

Reach Out and Touch Someone—with Caution

Touching is a form of nonverbal communication. The quality and quantity of touch makes a difference. Is there such a thing as "good" touching in the workplace? A handshake, a peck on the cheek, a pat on the back—what do these touches mean? Does a written office policy dictate what type of touch is okay, or is it more of a societal norm?

Touch varies from physical abuse at one extreme, to a soft caress at the other. Girls learn their role as nurturers by the way they are touched and how they observe the adults around them touching girls. Likewise, boys learn their role as protector and provider by knowing how they are touched and how to reciprocate to protect themselves or others. As adults, women continue the nurturing aspects of touch, generally touching to support and console others. Men often use touch to show sexual interest, dominance, and clout.

You may think that touching someone is good because it establishes a connection between the two of you. But it can also be presumptuous. It could be seen as inappropriate to touch a colleague that you think you know or a workshop participant you just met.

Consider two things before you touch someone:

1. Is the behavior reciprocal?

2. Is it acceptable in the culture where you are?

If the answer is "No" to either of these, keep your hands to yourself. Pay attention to how, where, and why you touch others. Does that touch have a positive purpose in the workplace or on that business trip? Are you encouraging or discouraging someone with that touch?

The amount of actual power—or even perceived power—we have influences how we touch others and how we react to being touched. People with power tend to touch others of lesser power more often and do not want to be touched themselves by people they think have less power. And men, who are generally viewed as having more status than women, touch women more often than women touch men. To add another twist, the amount and type of touch changes as men and women get to know each other better and develop a more intimate relationship. Chapter 15 looks at intimacy behaviors in the workplace in more depth.

This goes for physical space, too. An editor, Sue, said she rarely calls on one male freelancer, Jake, because the more she communicates with him, the more frequently he pops by her office unannounced, sneaking up behind her and putting his hands on her shoulders. Although Jake probably doesn't (consciously) mean anything bad by this small gesture, it bothers Sue. She says she doesn't understand what he's trying to communicate, but it feels too intimate for her. She can't help but wonder if Jake would do the same if she were a man.

Conversely, when is it appropriate for a male or female boss to touch a male or female employee? How would the male boss be viewed if he slapped his female employee on the back for a good job? Would he be viewed the same if he did this to one of the men in the office? We talk more about touch and sexual harassment, as well as its prevention, in Chapter 14.

First Impressions

First impressions are based on nonverbal communication. Before you even open your mouth to talk to people, they've made an impression of you, for better or worse, based on your looks (haircut, clothing), facial expression, weight, stance, smell, and so on. Various research on first impressions indicates that we tend to draw conclusions about someone very quickly, and those impressions are often accurate and not readily changed. Studies have looked at how quickly first impressions happen, often with several assumptions drawn by the onlookers. How fast does the mind work in determining a first impression? It took as little as one tenth of a second for people to form impressions of others, according to Princeton psychologists Janine Willis and Alexander Todorov in their 2006 research. Their study found that those impressions were as similar as those who spent a longer time looking at the person. Judgments were made about the person's looks, expertise, trust level, likeability, and hostility.

People form that first impression through three critical connections: eye contact, a handshake, and a smile. In American culture, making direct eye contact upon first meeting someone is generally viewed as a sign of trustworthiness and honesty. It helps connect with and begin a relationship with someone as a person. Averting the eyes often makes someone wonder if you're hiding something.

Here's an exercise Audrey often uses to illustrate the impact of first impressions. As the speaker, she's introduced to her audience by the meeting host; Audrey doesn't say anything. She then asks the group to write down on an index card five impressions they have of her. In a fury, the audience members write down items with no hesitation. This shows the power of first impressions and how ready and willing we are to judge someone. Audrey then collects the cards and reads them out loud to the group. Audrey is tall, thin, and angular, which garners adjectives such as "stern," "hard," and "means business." If she'd been rounder, she may have gotten comments like "jovial" or "good sense of humor." Instead, she's viewed as Nurse Ratched.

Many Baby Boomers in the workplace grew up learning what are now outdated office rules. Men were taught *not* to offer their hands for a handshake unless a woman offered hers first; she must initiate the handshake. Consequently, by not shaking hands, the woman was left out of important bonding. Smiling is the only universal sign among different countries and even generations; it shows our openness and friendliness when we first meet.

The touch of the handshake is important in establishing the relationship. By the time a boy is 5 years old, he has been taught how to shake hands: Extend your arm, use a full palm, and firmly grasp the other's hand. Regardless, some people still offer a "limp fish" handshake, which just screams negative nonverbal adjectives, like "lazy," "weak," "uncertain." At the other extreme is the bone crusher. This can be seen as a power play for A-dog status (are you shaking hands or having an arm-wrestling competition?) or overcompensation for a lack elsewhere.

Touch changes the tenor of an interaction most dramatically, and the handshake is the only sanctioned business ritual that employs touch. To participate as full partners, women also have to participate in this business code. Shake hands with both male and female business colleagues. Avoid "limp fish" and bone-crusher handshakes. Don't hold hands. Don't try to reel someone in like a fish on a hook.

code **SWITCH** *Consistently offer your hand and use a firm, full-palm handshake.*

Touch Around the Globe

What's perceived as normal male or female touching varies by culture. Do your research. Before you meet with international clients, learn what's acceptable in dress, touch, and courtesies such as a handshake. Some cultures might not consider it appropriate for a man to shake hands with a woman. In Saudi Arabia and the Middle East, two men holding hands signifies great respect and friendship; in San Francisco, the men would be perceived as two gay men expressing their close feelings for each other. Former U.S. President George W. Bush experienced these mixed messages in April 2005 when photographers caught him holding hands with Saudi Crown Prince Abdullah at Bush's Texas ranch. All in a day's work? The news item by Lana Berkowitz of the *Houston Chronicle* carried the title, "Hand-wringing over hand-holding: Saudi official says Bush, Prince showed respect." Berkowitz reported that in the rural South, especially Texas, it was unusual to see two men holding hands: "Good ol' boys tend to keep other guys at arm's length—unless they've just scored a touchdown."

As another example, consider Damien, a Polish man new to the United States. On his first day in the country, he offered a new colleague his elbow instead of a handshake because his arms were full. The American had no idea how to respond, so he put out his elbow, too. The American thought it was some "strange foreign thing." Turns out, Europeans often offer their elbows or fingers in lieu of a hand if their hands are full or dirty. But you're not supposed to click elbows together like two chickens. In this global market, being aware of cultural differences and expectations can mean the difference between returning home with a new client and returning with empty pockets.

Space Invaders

Levels of power and status influence what we view as appropriate space for others and ourselves. So the boss can invade an employee's space by sitting on the employee's desk or walking around the desk and standing next to the employee, but it would be seen as awkward and disrespectful for the employee to sit on the boss's desk or walk behind the desk, stand next to the sitting boss, and begin conversing. Studies have shown that men invade women's space more than women invade men's space. When challenged for that space by men or women, women generally give up the space or just leave instead of defending the area; men tend to defend their space.

The next time you're in a busy office building, take 10 minutes to observe people walking up and down the hallway or in the lobby. Watch and count how many times a woman moves to get out of the way of someone, compared with how many times a man moves out of the way. This is not trivial: this behavior contributes to women being seen as having lower status than men— therefore, it's perceived as okay to invade women's space.

"Hey, Do I Know You?"

That personal bubble or body buffer zone is the personal space immediately surrounding you that you carry with you all day. When someone enters your personal space, it signals familiarity. Intimate space is generally reserved for family. Anthropologist Edward T. Hall pioneered the study of how people use their personal space, known as *proxemics*. He argued that culture influences what people learned was appropriate personal space, and differing perceptions of space could develop into communication breakdowns and misunderstandings in different cultural settings.

Different cultures use space differently. Personal buffer zones frequently convey a culture's values and interaction patterns. In certain Latin American and Middle Eastern cultures, it is appropriate to interact very closely—within inches. It's good to feel the warmth of people's breath on your face as they talk and is considered rude to back away.

In other countries, such as the United States, people interact from farther away. A social distance in the United States for impersonal business conversations or when waiting on the public subway platform is about 4 to 12 feet.

Imagine that you're the only one in the doctor's waiting room, which holds about 12 empty chairs. Someone comes in and sits in the empty chair right next to you. You think, "What the heck is wrong with this person?" He's violated your social distance zone. He's in your space. This happened to Joan when she moved to Germany to work and study. She was sitting at a table in McDonald's with coworkers when several Germans sat in the empty chairs at the table. This stopped the Americans' conversation. Other tables were available; Joan's group thought it rude of the strangers to break up their lunch discussion. The Germans were probably just conserving chair space, anticipating the lunch rush.

Space and Power

Studies have shown that women generally use less space than men and give up their space more readily to men, as a function of learned social behavior, power, and gender roles. The next time you're in a meeting at the office, check out who has their belongings spread out everywhere on the table; who physically takes up the most space sitting at the table; who leans back in their chair, brings their arms up and folds them behind their head, or puts their feet up on the table. These are all power plays—the person takes up more space to show he has more power than others in the room. Generally the boss exhibits this behavior, or maybe it's someone vying for the boss's job or trying to impress the boss. This is usually male behavior, but some women mimic men, especially in a male-dominated work environment, where it may seem that the only way to get ahead is to mimic the male boss.

Space and territoriality also communicate messages. In the United States, women have a smaller personal space than men. Women unconsciously make themselves appear smaller when sitting, folding their arms across their chest, crossing their legs above the thigh, keeping their legs close together, and often wrapping one ankle behind the other. It's almost as if women are non-verbally condensing and saying, "Look how small and insignificant I can become." What's more, women also talk in little voices. Men expand their space as they puff up their chest and sit with legs spread apart.

code SWITCH *Make a play for more power by taking up lots of space at the meeting table and sitting without crossing your arms and legs.*

The seat you select at the meeting table indicates power, too. The head of the table position lets people know you're most likely the person in charge, and people will treat you that way. If you're running the meeting, make sure you get there early enough to select the seat at the head of the table, especially if you're running a more authoritarian type of meeting. If it's a collaborative meeting, it's okay to sit in a seat on the side of the table, but be aware that your team members may unconsciously be looking toward the person at the head of the table for directive cues. Subtle changes in your seating choices and behaviors can contribute to others perceiving you as more powerful.

> ## SWITCH IT UP!
>
> Audrey was hired by one of the largest law firms in the western states to look at several internal communication problems. The 45 partners sat in a U-shape in a large conference room. It was important to Audrey to keep charge of the meeting. She did two things to purposefully signal that she was the leader of the meeting. First, she sat at the head of the table, not in the middle. Second, when she began talking, she stood up and walked around the group behind their seats, and ended up full-circle in front of the room. During the break, one of the women attorneys mentioned to Audrey how powerful that was. It's an example of what you can do to show your control of a meeting.

Watch Your Signals and Expressions

Body language includes everything your body does, from head to toe: facial expressions, eye contact, gestures, posture, position, and fidgeting.

You won't find the exact meaning of folded arms in any dictionary. This posture could indicate any of the following:

- I'm cold.
- I'm uncomfortable with what the speaker said.
- I threw down my breakfast burrito too fast.
- I'm comfortable.
- None of the above.

Furthermore, men and women have different repertoires of behaviors. Kay Payne, communication professor and author, says that when talking with men, women generally use more passive or subservient behaviors. They use less body space, tilt their heads, frequently keep their hands in their laps, cross their legs, sit on the edge of their seat, and lower their eyes, Payne says.

Conversely, Payne found that men generally do not tilt their heads and use as much space as they can. Men "stare more, point more, take up more space, keep their head straight, stretch their hands, stand with their legs apart, sit in more outstretched positions, spread their knees while sitting, stroke their chin more often, use larger and more sweeping gestures, sit back in their chair, and hold their arms away from their body," Payne says.

Using your arms and hands as you talk is fine, but you don't want the behaviors to detract from your message.

code SWITCH *Use gestures such as pointing to emphasize a few key issues.*

Don't tilt your head unless you are purposefully doing so to indicate that you're sympathetic or nonthreatening. The tilt of the head is good when we are signaling empathy, but it also cues submissiveness. Think of your pet dog. When she meets a larger, more aggressive dog, they'll bark at each other at first, but then she'll tilt her head and quiet down in a submissive manner.

Hold your head high. Keep your chin up. Why do we have those sayings? They're signals that you're in charge of the situation—whether it's your pride or your emotions.

code SWITCH *Choose when you tilt your head according to the situation and message you want to portray. Keep your head on straight.*

The Face Says It All

The face is the richest source of information, adding meaningful nuances to the words you say. A lot happens in the face to provide information about a person's feelings. Women tend to display more facial expressions than men and to more accurately interpret facial expressions. Some suggest that because women are viewed as having a lower status, they must rely on all clues to understand those with greater status, and part of those clues are facial expressions.

Ever wonder why a woman is smiling at work? Women not only smile more often than men do, but some seem to smile all the time. Happy, sad, stressed, confused—some women have learned to smile to please others.

Does your workplace have an office cheerleader or office mascot—cheery, bouncy, and always smiling? Coworkers are sometimes left wondering if she ever has a serious or pensive thought. Women are usually the caregivers in the workplace, making sure that everyone's happy, no one's fighting, and people are getting along with each other. A woman's smile can tone down a conflict, start other people smiling, show agreement, and even be an attempt to ingratiate herself with others.

Watch it! If a woman smiles too much, it begins to impact her credibility and she risks not being taken seriously. That constant smile will be seen as a fake, meaningless expression.

Men learn to hide their emotions using fewer facial expressions and to smile only when the occasion calls for it. People who already have power and status positions (generally men, in many workplaces) don't need to smile. Use the smile as another tool to consciously convey a message or positive connection.

Women who don't meet the cultural expectation of smiling all the time have been viewed as more unhappy, more tense, and not as carefree as men who don't smile. Some people may even ask what's wrong; they've been conditioned to look for women's smiles. According to communication and English professors Teri and Michael Gamble, in the United States African American women smile less than African American men; Caucasian women smile more than Caucasian men. Asians may smile and laugh to hide their real emotions, such as shock or anger.

Consider a few code switching tips:

➡ Smile selectively. You don't have to be smiling all the time—you'll only diminish its meaning when you really do want to smile.

➡ Be congruent. Never smile when you are delivering a serious message.

Numerous studies on eye contact and gender have concluded that maintaining eye contact during conversations and looking at the speaker's face while talking are women's behaviors. Why? A woman is connecting with others. She's looking for information on how she's being received, and she's looking to bond with the person. Women, viewed generally as lower status than men, have learned they need to pick up as many clues as possible about the message's meaning. To do so, women tend to look at a speaker's face and eyes to see and hear both verbal and nonverbal messages.

Studies also conclude that men tend not to sustain eye contact during conversation. Watch two men talking. When speaking with other men, they tend to move their bodies so that they are standing shoulder to shoulder next to each other. They generally are not looking into each other's eyes or looking at each other's face. This is also an indicator of status and power: a higher-status person (usually a man, in many workplaces) doesn't think he needs the additional information gained by eye contact and facial expressions. Having said this, remember that there are exceptions. Both men and women can stare you down when needed. Professionalism and confidence may be displayed by direct eye contact just as easily as intimidation.

> ## SWITCH IT UP!
>
> When speaking with a male coworker who had taken the shoulder-to-shoulder stance with her, Claire physically moved to face the man speaking, to make eye contact. She noted his discomfort at having to talk with her face-to-face. He began moving to get back to the side stance again, while she followed him to keep eye contact. It looked like they were dancing badly! Some men are more comfortable talking with a woman face-to-face and adopt the shoulder stance only with other men. Be aware of your needs. Gain information through facial cues or by talking with a man in his comfort level.

For both men and women, staring can be viewed as a challenge. Maintaining eye contact and not looking away is generally viewed as a power play.

When you keep that eye contact going, a man may unconsciously accept a woman into his playground and view her more as an equal. A 2005 Dartmouth

College psychology study looked at people who purposefully made eye contact. Women who intentionally directed their gaze at a man were considered more likable and attractive by that man than women who looked away. Use eye contact to signal support. Use a direct gaze to signal that you've got power, too. Be aware of how and when you challenge others with a stare.

It's Not What You Say, but How You Say It

Vocal cues are associated with verbal communication. This includes voice pitch and variety, vocal quality, articulation, pauses, sarcasm, and inflection.

Male voices sound deeper, louder, and more robust as a result of shorter, thicker vocal folds; larger chests; and larger larynxes and pharynxes, according to communication professor Kay Payne. By contrast, Payne says, female voices sound higher and smaller because of their longer, thinner vocal chords; smaller chests; and smaller larynxes and pharynxes. The late actor John Wayne demonstrated the perfect example of the male's strong, deep voice, and he often played the ultimate "man's man" type of hero roles in movies.

But physical differences don't explain all the vocal differences between men and women. After all, we have most likely grown up knowing that it's impolite to raise your voice—but more so for a woman (who would be seen as a bossy witch) than a man (who'd be seen as forceful, direct, and assertive).

Samantha was tired of her manager yelling at her. Hank, her manager, argued that he wasn't yelling or even raising his voice. Samantha heard his forceful, direct approach as yelling; she felt scolded like a child. To Hank, yelling meant raising his voice loudly and shouting. To him, he wasn't shouting; he was just telling it like it is—no sense beating around the bush. Women tend to use more of a sing-song pattern to their speaking and may make statements that sound more like questions, which decreases how others perceive their confidence and credibility. When speaking, a woman might sound like, "I have four brothers?" and "I come from Kentucky?" A man might reply, "Well, for Pete's sake, if you don't know how many brothers you have or where you come from, you've got serious problems." He'd walk away thinking she'd lost it.

And here the woman was looking to build a relationship. She'd walk away thinking she'd failed to connect with him. Just as men and women say "How are you?" as a generally meaningless greeting, she was trying to bond by talking about unimportant trivial things. The sing-song pattern in her voice just made her look confused.

Sexy Voices

Do you like that throaty, breathy whisper from your significant other? Should you use that same breathy whisper at work?

David Addington published a study in which individuals' personalities were judged based on their vocal qualities. He found, "Women with breathy, tense voices were judged to be pretty, feminine, petite, shallow, immature, and unintelligent. Men with throaty, tense voices were judged to be mature, masculine, intelligent, and sophisticated." From Marilyn Monroe to Jackie Kennedy, women have used the breathy voice to show femininity, yet have been perceived as unintelligent or shallow. A sexy, low-toned tigress voice (think of Batman's Catwoman) isn't what you want to use, either, when you're asking the boss for the tax report.

Does it help when women sound more like men? Some women take voice coaching to lower the pitch of their voices. The U.S. business world tends to value men and their behaviors more highly. Although this is changing, you still find these attitudes in male-dominated work environments. A man's deep, loud voice is viewed as commanding and confident, a sign of strength. Men with a high-pitched or soft voice are sometimes labeled effeminate. On the other hand, women with a stern-sounding, low-pitched voice often have their femininity and sexuality questioned.

Women, watch what you do and how you play with the boys. We're not suggesting that you act like a man, but you must be in control. Select behaviors that will help you succeed on the job. How we say words—soft or loud, with a shrill or deep sound, cute and playful like a child, or soft and alluring like a porn star—influences how others perceive and respect us and how they accept and value our messages.

Of course, if you select the soft, alluring voice and you happen to be an aspiring sexual porn star, well, more power to you. The key is to choose what works best for you in your particular situation to meet your goals.

The Quiet She-Mouse

What does being quiet say about you—and about your work? Silence is another tool that can make you appear thoughtful and get others to do the talking. As trainers, we pose questions to our audiences and sometimes have to wait in silence for someone to respond—which they generally do (thank goodness!).

Most U.S. audiences are uncomfortable with spaces of silence and blurt out words just to break the stillness. Police officers and interrogators sit quietly after they ask a question because they've learned that the person they are questioning will eventually start talking to avoid the uncomfortable silence.

However, it's important to note that perceptions of silence vary with cultures. In some Asian countries, people do not perceive silence as awkward.

> ▶ SWITCH IT UP! ◀
>
> Learn to control silence and make it your friend. When Claire investigated potential discrimination cases, she prepared a list of questions and then spoke with the person who had allegedly committed the damaging behaviors. Sometimes the person readily provided answers. Other times she was met with silence. Once when she was interviewing a man, they sat in silence for what seemed like forever. Claire chose to continue the silence. After all, she had plenty of time at her end. He looked at her, looked down, looked away, and then finally replied, "Well, I don't know quite what to say." This opened the door for Claire to ask more about his role in a particular situation. She eventually got the information needed. She truly believes that sitting in silence helped him collect his thoughts and understand the severity of the issue so that they could move forward. If Claire had jumped right in to cover up the silence, she might not have gotten to the information needed.

Ever heard of the strong, silent type? That's a description of a man, right? We don't describe women as strong, silent types—it sounds silly to even think of it. But this is a positive value for a man. His silence creates a mysterious vision of a man who has many secrets that we are left to imagine, sort of James Bond–ish.

Because women are basically relational, they have a need to dig into that silence and find out what's going on. Women are faced with a double whammy. They have been taught that it's better to be seen than heard, to speak only when spoken to, and that it's not feminine to raise your voice. Yet in the workplace, if a woman doesn't speak up, she's viewed as uninterested in the project, unable to do the work, and not wanting to advance herself.

code SWITCH *Try out a little James Bond. Use silence to your advantage. Sit quietly for a few seconds before you respond to a question. You may be viewed as an intelligent, thoughtful person who chooses words carefully before replying.*

Verbal and Nonverbal Snubs

Feeling uncomfortable in the workplace? You've probably been at the receiving end of *microinequities*, a term conceived by Massachusetts Institute of Technology ombudsman Mary Rowe in the early 1970s. These are subtle behaviors that leave you feeling less than the others in the office: put-downs, hurtful remarks, slights, snubs, unintended insults, or rejections. They can be subtle or covert, leaving you wondering, "What just happened?" Those behaviors, verbal and nonverbal, make you ask yourself, "Am I being too sensitive, or did he really totally ignore me as he walked by? Maybe he was busy. Yeah, he's got a lot on his mind and didn't even see me—although he did look directly at me."

These behaviors often leave women and minorities feeling left out, ignored, devalued, and excluded. The bosses verbally give the right messages, but the nonverbal messages say that you don't belong here or that you don't fit in. These behaviors include being interrupted, left out of the friendly office banter, mistakenly not invited to a work meeting, or treated like a second-class worker and not primo management material.

Psychiatrist Dr. Chester Pierce calls them *microaggressions*. They happen automatically to keep certain people in an inferior position. Years of receiving these behaviors on the job frequently culminate with employees either shutting down so they won't get hurt anymore or leaving the organization. ("I wonder why Jane left. I guess the work was just too hard for her.")

Imagine this. You're sitting at a meeting, and just as you get the nod to begin your presentation, two people across from you whisper to each other and laugh. Another person pushes his chair away from the table and starts checking his BlackBerry for e-mail. You start to talk, and your boss looks down at his watch and then shakes his head. A colleague fumbles through her pockets, pulls out her wintergreen mints, and starts passing them around the table. Another person's heavy sighs echo through the room. Been there, done that? You've been blasted with microinequities. These messages covertly (or sometimes not so covertly) let the speaker know that he or she is "less than" and has nothing important for the audience to hear.

Don't despair! You may also pick up on *microaffirmations*, supportive behaviors that encourage you. A smile, a head nod, or a look of approval will let you know you're on track. Microaffirmations confirm that you're doing something right, you've been given approval, and you're on your way to being part of the "in" crowd. In other words, they make you feel warm and fuzzy; you want to hang around this workplace and do your best.

Let's go back to that meeting. You get the nod to begin your presentation, and two people across from you smile and nod with approval. Another person picks up his BlackBerry and puts it away in his briefcase. You start your remarks and your boss turns his chair so that he's facing you, increasing his eye contact. A colleague goes through her pockets, pulls out a pen, and starts taking notes. These microaffirmations are all positive behaviors letting you know you're doing a great job. Microinequities and microaffirmations are critical behaviors that influence your decision to stay or leave a particular job.

Mimicking the nonverbal behavior of someone else is a helpful tool. Unconsciously, we often mimic the person with whom we're talking, especially if it's someone we agree with. She crosses her arms, you cross your arms. He uncrosses his legs, you uncross your legs. Mimicking behaviors isn't an adult phenomenon. Girls generally grow up watching their moms and copying their caring behavior. Boys grow up mimicking their fathers' competitive behavior.

Knowing that mimicking behavior often shows a sign of support, agreement, empathy, or increased liking, you can use it as a tool to enhance rapport. Experienced salespeople often do this to make the customer comfortable and establish a link between them. Reflecting the behaviors of the other person can help build relationships.

code SWITCH *The next time you're talking with the boss, don't sit there with arms and legs crossed, all wrapped up in a tight little ball. If he touches his chin, you touch your chin. When he changes position in his chair, slowly change your position to match his. If you disagree on an issue, mimicking may move you closer to a sense of accord.*

Lying Words versus Nonverbal Leakage

Nonverbal leakage. Sounds nasty, like maybe something that can be cured by wearing adult diapers. Wrong! Nonverbal leakage refers to the nonverbal messages that seep out below our verbal messages. They provide additional information to either support or contradict the verbal message. What message do you believe when the spoken words and nonverbal leakage contradict each other? Generally, we go with the nonverbal. These behaviors happen so quickly that they tend to be free of malicious intent or distortion.

Nonverbal behavior may indicate that someone is lying. Interestingly, the harder someone tries to not show that they're lying, the more obvious the lying becomes. Signs to look for include shifty eyes, diverted eye contact, a gaze turned away from the speaker, excessive blinking, a nervous tapping of the index finger, a rigid posture, signs of stress and anxiety, a motion to cover the mouth with a hand, and a change in the sound of the voice.

Looking away generally creates an uneasy psychological distance between the deceitful person and the other. A person who is telling the truth tends to lean forward, appears open and comfortable, and directly answers a question.

A liar often pushes away from the table, leans back, hesitates or stammers when responding, and assumes a closed position by crossing the arms or legs.

You can try to read some of these nonverbal cues in others, but it won't be 100 percent accurate. Many people tell lies, from small ones to big whoppers. Some people are good at lying—so good that they begin to believe it themselves. They make sure that they have direct eye contact and don't shift their eyes, to "prove" they are not lying.

Even when we're telling the truth, we may be nervous when answering tough questions at a job interview and stammer a bit. Here's a reminder: tell the truth. Simple. Don't get caught up in lies or office rumors. It's less stressful for you not to have to keep a running tab of what your story was the last time.

Don't Let Them See You Sweat

Convey confidence. Stand up straight. Sit up straight. Don't slouch. Keep your shoulders back. Throw out your chest. Speak up. The higher-ups at the office are looking at you and want to see behavior that shows you're ready for the executive suite. Don't act cute, coy, shy, and bashful. Women who act this way at the office are often viewed as not being management material. You could be sending nonverbal signals that you're not confident or that you have low self-esteem. Sure, you're not the CEO yet, but there's nothing wrong with sending signals that you're a take-charge person.

code **SWITCH** *Try out some new nonverbal behaviors. Become a supersleuth as you observe and take note of nonverbal behaviors all around you. Check out the boss's nonverbal behavior, or that of the boss's boss. Experiment and learn what works best for you.*

8

Are You Wearing That?

Behaviorist Desmond Morris wrote in *Man Watching: A Field Guide to Human Behavior*, "It is impossible to wear clothes without transmitting social signals." Like it or not, our dress conveys messages of how we want to be seen. Fifty years of research tells us you can change perceptions of a person by changing his or her clothes. Clothing has a profound impact on others' perceptions of you—your profession, level of education, socioeconomic status, personality, trustworthiness, level of sophistication, and personal values.

The effect clothing has on perception makes it critical that you consider the appropriateness of dress, the context for the outfit, and the image you wish to communicate. Audrey conducted a training session for a John Deere manufacturing facility in Wisconsin. She was instructed to dress for the context. Suits (Audrey's "uniform" for conducting training sessions) would not be appropriate. She did not need to dress to impress; she needed to identify with her audience. The audience and occasion should dictate whether you dress up or down.

What Signals Are You Sending?

You hate to admit it, but don't underestimate it: we judge a book by its cover. Not fair? Nope. But it's human nature. We look at people and size them up. And women are judged more harshly and by a different yardstick than men. A woman's credibility can be on the line with her hemline.

Linguist Deborah Tannen explains, "Because we are so much judged by our appearance, women don't take lightly any indication that our weight, our looks, or our clothes are less than perfect." Matters of our personal appearance and dress are lightning rods for most women. Culturally, women learn that they should care about how they look more than men do. The roots are in our social expectations of femininity. Just as a man can sprinkle a few profanities into his speech and get away with it, he can relax in his dress and not be judged harshly.

Looking at the men and women sitting at the table of a recent management team meeting, it was apparent that men don't have the range of choices and, consequently, potential dress code violations as women. That also means men don't have the same freedom women do to express their "uniqueness" or personality. So many men, so many drab blue and gray suits.

Women's style is more complex and has more variations. But that simple fact contributes to how vulnerable women are to sending the wrong fashion messages. In the United States, women's clothes are more decorative, whereas men's are more functional.

Consider the famous case of a successful stockbroker—a top producer in her company who was denied a promotion because her clothes and appearance were not up to the company's standards. As the single head of household with two small children, the woman sued the brokerage company—and won. She claimed that more emphasis was put on her attire than was placed on the appearance of men in the firm. This case confirms that women are not judged just by performance; they are sometimes judged much more harshly on their hair or hemlines. Remember the running commentary on Hillary Clinton's headbands when her husband was president? How about the constant discussion of Sarah Palin's hairdos, the pins and accessories she wore, and the controversy over how much money she spent on her campaign outfits? We didn't hear similar criticism of any of the male candidates' price points and style choices. And could Palin's choice to spend that much on her clothes to begin with have reflected the intense pressure women are put under to look "perfect"? Maybe we should have been shaking our heads not at a politician who would blow that much money on a dress, but rather at our society, which teaches that an expensive dress is the only way a woman can rise to the top.

No Second Chance to Make a First Impression

We judge a company's image and credibility partly by how employees are dressed.

As we mentioned in Chapter 7, there's no dress rehearsal for a first impression. Right or wrong, the average person you meet forms several stereotypes about you within the first 30 seconds, and most of these stereotypes are formed by nonverbal cues of your appearance. First impressions help determine whether we close the deal or win the contract, and also can dictate the future of a relationship.

First impressions are difficult to change. They have a certain "sticking and staying power." Remember that audition that occurred behind a screen (see Chapter 6)?

Today, when many people think men and women have equal opportunities to succeed, using the screened auditions and eliminating the stereotypes creates a more honest first impression.

Dress Code Violations

Another critical consideration is the violation of dress codes. Is it a gender equal shared opportunity? Absolutely not. If a woman wants a man to listen, she has to remember how she "packages" herself will be a deal maker or breaker. Look around at your office. People looking more than casual? Do they look like they are ready for a night at the club, especially women? Thank you, Hollywood.

How did we get so sloppy and out of control? Casual Friday began in the late 1950s, originally as an attempt to raise worker morale in the new white-collar office environment. The idea was to get employees to relax and become more productive. At that point, only a few companies encouraged casual attire, and it was not widely accepted.

Casual Friday (followed quickly by Casual Monday through Thursday, for many companies) became prevalent during the dotcom boom of the late

1990s and early 2000s, particularly in the Bay Area. (Think about every time you see Steve Jobs from Apple roll out a new product—he's always wearing jeans.) Then things got out of control. Employees started wearing shorts and flip-flops. For many men wearing a tie every day to work is dead, and for lots of women wearing pantyhose just isn't happening as often; suits are generally not the norm at work unless you're in law, a financial institution, or a related industry.

When the dotcom industry crashed, the Casual Friday dress code experienced a backlash. Some organizations are now moving back to more formal business-casual; for other organizations, it's straight-up business-formal. Retail store Target requires business-formal dress for all employees at their corporate office in Minneapolis, Minnesota.

Thomas Vinciguerra, an editor for *The Week* magazine, referred to a startling statistic of the toll of Casual Friday: the loss of men's ties. He writes: "When I first saw this statistic, I was so startled I could have spilled my soup on my tie. But I wasn't wearing one—and there's the rub. Only 6 percent of men now wear ties to work everyday. The ripple effect of Casual Friday has taken its toll. U.S. sales of ties plunged to $677.7 million in 2007, down from $1.3 billion in 1995. ... I can't help feeling something important is being lost."

Unfortunately, this trend toward casual dress has a more harmful impact and negative implications for a woman's credibility. In other words, men can get away with a more casual dress code; women simply cannot afford to break the dress code rules. The perception of credibility is at stake for women here. Women need to keep that jacket on because it is the authority symbol. If she does not abide by a business dress code she will not be taken seriously by men. They will not listen if she is dressed for a night of clubbing. They may think she looks sexy, but not credible.

We asked our clients what they think is the most inappropriate office attire for women. Here are the results:

- Extensive tattoos
- Facial piercings
- Nightclub makeup

- Bras that let your nipples show
- Underwear that is visible when women bend over
- Cleavage
- Miniskirts or tight skirts
- Sheer dresses
- Slip-style dresses
- Anything strapless
- Revealing tops or see-through blouses
- "Muffin tops" (a product of too-tight and too-short shirts)
- Tank tops
- Shirts that gap between buttons
- Belly shirts
- T-shirts
- Halter or tube tops
- Sweatpants or athletic pants
- Navel-exposing pants
- Shorts
- Jeans, especially unzipped and folded over, low-cut jeans, or beat-up, faded, ragged jeans
- Open sandals
- Flip-flops
- Anklets

Pop singer Britney Spears might flaunt her midriff and belly ring, but that's part of her image marketing. Unless you're banking on selling (out?) yourself sexually, don't model your own self-marketing after her.

Apparently, some women must be working on their own remixes of "I'm a slave for you." Either that, or they missed an important message. On one recent trip to the bank, a teller's thong was in plain sight. There she was, perched on her chair handling large transactions of cash and giving financial advice, and her thong was playing peek-a-boo with the customers. Were we supposed to leave her a tip after making our checking account withdrawal?

Ah, the Britney Spears phenomenon. Less clothing equals less credibility in the workplace. Sometimes women look more like they are dressing for access than for success.

This is a female problem. How is a man going to dress sexy at work? Tight leather pants? A mesh shirt? Better yet, he could go for the 1970s John Travolta look: tight poly pants and a big-collared shirt unbuttoned to his waist, revealing his hairy chest. Throw on a couple of gold stud chains, and he's good to go. What message do you get when your cubicle-mate dresses like Austin Powers trying to find his mojo? A real turn-on. Yeah, baby.

Any woman who thinks it's acceptable to flaunt her body 24/7 is, to put it mildly, confused. Understandably, the workplace dress code is still ambiguous. It's easy to make mistakes when Casual Fridays have leaked into the rest of the week. Plus, celebrities are setting unreasonable standards. But remember, they go to premieres, not offices.

code **SWITCH** *If a person's dress is affecting your productivity, share this with your human resources department. You need to air your concerns. If this person's attire is offending you, it may be offending other employees and clients.*

A Sexually Charged Workplace Environment

Napoleon said, "A man becomes a creature of his uniform." This was driven home recently when Audrey was called in on a sexual harassment case at a dotcom company. As she walked up to the reception counter for initial interviews with the alleged perpetrator, the victim, and the CEO, her eyes quickly flew past the front desk to the cubicle behind it. There sat a barefoot guy in khaki shorts and a Hawaiian shirt. It looked like he was on vacation. All he was missing was an umbrella drink.

We believe the lax dress code at this company contributed to the frat-house behavior that many of its male employees exhibited. Loose and lively may be a climate ideal for spring break and wild parties, but at this office, it contributed to a sexually charged atmosphere that set the stage for salacious comments and antics.

Do you dress for access or to impress? Our appearance can have a definite impact on others. That's bad if you don't like to take care of your appearance, if you're lazy, or if you're particularly obsessed with Hawaiian shirts. But that's good if you realize that you have major control over this avenue of nonverbal communication. It's much easier to comb your hair and button your blouse than to control every nonverbal facial expression that passes through your eyebrows.

And don't say you can't afford to dress nicely. A button-up shirt and a T-shirt cost the same at most stores. Organizations in many cities sponsor clothing swaps and business attire give-aways. Stylists agree that if you buy just a few high-quality items of clothing, such as a suit or a blazer, you end up spending less in the long run than if you buy many cheap, lower-quality items for your wardrobe. Consider it a cost-to-wear ratio; the more you wear something, the less each individual wear costs. So over several years, that $200 jacket that you can wear all the time ends up a lot cheaper than that $15 T-shirt you wore twice and stuffed into the back of your closet. It's not about how much you spend, but about how *smart* you spend—and how you put it all together. Your wardrobe is your storefront to selling yourself. So what do you look like you're selling? (*Hint:* It shouldn't be your body.)

Look around at your office. Are you impressed yet? There's a huge sex difference in dressing for "access." For obvious reasons, women's clothing has more potential for violating appropriate dress for the workplace. It's hard for a man to dress sexy at work.

A double standard might be at work here. Do we have different dress codes for men and women? For example, could we have dress codes that could prohibit a man from wearing pierced earrings or long hair? Could we insist on the same for women? Disney allows one hole in each woman's ear and no pierced earrings for men. As a general rule, corporations can have different dress code rules for men and women.

Most employers realize that social norms, business needs, and safety should guide dress codes. If a dress code is applied uniformly, it does not violate a person's civil rights.

Consider a few specific guidelines for women:

- Lean in toward a mirror. If you see cleavage, change your top.

- The "2-inch rule" applies to hemlines and height of heels. Any hemline that is more than 2 inches above the knee (we have seen 3 to 5 inches in some Fortune 50 companies!) is simply too short. If a heel is higher than 2 inches, it's simply too tall. Most shoes for women are designed to call attention to their legs, at the cost of comfort and safety. If the building catches fire, how fast can you run to safety in heels? Stilettos—heels that are 3 inches and up—are specifically designed for sex appeal, to push up the calf muscle and draw attention to the leg.

- Say no to spandex. Work is not the place for provocative, tight-fitting apparel.

- Feel a draft at your midriff? Close the gap. Skin showing between your shirt and waistline? Don't wear it. It may be okay for a club, but it's not appropriate for work.

Be aware of brand names or words on shirts that could be inflammatory or offensive, or that could hurt your credibility. Bridget, a journalist, wore a shirt that said "Jesus is my homeboy" underneath a blazer to work. Then she was sent out to cover a religious-based abortion protest. Bridget's shirt, although not offensive, tainted her credibility as an "unbiased" reporter; she looked like she was part of the protest. The truth of this was driven home when another journalist asked her if he could ask her a few questions. She had to explain that she was a professional, too.

Several trends have evolved to come to the aid of women. One is a "Peek-A-Boob-Strip," which is a double-sided fashion tape. We vividly remember watching a woman making a presentation, and with every gesture, we got a full visual of her leopard-print bra. Everyone remembered the bra; no one could recall what she said. These strips eliminate the unsightly blouse gap—no more tacky bra-viewing. (Another simple solution that many women forget: alterations. It's surprisingly inexpensive to get your clothes tailored to fit you, and then you don't have to worry about any awkward bulges or gaps.)

Another recent movement is organizations setting up meetings with their female employees and local department stores like Nordstrom. They use personal shoppers to educate women on appropriate bras with enough padding to keep nipples from showing.

The Worst Offenders: Gen X and Gen Y Women

Generation X and Y women have created interesting trends in appearance, and they bring those trends to work with them. These women aren't pleased to hear us remind them that employees give up some First Amendment rights when they come to work. As children of the 1960s, we remember well the freedom of expression in dress. However, an employer can dictate a standard of dress. Few organizations have a specific and detailed list of dress code and appearance violations, a crucial proactive measure for all of them. If organizations had these guidelines, it would help eliminate violations. But there are always a few who will push the boundaries despite being told what to wear and what not to wear to work. Gen X and Y women are presenting a challenge for ill-prepared organizations.

You might not agree with the rules, but that doesn't change them. Sarah, a 22-year-old employee fresh out of college, was infuriated when her boss told her she couldn't wear colored tights to work. Sarah took great pride in her appearance, always wearing blouses and blazers and modest dresses. In the winter, she liked to wear colorful tights; they were warmer than pantyhose, and they were also in style. But her boss said they violated the dress code. She had no choice but to leave her colored tights at home.

Now city governments are getting in on the act of enforcing dress code rules. Lynwood, Illinois, wants its bottoms covered. Lynwood passed an ordinance stating that people who expose 3 inches of their underwear will be fined $25, making Lynwood the first Chicago-area town to crack down (no pun intended) on low-slung pants. Following suit, in Riviera, Florida, the fine is

$150, and in Flint, Michigan, offenders can be fined $500 and face time in the slammer.

Body Piercing and Tattoos

Another Gen X/Y trend is what we call the *pin-cushion syndrome*, body piercing in any and all parts of the anatomy. But body "art" doesn't always work at work.

Although body art is common in college communities, twenty-somethings who adorn themselves with multiple piercings might find themselves on the wrong side of corporate dress codes.

And then there are tattoos. Although tattoos today are prevalent on everyone from grandmas to preachers to CEOs, the stigma is not entirely gone.

One woman, Deana, had one full arm sleeve and several facial piercings and had a hard time finding someone who would hire her. The only places that she could find work were at an alternative barber shop, as a plumber, and with a tow-truck service. (Granted, we weren't there for her interviews, and we didn't talk to her references about her work ethic.)

One restaurant chain failed to check any of its servers or bartenders for felonies (several had long rap sheets), but it required staff to cover all tattoos and remove piercings. The body mods might offend or repulse customers, the policy stated. (As if the customers wouldn't be worried by a sex offender serving up their soup.)

On the other hand, many tattoo shops will attest that some of their best customers are law enforcement officials, firefighters, and military men and women—jobs with high social regard but apparently less strict policies on tattoos. And one IT manager, Edward, says the small tattoo on his arm once opened up a conversation with a colleague that eventually brought him a promotion.

Tattoos also bring up problems when they go beyond simple markings. One woman, Brenda, says she regrets her choice to get a large tattoo on her bicep one night when she was drunk on spring break: a Looney Tunes character with devil horns and a tail dancing on a stripper pole.

A decade later, Brenda landed a job as a high-profile attorney. She says she always wore long-sleeved blazers to hide her embarrassing mark. One day, she was sitting in her office working on papers and she took off her jacket. Just then a client burst through the door, unannounced. Brenda says she spun around in her chair and dove under her desk. She says she didn't want him to see her tattoo because she thought it would discredit her—not to mention open up a story she didn't want to touch.

When the case was over, the client confessed to Brenda that he had seen her tattoo. And it made him keep her as his attorney. He said it had impressed him because he figured she was "tough" and "fearless," qualities he wanted in his lawyer.

Still, Brenda keeps her Looney Tunes stripper devil under cover. And she can't wait to get it removed some day.

Unless you work for one of the handful of surviving Internet start-ups, wearing vintage Pumas and a ratty band tee to work may no longer cut the mustard. According to the American Industry Dress Code Survey, a national poll of 201 senior executives at companies with more than $500 million in annual revenue, more than half of large businesses (56 percent) maintain a business attire policy. That means a suit and tie for the guys and a suit or dress for the gals.

Of course we all know different professions have different dress codes. For example, a barista or hairstylist dresses by a different set of rules.

Why Organizations Need a Dress Code Policy

A crucial proactive measure for all organizations is to have a specific and detailed punch list for dress code and appearance violations. Few of our clients have this in place. Consequently, they often create more problems and potentially embarrassing situations—not to mention driving customers and clients away. Recently, Audrey tried to buy a bagel at her local shop and she was unable to look the employee in the face due to his heart-stopping body art.

Our single biggest piece of advice: when in doubt, don't wear it! If you're questioning whether a blouse is too transparent, it probably is. Err on the side of dressing conservatively at work. This goes for company picnics and outings, too. Audrey was leading a company retreat at a luxury five-star resort in the Caribbean. Much of the time, she worked outdoors with the group, either around the pool or at the beach. One of the female attendees wore a tiny bikini. It seems Melissa forgot she was supposed to be at work; she thought she was on vacation. She was the talk of the retreat and the brunt of snide jokes for months thereafter. A one-piece or modest two-piece bathing suit was in order, not a sexy thong, especially when hanging out (literally) with coworkers.

Although the right clothes won't necessarily get you hired or promoted, the wrong ones can sure get in your way. Trying to decipher today's dress code is tough business. All clothing is context bound. That sassy spandex skirt is fun—at the club; it's a mine field at work.

Now, we're not trying to play fashion police. But we do care about your professional health and the image you're projecting. Remember, the wrong choice when you go to your closet in the morning can threaten your credibility and be a distracting barrier to successful communication. You cannot *not* communicate in your dress. We are constantly broadcasting who we are through our attire. What are you broadcasting?

9

Fight Fair and Get What's Yours

Generally, nice girls don't cause conflict. Conflict is not feminine. Women are supposed to be the peacemakers, both at the office and at home. Women are taught to be cooperative and play the role of peacemaker. Their job supposedly is to not rock the boat; men get that role. A woman's world revolves around connection and relationships, and they place a premium on interdependence—so high, in fact, that women tend to avoid and accommodate others in conflict situations. They often say "yes" when they want to say "no." They go along to get along. They sacrifice what is important to them and don't get their needs met. The myth many women live by is "Harmony is normal." If harmony is normal, conflict is abnormal.

Do any of these themes resonate with you?

- Taking care of others
- Taking a back seat
- Acting dumb
- Being the power behind the throne
- Suffering silently
- Waiting to be saved
- Playing nice
- Being seen, not heard
- Sacrificing yourself for others

➤ Being a people pleaser

➤ Not rocking the boat

➤ Making peace

These themes become blueprints for how we handle conflict and the roles we play.

Using Playground Skills to Battle in the Cubicles

From childhood to adulthood, men are taught to be aggressive, competitive, and independent (they actually score notches on their macho belt for standing alone on an issue). Men are interested in power—how to get it and use it. Women are taught not to hurt people's feelings, so they will go along to get along.

Bullying and Bantering: It's a Boy's World

If you're a girl, the playground isn't a bully pulpit. If you're a boy bully, you're not only accepted, but you're among the more popular kids in school.

Hang on a minute. Does this sound like a double standard?

A study at Purdue University by child development expert Laura Hess shows that a marked sex difference exists as early as elementary school when it comes to styles of handling conflict. According to Hess, "Woe to the girl who is overly aggressive. ... Our research shows that girls who are disruptive and aggressive are at a much greater risk of being rejected by their peers than are their male counterparts."

Boys are indeed more aggressive than girls. Drive by an elementary-school playground and watch the boys throwing each other to the ground, grabbing and hitting each other. Boys and men often compete and confront each other with banter, joking, and playful put-downs to avoid the one-down position.

Most boys and men like to fight. They start when they're young and keep it up to the grave. For many men, fighting is part of the game—it's sport. We see it all the time in corporate America. Men verbally duke it out in the

Monday morning staff meeting, only to be slapping each other on the back in the company cafeteria at lunch the same day. They're ready to go at each other again tomorrow. This is an alien world for most women.

As boys enter high school, banter and playful insults replace the hitting and punching. Linguist Deborah Tannen suggests that banter is a form of "verbal mock attack." Among men, this is often how they express "intimacy" toward each other. Yes, intimate attacks.

Girls and women are caught off guard when boys and men banter. Women take the banter literally and misread it for a "real" fight. Women seldom banter. It is almost nonexistent in female culture and can often cause moments of discomfort for women when men engage in this predictable ritual.

Audrey recalls a managers' meeting she was attending for a client. In the middle of the meeting, the conversation turned to the failure of securing a big contract. Bill was addressing his disappointment when Mike jumped in and said, "Maybe next time you'll know what you're doing!" Bill didn't skip a beat and retorted, "Well, I couldn't have lost this big fish without your input, pal!" Audrey learned that Bill was the lead and Mike was on the team that had courted the contract. They were good friends, and this was a way of expressing their disappointment, as well as confirming the friendship. Audrey learned from talking to other members of the management team that Bill and Mike engaged in this bonding ritual of banter at almost every meeting.

But the scene is different when it's male and female coworkers. At a work book-sale fundraiser, Gregg was collecting money for the purchases. Brittany owed him $9.50 for her books and handed Gregg $10. She waited for him to give her change, and he jumped in, "What, you can't spare 50¢ to donate to the cause? What's wrong with you?" He was smiling and meant the comment in a friendly way. But Brittany's face dropped. She walked out and began to cry. And you can bet she talked about his comment for months among her female coworkers. In fact, she probably still holds it against him today.

Men enjoy and appreciate an adversarial stance. It is a form of a compliment: "You care enough to fight with me." They see challenge as a way of honoring someone's knowledge or position. Men like to play devil's advocate. They like to take someone's idea and rip it apart and turn it upside down. Men never get over ritual combat. Women would prefer for everyone to play nice, and they want everyone to agree in a discussion. Look around the room next time a heated debate begins; you'll observe women getting uncomfortable. We've seen women excuse themselves from a meeting when things get too hot.

SWITCH IT UP!

The next time a man is play-fighting and you're thinking this is war, remember that it's only a little rumble. He enjoys the process more than you. That's motivation for you to get over it quickly. Men often turn business into a game, and they want to spar with their opponents. This isn't an emotional crisis—just a little fun. Lighten up!

Girls and Relationship Currency and Retaliation

Girls generally play cooperatively in groups. Boys organize themselves into *hierarchical* groups more than girls do, with one designated leader. The rest of the boys are left to jockey for second and third positions by acting tough and aggressive.

When a new shop opened in town—with five male employees—the first three months were spent trying to establish hierarchy. When Jonathan put on a CD, Zach always walked back and changed it to something he liked. Then Jonathan refused to help Zach with his work; in turn, Zach made snide remarks about Jonathan and picked fights with him. When Jonathan's girlfriend saw what was going on, she was upset.

"How can you let him treat you like that? What kind of friend is he?" she asked.

Jonathan just smiled. He knew this was just a typical struggle to determine A-dog. And he knew he was going to win.

When girls want to seek social justice on the playground, they usually act out through indirect aggression. For example, a study by child psychologists Jessica Giles and Gail Heyman revealed that when a girl wants to be mean to a boy, she often resorted to "I'm telling." This is a social action of *retributive justice* and a form of indirect aggression. Boys demonstrate more direct aggression by attempting to physically hurt others. Girls employ what they have already learned and do well. They use *relational methods* to damage the cohesion or intimacy goals of the group, especially if it is a group of other girls. Boys are socialized to value status and seek victory. The training ground is often the playground, where adult supervision is not as intense as in the classroom. Boys are freer to test the norms of dealing with conflict. From the playground to the workplace, we see this scene played out.

A woman who had worked on a team for five years was promoted to manager of another division. Many of the women on her team envied her promotion. As social retribution, they excluded her from the baby shower for one of the women team members. They were punishing her by not inviting her, and this leveled the playing field. She got the promotion; they got to exclude her. The exclusion was the power equalizer. She was now outside the "community" of the female team members.

In their book *Why Men Don't Listen and Women Can't Read Maps*, Barbara and Allan Pease quote an interesting study. This study, conducted in five Western countries, asked men and women to describe the kind of person they would ideally like to be. Men overwhelmingly chose adjectives such as *bold, competitive, capable, dominant, assertive, admired,* and *practical.* Women chose adjectives such as *warm, loving, generous, sympathetic, attractive, friendly,* and *giving.* Understanding what each gender values can affect your conflict communication with your coworkers, boss, and customers. When men engage in conflict, we see the bold and dominant characteristics play out. Likewise, with women, we see attempts to maintain a warm approach, to foster the relationship.

Nice Girls Don't Do Conflict

Engaging in conflict is perceived as unfeminine. It requires a great deal of assertiveness, which may include rocking the boat. A woman's role is to be the peacemaker, master negotiator, Office Mom, and smoother of all ripples of conflict at work. Girls receive the message early: sugar and spice and everything nice are the ingredients from which they are made. When a woman expresses anger, she is questioned. Are hormones driving this outburst? Is she being emotional? For men, expressions of anger are sanctioned. In fact, anger is one of the few emotions men can express publicly. We look to men to lead us into battle and women to heal the wounded and minimize the fatalities.

Women Try to Get Over Anger Like They Have the Flu

In *The Princessa: Machiavelli for Women,* Harriet Rubin claims that "when the tension is overwhelming, women often withdraw, or react in anger, then regret the outburst." Women try to shake off anger like a bad cold. Then they apologize or compromise. They go back to their cubicle and start undoing— they try to convince themselves that it really wasn't that important; it just isn't worth it. Look what they do with children: they cuddle the anger out of the child. Any tension women feel at work can paralyze them.

But anger is a natural human emotion that means you have boundaries. Anger is life affirming; it calls for change. Anger is a signal that something is wrong. If women hold back anger, they deprive themselves of dealing with issues within us and other people. Holding anger back does not make it go away.

Not only is the "nice girl" syndrome unhealthy, but it also earns women no respect from their coworkers by staying silent, acting hurt, crying, and playing the martyr. Instead, women store up a warehouse of anger.

So begins a self-perpetuating cycle that leads to other dysfunctional behaviors, like guilt. We are so concerned about being nice and "Queen for a Day" that we will be popular at any cost. Women have a high need to please. In conflict, it is an adaptation. Girls and women are expected to comply with the "rules" and socially controlled behavior far more rigidly than boys. When men break the rules in corporate America, they are mavericks. When women break the rules, they cross the line. Male behavior enjoys a larger latitude of acceptance: boys will be boys.

Women learn compliance as a primary method of coping because they need to please other people to feel okay. "Make everyone happy" becomes their mantra. Many women anxiously mold themselves to fit what they believe everyone wants them to be at work. Now we lose women's objective opinions and the team suffers from their lack of input. They have no opinion because they don't even know what it is anymore; they've spent so many years pleasing others and trying to say what they want to hear. Of course, this is a trap. No matter what a woman does, often it is never enough; she will never receive total approval from others.

> Audrey had a 2-year consulting contract with a major telecommunications company. The CEO wanted to make his organization more "female friendly," to attract and retain women engineers. He organized an all-hands-on-deck managers' meeting for Audrey to deliver the good, the bad, and the ugly on how the organization treated women. Her report was controversial, and the CEO was concerned that some managers would miss this critical meeting. He instructed her to get the session videotaped so the missing managers could get the report. When Audrey consulted with the company's operations manager, he hesitated because the legal department did not think it was a good idea to have this report on record. She followed the "rules"; she didn't even think about breaking the rules and having the session taped, despite the warning from the legal department.
>
> When Audrey and the CEO walked into the meeting, he looked around for the videographers. He asked Audrey where they were. She replied that his legal department hadn't thought it was a good idea, so she'd acquiesced. He retorted, "Since when do you listen to lawyers?" It was a poignant moment for Audrey. Is this how CEOs operate? They don't always follow authority. They question it and make up their own rules.

For women, the situation often boils down to "See no evil, hear no evil, speak no evil." Harriett Lerner, a psychotherapist at the Menninger Foundation, explains the difficulties women have expressing anger in her book *The Dance of Anger*. She writes about the "bitchy woman":

> Those of us who are "bitches" are not shy about getting angry and stating our differences. However, in a society that does not particularly value angry women, this puts us in danger of earning one or another of those labels that serve as a warning to silence us when we threaten others, especially men. Like the word "unfeminine" but even more so, these labels may have the power to shock us into silence, or to further inflame us by intensifying our feelings of injustice and powerlessness.

About three decades of psychological research tells us that women have higher rates of depression than men. The operational definition of depression is anger turned inward. Women suppress their anger, and men express it. A woman can take the anger out on herself by feeling guilty, depressed, and self-doubting. The cost is high, and the taboo on showing anger is too great.

The Learned Helplessness Syndrome

Women learn at a young age that they get more strokes for being childlike. They get rewarded for acting helpless, weak, and dependent. The image of a John Wayne character often played by male colleagues and bosses comes to mind.

She acts helpless: "I just can't figure this out. This is too hard."

He steps in and plays his role: "Hey, little lady, step aside and let me take care of this."

In fact, Amber has found that her occasional helplessness at work improves her male boss's attitude so much that she intentionally asks for help, even when she doesn't need it. When she is "too competent," he begins acting aggressive and grumpy—maybe even threatened. But after she asks for his help on something, he softens and becomes less confrontational. He literally sits at his desk smiling; Amber notices that and feels like she has done something right. She considers this just part of the game. But at the end of the day, it makes her angry at herself.

In the 1950s and '60s, a popular idea arose that women could get things done by acting helpless. A man always wants to rescue a damsel in distress. Talk about a sick relationship. The only way she can get things done is by acting weak. This certainly does not promote capable women. Some men suspect the manipulation and resent it. It certainly is an unequal and unbalanced relationship: you act weak, and I can act strong and save you.

Of course, when a woman acts strong and independent, she doesn't need help, and he doesn't have the opportunity to realize his power.

Some men are known to treat women at work like their daughter. A paternal role develops. This learned helplessness syndrome undermines her ability to handle conflict issues. It pries women from their own core of healthy self-centeredness and opportunity to achieve what is important to them and to get their needs met.

The Queen of Passive-Aggressive Behavior

Women often exhibit more indirect ways of expressing their anger, like passive-aggressive behavior. A woman might get mad at someone not directly, but indirectly. Passive-aggressive behavior may appear innocent on the surface (conveniently misunderstanding something, forgetting something, being tardy), but underneath the behavior, a rage flows. Passive-aggressive behavior is like a big fluffy dog that licks you and pees on you at the same time. I smile as I stick the knife in.

The danger is that the conflict is never addressed directly. It isn't discussed or explicitly recognized, and everyone makes nice.

Consider some of the more common passive-aggressive games women play:

- Sarcastic sniping (hostile sarcasm)
- Convenient misunderstandings
- Convenient forgetfulness
- Mocking (appears to be playful)
- Silent treatment
- Crimes behind the scenes (sabotage work)

Audrey was addressing a group of women support staff of a Fortune 50 company for Secretaries' Day and asked them how they handled anger toward their bosses. One woman reported that she had been angered by her boss's orders, especially to get him a cup of coffee. So she just spit in it before she gave it to him. While the audience collectively gasped, she explained that it took care of all her anger toward his demeaning orders. She couldn't directly address the issue with him, but she took care of it indirectly.

Barb has her own method of passive-aggression: a sort of martyr game. She felt like she wasn't paid enough at work, but instead of asking for a raise, she got a second job. She spends a lot of time at her first job complaining about how busy she is, how tight money is, and how much she hates her other job. She somehow thinks this will guilt her boss into giving her a raise or make him feel bad about how hard her life is. But really, the only person she is punishing is herself. And her boss gets away with still paying her so little.

Anger is an important signal in conflict that cannot be ignored. Anger can signal a crossed boundary, express frustration that things aren't right, and, most important, maintain the integrity of our self. Women who openly express anger at men are especially suspect. An angry woman is undesirable. Just the act of directly expressing anger, especially at men, makes women unladylike, unfeminine, and unmaternal. After all, women are here to take care of people, both at work and at home.

One of the greatest challenges in conflict is allowing the productive expression of anger. Women may have to be coached that it is "safe" to express anger without jeopardizing their femininity.

The Crying Game

Women are taught to be "highly expressive"—that is, they can express all their emotions, especially by crying. Emotions are a female trademark, but men report having feelings just as often as women. They just don't express them.

In an analysis of 500,000 adults, men rated just as high as women in emotional awareness. But men process and express emotions differently than women, and they have no roadmap for how to combine the masculine requirement of being strong and emotional at the same time. A woman cries and a man loses his temper; that seems to be the pervasive theme in many conflicts. Men and women react differently; she shows her vulnerability and he must remain in control.

Yet a woman gets into risky business when she cries. She is often perceived in one of two ways. First, she is weak, emotional, and out of control. Second, she is using her tears as emotional blackmail, a form of manipulation, and he resents it. For a woman, crying is a no-win situation.

This is a dilemma for women, because the tears may flow naturally when we are worked up.

Audrey had a client who claimed that a pressing problem at work was causing her to lose sleep and become anxious. When Audrey asked, "Why haven't you approached your manager?" The woman replied, "I'm waiting until I'm sure I won't start crying."

A useful technique for women in this kind of situation is "pre-cuing." Set up the conflict communication, and possible tears, for a win. Tell the person that you're very concerned and upset about what you're preparing to discuss. If you subsequently get upset, say that you will take responsibility for your tears and you want him to take responsibility for what you are saying. Many women have reported that when they indicate that they may "lose it" and start to cry, they actually gain a sense of more control and end up not crying. This pre-cuing technique handles the credibility issue for an out-of-control woman and also eliminates the perception of manipulation. The receiver knows that the tears are a product of concern and frustration.

One of the biggest mistakes men make in conflict is perceiving a woman's tears as an indication of sadness. Then the man begins to console the woman. She may respond by getting snappy, because he has misread the cue. Underneath a woman's tears is seldom sadness—but rather anger! Although the man is experiencing a high discomfort level with her tears, he needs to get at the anger she is feeling.

Big boys don't cry, except if you are President of the United States. Elizabeth Bumiller, a columnist for *The New York Times*, documented that the "bawler in chief" may be setting a new standard for men. She cites several accounts, some almost back-to-back, of George W. Bush shedding a tear: "George W. Bush became the first American president to weep in Iraq. Reporters ... noted a very visible tear dripping down his cheek when he was greeted by whooping American soldiers. ... The fact is, Mr. Bush cries all the time. Two days after Sept. 11, 2001, his eyes welled up during a phone call with Gov. Giuliani. The following day, he nearly lost his composure while speaking to the nation from the National Cathedral. The president ... has helped make it safe for men to cry in the open."

Former President Bush is said to have asked his doctor if he could "prescribe anything to dry up his tears." True, we see more men crying publicly. However, the context has to be highly defined and emotionally charged to warrant such a display. It takes a war—an act of terror, in the case of President Bush.

Same Ends, Different Means

Men and women have different conflict styles. Communication professors William Wilmot and Joyce L. Hocker summarize some of the key issues for men and women in conflict:

1. Interdependence vs. power over others

2. Mutual empathy as the basis for understanding and communicating

3. Relational self-confidence vs. separate self-esteem (autonomy)

4. Constructive conflict vs. domination

5. Level of engagement with others while in a conflict

6. Separate knowledge vs. connected knowledge

7. Report talk vs. rapport talk

8. Continuation of dialogue during disagreement

We know that women value connectedness and feel interdependent in conflicts. Men, on the other hand, tend to dominate and try to gain power over others. During a conflict, a woman's self-esteem and confidence ride on her ability to maintain a workable relationship. Women do a lot of rapport talk to check in on how the relationship is surviving the stress of a conflict. A woman may say things like, "I know this is hard for us now, but we can figure this out" or "You are important to me and so is our working relationship. I want you to be satisfied with this decision." This is difficult for women sometimes because men do little of that rapport talk or relationship maintenance. A man generally focuses on reporting the "facts" and pertinent information. A woman views this as being removed and thinks he may not be as invested in staying engaged in the relationship. Many women wish men would do more of this psychological stroking in a conflict. But this is often women's work.

Power: The Center of All Conflicts

All conflict revolves around power. Always. There's no getting around it. Who has the power? How do they use their power?

Power bases also can shift during a conflict. One moment, someone is in the driver's seat; then something can happen to usurp that person's power and put someone else in that position. If you strip away all the issues, topics, and details of a conflict, you will always find a power struggle underneath.

Power and gender are interconnected. Traditionally, men have had power over women in the workplace. More men than women hold legitimate power positions (president, CEO, chair, and so on). Men have followed a tradition of denying women access to power positions. Women who have little or no power are not really free to say what they think. Consequently, in a conflict, women often feel that their viewpoint often is not represented, is minimized, or is ignored, both in the workplace and at home.

"Hey, that was my idea! But nobody heard it until he said it!" This is a complaint we've heard from women for decades. A woman expresses her viewpoint, and the committee goes on to the next agenda item without acknowledging her input. Then 10 minutes later, a man says the exact same idea and the group acts like it's the best thing since baked bread. The woman is furious. Does she play nice, keep her mouth shut, and act like nothing happened? No, she steps up and gets the credit she deserves while helping the group save face. It sounds something like this: "Hey, Bob, thanks so much for bringing up my point again. I am glad the team is willing to consider the merits of my plan."

Instead of repressing that moment of anger, channel it to your advantage. Be calm. Eliminate vocal cues of resentment. You're simply taking care of business—the business of your gaining respect and credit when you deserve it.

When It's Over, It's Over!

One of the most common complaints I hear from men about how women handle conflict is that they don't let go and move on. A male manager had a female coworker bring up a mistake that happened a year ago on their respective projects. It was an honest mistake that had impacted her. Everyone felt bad and apologized to her. Apparently, that wasn't good enough.

For a woman, if the conflict is addressed on the content and issues but not on the emotional level, she'll hit you over the head until she's satisfied that you have truly empathized with her feelings. If the conflict doesn't go to this depth, she will continue to be annoyed. This becomes cumulative annoyance. She begins compiling secret mental lists of grievances known only to her. This progresses to gunnysacking. She stores it up and keeps adding to the sack of complaints. Then one day, look out. She comes unglued and unloads. This is really a sophisticated form of avoidance. It is also not productive. The woman appears to be out of control when she goes on her tirade and spouts off an endless list of complaints.

code **SWITCH** *Let your coworkers know it's important for them to realize how frustrated, disappointed, and disregarded you feel. Spell it out. Tell them the issue is not as relevant as their ability to understand how you feel about what happened. Be firm. Use a serious tone. Don't soften it with a smile or contradictory behavior. Be respectful but forceful.*

It's Okay to Say "No"

Women often create more conflict for themselves because they are not proactive. Every day our boss and coworkers will test our boundaries. Just like your children, they will push, push, push you to see how far they can go. The ability to say "No" is critical in our daily lives. But, again, it is difficult for women to say "No" because they want to be liked and don't want to rock the boat.

Leigh, a reporter, was heading home from work one night when her boss stopped her.

"Is your column in?" her editor asked.

"What column?" Leigh hadn't been told that she was supposed to write a column that day, and the package they were talking about wasn't scheduled to run for weeks.

"I need you to write a column," the editor responded.

Leigh could have said "No," or she could have easily done it the next day; she had plans that night with friends, and she hadn't had a free night for weeks. But instead, she sulked back to her desk and spent her evening writing something she hadn't even known she needed to write and didn't need to write that night. She was too afraid of upsetting her boss. And you can bet that she wrote that column with fingers fueled by passive-aggression.

The yes-no-yes sandwich works well for women because of the relational component. When Audrey presents this formula to audiences, women buy into the ability to say "No" because it establishes and ends with an emphasis on preserving the relationship. William Ury, who directs the Global Negotiation Project at Harvard, states in his book *The Power of a Positive No: How to Say No and Still Get to Yes* that the wrong "No" can alienate people. The secret to saying "No" without destroying the relationship is a technique that recognizes that saying "No" isn't easy and can put relationships in jeopardy. This appeals to women's need to maintain the relationship.

The first "Yes" is a yes to your needs—your boundaries, wants, and desires. If that "Yes" is grounded and uncontaminated, saying "No" is easier and clear. The last "Yes" in the yes-no-yes sandwich is a "Yes" to the relationship. Ury suggests if we forget to do this, it destroys relationships. After all, we have to go to work with the same people every day. We need to maintain the relationship.

A technique for saying "No" is to frame it with "I have a policy." Here are some examples:

- "I have a policy of not loaning money to coworkers."
- "I have a policy of not serving on boards."
- "I have a policy of choosing educational groups for charity."
- "I have a policy of not dating my coworkers."

When you have to say "No" to demands or a request, always try to offer an alternative. That is a "No" with a positive solution that addresses *their* needs while still meeting *yours*.

Imagine that you are a manager and one of your best employees comes in and asks for a raise. You indicate that the budget will not allow for this increase. You have to say "No." The employee walks out of the office looking disappointed and defeated. Instead of risking losing such a good employee, you brainstorm about other options that would stay within your budget and address the employee's needs. Maybe he would like to be appointed to a prestigious committee or get specialized training, a new computer, or additional responsibility. The goal is to invent things for mutual gain.

Do You Want to Take It Outside?

Carly Fiorina has been the female poster child for breaking barriers in the corporate world. She took a big fall, but she's back. She was the unofficial attack dog on women's issues for the GOP, speaking out on gender whenever the occasion required. During her early days at Hewlett-Packard, she remembers the blogs circulating in Silicon Valley: "I was routinely called a bimbo or the other b-word. This happens to women all the time. ... I don't think we have enough practice with women in positions of authority."

Fiorina's very public six years as CEO of HP were a prime example of a woman in a power position taking risks. When she confronted two board members for leaking confidential conversations, she confronted them directly. Head on, she said, "We cannot operate this way as a board. We need to talk about why you felt it necessary to do that."

Ten days later, Fiorina was fired. Sometimes women are scrutinized more for doing battle. Sometimes women pay the price. A woman who puts herself in positions of power must be able to take on conflict and know that when the gloves come off, she may not win.

But as in the case for Fiorina, one door closes and another opens. Life goes on. It is risky business, and if you can't stand the heat, get out of the kitchen— or the boardroom.

Let's Come Together

Women value community and connectedness. Often they sacrifice their own needs and wants for the sake of the relationship. Women rationalize away the real importance of the issue and harbor an unhealthy anger. Maybe that is why in our gender communication seminars we hear men ask, "Why do women never forget and drag stuff out you did two years ago?" Well, she never addressed the conflict. She chose to internalize it. She also strives to empathize and believes that building rapport and continuing dialogue is the way to manage the conflict. "Let's talk it out" could be a mantra for women.

In contrast, men can become like hermit crabs. They pull in when they feel threatened or when they begin losing in a conflict. Men don't want to be bullied or cajoled into sharing emotions. They feel more comfortable with report talk, not rapport talk. He wants to "report" the circumstances and offer logical and unemotional ideas. She wants to talk about her feelings and, most important, check on the relationship through rapport talk.

Men want solutions to problems, and women look for understanding of their problems. Men believe expressing disagreement is a sign of intimacy. Women think expressing disagreement is a threat to intimacy. Men like to play devil's advocate, and women want to be the angel who helps everyone agree in discussion. There's no right or wrong to these approaches—just differences. If we understand how men operate in conflict, it can help women reframe the conflict.

Conflict is inevitable. It is a natural, normal part of life. Where there are relationships, there will be conflict. A component of successful relationships is the ability of women to handle conflict in the boardroom. In fact, a couple's ability to handle conflict is often considered one of the keys to a successful marriage.

A strong measure of managers' success is their ability to deal with workplace conflict, not act like it doesn't exist. No workplace is without conflict. When women lack productive conflict-management tools and don't understand gender differences, costly problems can result, such as retention problems, low morale, and poorly functioning teams. Women can learn more productive responses and help others resolve their disputes.

The Chinese character for conflict consists of two different symbols: one for "opportunity" and the other for "danger." All conflicts have the potential to pull people apart or bring them closer together. Women have the opportunity to take the bull by the horns and express the ultimate talent of creating a bridge and bringing people together. That is what we do well.

10

Ask for What You Deserve

Who negotiates better, men or women? On one hand, some may argue that men have a more competitive nature, are more aggressive, understand how to use power to their advantage, and appear more business savvy than women. On the other hand, others may argue women bring the relational aspect into a negotiation and look to create a win-win for both parties.

But does a woman's need to maintain the relationship impact her desire to fully negotiate? The desire to be nice—to not hurt anyone's feelings or look too selfish even when the things she's asking for are rightfully hers—may influence what a woman asks for or feels she deserves. Gender does impact the negotiation process. Assumptions about who's the "better" negotiator and other such factors can affect the process and, ultimately, the outcome of a negotiation.

Why Negotiate?

Negotiating is a way to ask for, discuss, and arrive at a settlement—hopefully what you set out to get. When someone else has something that we want or controls what we desire, negotiating is a way to exchange ideas or products to meet our needs or wishes.

U.S. culture teaches us that prices for items that we see in stores should not be questioned; there's no bargaining here. Negotiating is acceptable on only a few set items, such as the price of a home or car or a job's salary.

Most other cultures around the world have learned that the prices on almost everything can and should be negotiated. Just about anything can be negotiated.

Whether we realize it or not, we're negotiating all the time—from how many cupcakes you need to bring to the school's bake sale, to the how and when of your first sexual encounter with a new partner, to who's getting the new office furniture. We even negotiate with ourselves.

Bargaining with the Devil and Angel

You can almost see the devil and angel sitting on each of your shoulders, going back and forth: "You should stay one more hour and finish the budget report. No, you don't have the time. Yes, but if you stay now, you can sleep in late tomorrow because the report's done. Okay, you'll stay." Claire has had that conversation with herself a few times, except that her bargaining chip is usually a stop at the local ice cream store for a scoop of chocolate chip mint. Works wonders.

We bargain with ourselves in other ways, too. One woman, Jane, used to force herself into self-bargains. When she was up against a deadline at work, she bought four or five Mountain Dews and chugged them at her desk. Sure, the extra caffeine helped her crank out the pages. But Jane did this because she knew it'd turn her bladder into a time bomb. She had about 35 minutes to finish the report before she'd need to go to the restroom—and she wouldn't let herself go until she finished her work. Needless to say, Jane never missed a deadline. Of course, this could be looked at as self-abusive and in the long run, do some kidney and bladder damage. We're not recommending that anyone chug empty calories and get a caffeine high. It does illustrate what some women will do when negotiating with themselves as the winner *and* loser.

Just about every business transaction includes negotiation. When you're first hired, you have to decide upon the starting salary. Thereafter, there are promotions, salary increases, transfers, job assignments, project assignments, workloads, presentations, office equipment, reprimands, performance ratings, business trips, the corner office, ergonomic chairs, the number of vacation days, when you take vacation, deadlines, working weekends, signing contracts—ah, it never lets up.

This reminds us of one episode of the TV show *The Office*. The boss found that the business had a surplus, but they had to spend it that day. When the employees found out, they waged a battle among themselves, half in favor of a new copy machine, the other half rallying for new chairs. They tried to negotiate with the boss, down to bribing him with lunch and complimenting his tie.

Negotiation Skills = Successful Career

Good negotiation skills are tantamount to a successful career, starting with understanding the process of negotiation. First, there's preparation: understanding wants, needs, positions, interests, and your desired outcome, as well as that of the other side. Then you must communicate your views. You analyze your goals as the negotiation progresses. Eventually (hopefully sooner rather than later), you reach an outcome that is agreeable to both sides. A win-win is an ideal ending to a negotiation. Otherwise, it feels more like a manipulation, suppression, or resignation.

In *Getting to Yes*, authors Roger Fisher and William Ury of the Harvard Negotiating Project make a distinction between position and interest. A *position* is what people state they want. An *interest* is what they really want, the root that underlies their position. For example, Sue may state that her position for the negotiation is to increase her vacation days, but her interest is that she needs more time off to care for a sick parent. Knowing her interest, the other party may either grant Sue vacation days or offer her information from the human resources department on elder care services.

Fisher and Ury say a negotiation settlement is successful based on three things: "It should produce a wise agreement if agreement is possible; it should be efficient; and it should improve or at least not damage the relationship between the two parties." A wise agreement is one in which both sides believe that their interests have been met and have a feeling of fairness. As in conflict resolution, Fisher and Ury recommend focusing on the issues, not the individual people involved. This helps both parties understand each other's perspectives and better meet each other's needs.

Competition and cooperation seem to be duking it out in a negotiation. The competitive side wants to get what's best for its side and win. Meanwhile those who cooperate are looking for an outcome that both parties can live with. For a negotiation to succeed, you must find the best balance between cooperation and competition.

A cooperative strategy might involve brainstorming with the other side to develop possible options for resolution. Fisher and Ury recommend using *brainstorming*, with both sides contributing as many ideas as possible without judging them. When the brainstorming time is up, they review the list of ideas and focus on the ideas that best apply to the negotiation. They then review the selected ideas as part of the negotiation. Brainstorming is valuable since it not only provides information about each side's interests, but also generates more potential solutions.

Maintaining the relationship is of utmost importance in a win-win negotiation. Treating each other with respect and feeling that the outcome respects your goals impacts the relationship's future. Preserving the relationship is key because that's where future business may develop. Negotiating opens new doors that can solidify relationships and build admiration and self-respect for both parties.

Running Toward Negotiation Instead of Running Away

Do you have to win? Do you need a Vegas poker face? What if you feel unprepared compared to the know-it-all you're up against? Are your negotiating skills on par with those of your boss? Just what are negotiating skills? Think about this one: do you run *toward* negotiating or run *away?* Why?

Understanding your feelings, motivations, fears, goals, weaknesses, and skills helps you become more conscious and deliberate in your actions. This is the first step in growth and improvement.

Breaking the Hype

A stereotype holds that women are bad at negotiating, whereas men are great negotiators. Because of this, women often believe that they don't have the skills to successfully negotiate. If women act assertively and work for what they want, they may fear getting labeled negatively for acting outside society's expectations. Even worse, if you buy into this hype, you may set yourself up to act as if all this hype is true. It's a self-fulfilling prophecy. Unfortunately, the person you are negotiating with—man or woman—has been exposed to society's same assumptions and will react to you accordingly.

For example, imagine that a woman employee approaches a male supervisor. He's already thinking that women are not good negotiators and will react to her in that manner (no need to give in—she won't fight, she'll walk away with less and be happy, throw her a couple hundred bucks and we're done). Same goes for a woman approaching another woman to negotiate.

When the supervisor negotiates with a man, he reacts according to that hype, too (this will be tough, let's see how he plays the game, he'll ask for everything).

code SWITCH *Recognize that you and the person on the other side may have some assumptions about women's ability to negotiate. Move beyond the stereotypes. Prepare by knowing your interests and options, and knowing the other person's interests and options, too.*

Driving a Bargain

The first time Claire purchased a car, she did all the preparation: she talked with several colleagues and checked prices at different dealers. When she settled on the type of car she wanted, her friend, Jill, suggested that she talk with her friend, Sarah, who was a salesperson at the Chevrolet dealership.

Claire met with Sarah, who showed her the model and gave her the bottom-line price. Claire told her it was too high. Sarah left the room to "speak with her manager to see what else she could do." Sarah came back and told her that the offer she'd made was the best. Claire said that it was still a bit too high and that she would think it over.

The following week, Claire went to a different Chevrolet dealership and this time brought a coworker, Ken, with her. The salesperson gave them a price, Claire said it was too high, he checked with his manager, and he returned with a lower price—even lower than Sarah's price. Claire signed the papers and drove off in her new Chevy.

A few weeks later, Claire met up with Jill and Sarah. When they saw the new car, they felt shocked, hurt, and even betrayed that she had bought a car elsewhere after Sarah had taken the time to show her the model.

"Sarah gave me her bottom price, and it was too high," Claire said. "Don't you know? It's a game," Sarah replied. "You're supposed to keep asking me for a better price, and then I finally give you the real price. But you just left."

Did it help to have a man with Claire to get a better price? We don't know, but it did make Claire feel more confident as a 25-year-old purchasing a car. A lesson on negotiation: don't be afraid to demand more so that you can leave feeling comfortable and confident, and with a good deal.

Also beware of the other side's motives and techniques. Don't fall for the staged tug-of-war, the good cop/bad cop spiel. That's likely what's behind the whole "Let me go talk to the manager and see what we can do." This is probably designed to make the buyer feel like the salesperson is going out of their way to fight for them, but it is just another (predictable) negotiation strategy.

While shopping for a car, one woman, Angie, grew sick of the back-and-forth. The salesperson kept going back to the "manager" and coming back with a number circled in black marker. Angie, who had done her research and shopped around, knew the going price and shook her head. After another manager visit and a lower circled number, Angie finally asked, "Why can't I just talk to the manager firsthand? Cut out the middle man. The car lot is dead empty, and it will save us all a lot of time if we can both write down bottom-line numbers and see if they match." The salesperson was shocked and explained that it didn't work that way. Angie was forced to play by their rules or buy elsewhere.

Many women don't run toward an opportunity to negotiate. Some run away. Some stand still. The stereotypes may be holding you back from reaping the benefits you deserve.

Right out of school entering their first jobs, more men than women negotiate their starting salary. Does that mean women are being offered a higher starting salary and don't feel the need to negotiate? Not with the gender gap of unequal pay. Women get paid 77¢ for every $1 men earn, according to the U.S. Census Bureau. This pay gap is expensive—it can cost a working woman an estimated $700,000 to $2 million over the life of her career. If you narrow it down further, the earnings are even less; African American women earn 68¢ and Hispanic women earn 57¢ per $1 that men earn.

Why Ask? They'll Only Say No!

Part of the issue with approaching a negotiation is that women have been socialized to not ask, to accept what they have and be thankful. "You're lucky to even have a job. Don't rock the boat." "Don't cause any trouble, be nice, follow the rules, and make sure everyone likes you." Women may feel, "My boss is my friend. Surely if she could get more money for me, she'd do that. That's part of her job. She'll take care of me. I shouldn't have to ask."

Whether the boss is a man or a woman, women assume that the boss has their best interest in mind. This may be even more pronounced if your boss is a woman. You begin to think that you have some sort of female bond with her and that she automatically knows that you need a bigger raise, more vacation time, or an extra personal day, without your asking. Yet those things never happen. Because you never ask.

In fact, the thought to ask never occurs. Many women assume that if they work hard, they'll be noticed and that the pay and recognition will automatically be there: "If I don't get the extra bonus, I'll be disappointed, but the boss knows how hard I work and will make the right decision."

Wrong. If the boss is managing 20 people and 2 of them keep bugging her for more money, guess who will get more money at review time (assuming that everyone is doing their job)? When women do ask, they often low-ball themselves and don't ask for the big bucks. Men ask for the big bucks; they don't always get it, but they ask for top dollar.

code SWITCH *Aim high—very high—when you ask; it's easier to come down than go up.*

Sometimes women don't know that they *can* ask for something. Not socialized in the male competitive ways, many women don't realize that it's okay to ask for more pay or an extra vacation day. And when they do, they often ask for less and accept less in their bargaining. Ouch! Add this to the stereotype that women are poor negotiators, and the other side goes into the negotiation expecting to offer the woman less.

SWITCH IT UP!

Sadie worked at the same company since it was a small start-up. Over the past five years, the company grew to close to 200 people, and Sadie's responsibilities as office manager increased accordingly. One day, she mistakenly received a memo from human resources that listed the salaries of a few newer employees in what she thought were comparable positions. They were all making more money than she was. She was livid but feared talking to her boss; she didn't want to appear emotional, although this was an emotional issue for her. Instead, she drafted a job description that included her new job responsibilities, delivered it to him, and scheduled a meeting to discuss it. Eventually Sadie did get more money, but it took eight months of meeting with human resources and rewriting her job description again and again. Still, she made it. Ask. Aim high. Don't give up. Be persistent.

Not only is it okay to ask for more, but you deserve more. Studies and reports such as the classic *Primetime* 1993 segment "The Fairer Sex" showed that women generally are given higher starting prices for cars than men, and women's final deal is often higher. This also happens to ethnic and racial minorities.

Salespeople sometimes discriminate—consciously or unconsciously. The salespeople also know that women are less likely to realize that they can negotiate, are less likely to do research on prices, and might be terrible negotiators anyway, per the stereotype. Women, start asking more often for what you want.

You've heard the saying "Be careful what you ask for; you might just get it." At one college training program, we met a woman who mentors female students. The mentor said she often tells the ones who hesitate to confront their professors to "strap on their girl balls and go for it." Not that women have to act like men, but it's a reminder that women deserve more and that it's okay to take the risk and ask.

I'm Afraid! Please Don't Hurt My Feelings

Are you nervous about negotiating? You're not alone. Many women express apprehension and extreme discomfort at the thought of having to negotiate. Some women never negotiate. Women tend to choose to negotiate less than men. Even when they are aware of the potential benefits (like a bigger salary), they often decide not to negotiate. Anxiety takes over.

Women worry about their skill level. "Will I succeed? Will I fail? What if I make a mistake, what if I give in, or what if they take advantage of me?" Women tend to be afraid of losing their friendship or relationship with the other person. "What if I ask for too much money? Will they still like me? If the other side is angry or mean toward me, will my feelings get hurt?"

For some women, it's almost like they need permission before they can request more. Some may lack confidence or not have enough self-esteem to realize that they should be asking.

It's not wrong to have some fear. Studies show that after negotiating, a woman's coworkers sometimes ignore her or give her a negative label.

Asking requires action. It's being assertive. Others may view the assertive behavior as unfeminine and may label her for that, too. It's not always pretty. It's a risk. But so is sitting back and choosing to do nothing.

According to Kathleen McGinn, a Harvard professor who researched negotiation, women do better when negotiating on behalf of others than for themselves. McGinn noted that the negotiation tends to be "demasculinized" when the woman feels that she's working for her group instead of grabbing everything for herself. Regarding salary negotiations, McGinn knows that women may be afraid of being seen as aggressive, but "the perception of you if you don't negotiate is much more negative than the perception of you when you do negotiate." Look at your situation. Keep the end picture in mind. We give you permission to do what's best for you!

> ## ➤ SWITCH IT UP! ◄
>
> When Claire left the corporate setting after 25 years and began her own consulting and training business, she attended a diversity job fair. While talking with a diversity manager from a local company, she learned that a vendor she had hired in her past role as EEO/diversity manager was now hiring trainers for sexual harassment prevention courses. She waited about a week to call, not knowing whether it was presumptuous to contact him, thinking about what he might say, and not knowing for sure how he would receive the call. She called on a Wednesday and asked to be added to the group of trainers. They talked, and he explained the guidelines and pay scale for training. When they hung up, things remained up in the air. That Friday, She got the call asking if she could be on a plane Tuesday headed for the West Coast to do training. Ask for what you want and see how the world unfolds to answer your request.

Men Play the Game

When entering the workplace men tend to use the aggressive and competitive behaviors they usually learned as boys. They set out to win, speak up, go after what they want, go for the kill, and fight to the finish. Competition is a game; someone wins, someone loses. Men learn that there's nothing wrong with asking. In fact, part of the game is asking to see how much you can get.

Linda Babcock and Sara Laschever, authors of the book *Women Don't Ask,* talk about a man who had been taught when growing up to always do his best. But that wasn't enough to get the promotions and excel the way he wanted at his career. Once he learned to "sell himself," regularly talk about his successes, persistently pursue his goals and let others know of his goals, ask for better projects that would specifically show his talents, and get the experience needed to move up the ladder, then his career started to move upward more rapidly. That sounds like a lot of work, and it can be scary at first. He admitted that he was initially afraid of what might happen. Not every request was met. However, management stayed aware of his goals and ideas. The more he asked and talked up his skills, the more secure he felt and the easier it got.

Babcock and Laschever noted that "women's greater reluctance to ask for what they want often prevents them from learning this lesson—or means that they learn it more slowly." Unfortunately, many women learn the importance of asking after they've been passed up a few times for promotion or lose out on the to-die-for assignment.

code `SWITCH` *Ask. If you don't ask, you won't get it. Ask for everything, and you might get something. And something is better than nothing.*

"Negotiation through data and banter" is another descriptor of men's negotiation style, according to Michael Gurian and Barbara Annis, authors of *Leadership and the Sexes*. Men communicate the how-to's and must-haves through bravado. Who's the best, mine is bigger and better, who's got the best data, aggressive talk—all in an effort to smash the competition. They tend to keep that poker face showing little emotion.

Think of the lyrics to rap songs, mostly written by men. If the song isn't about having sex, chances are, it's about how cool the singer is, how many cars he has, how he's better than his competition, or how everyone wants to be like him. The entire gist of freestyling or improvisational rap is to come off bigger and better, even if it means tearing down the other guy. Hello, bravado overload.

Women's style, on the other hand, is considered "negotiation through rapport." This emphasizes a collaborative approach to the solution.

Both are valid styles, depending on the situation. Competitive tactics, as Babcock and Laschever put it, feature behaviors such as faking your position, holding on to unrealistic shoot-for-the-moon positions, and refusing to compromise.

code `SWITCH` *Bring your data and be prepared to move to an aggressive style. Try on that poker face with less emotion, and see what happens. You may want to try this alternate approach away from the office, perhaps when arguing with the phone company about the errors on your phone bill. Give it a try. It can help build confidence to know that you have another negotiating style you can use to fit the circumstances.*

Women Share the Pot

Women are often naturals at the collaborative relationship-building style. They pick up facial cues, body movements, and vocal tones during the negotiation and try to ensure that everyone's needs are being met. Women generally do well using integrative tactics, which Babcock and Laschever identify as questioning, making an effort to hear the other's views, and obtaining end results that are agreeable to both parties. This integrative style is effective when several issues must be resolved. Both sides learn much about each other's interests and work to address those interests by swapping smaller items back and forth, suggest Babcock and Laschever.

With competitive strategies, the focus is on defending positions at all costs and not giving in to the other side. The integrative approach looks at creating that win-win. As Fisher and Ury recommend, you must realize that both sides share certain commonalities. A woman's approach often aims to share the results; both sides feel good about the end game.

What's the Trade-Off?

Many psychology, sociology, and communication studies have looked at different aspects of gender and negotiation. They agree that women frequently use a collaborative style and men use a competitive style. The former often achieves better results in the long run because the relationship between parties remains intact, whereas the competitive approach is more expeditious. The win feels good, but it can leave the other party battered, scarred, and unwilling to do business again.

The male competitive style still appears to be the norm by which we judge others. Both men and women tend to view the collaborative style as inferior to the competitive style. A woman's approach generally takes longer, since it demands more time to attend to feelings and ensure that all views and interests are heard.

Competitive negotiation places less concern on whether both parties feel good and walk away whole. Sometimes women risk being labeled as aggressive when they choose to use a competitive style. And when women are labeled as aggressive, that's definitely not a compliment.

code SWITCH *Be aware of the impact of the style you use, and go for the impact you want.*

Good News! Negotiation Skills Can Be Learned

Learn to negotiate. Start small and work your way up to the big-tag items. In a 2007 issue of *Negotiation* magazine, Iris Bohnet and Fiona Greig, both at Harvard's Kennedy School of Government, recommended that workplaces offer negotiation courses to benefit women and men. They found that women seemed more comfortable negotiating items related to where and how they spend their time, and men were more comfortable negotiating items related to their salaries and other finance-related items. Companies can support the integrative style that lends itself more to asking questions, listening, learning interests, and maintaining the relationship—areas where women tend to excel.

Don't Wait; Negotiate

First do your homework and be prepared. Know your goals and what you want to achieve. Know what you are willing to give up or trade in the discussion. Know as much as you can about the other side's goals, positions, and interests before the meeting. Here we're looking at a win-win negotiation in which both parties can walk away satisfied. Understand the differences between your positions and your interests.

Select a time and place for the negotiation. Depending on the topic, consider bringing others with you to the table.

At the negotiation itself, treat the other side with respect at all times. Work on mentally analyzing what the other side is telling you and reevaluating your views based on the new information you receive. Use the brainstorming technique to generate options. Don't feel pressured to cave. Most of the time, you don't have to make a decision right then and there. If you need more time to think over the options and offers, say so.

If the other side wants to play rough, you don't have to reply in the same manner. In fact, it often helps to keep a cool head and show that you won't move to an aggressive stance. Avoid personal attacks.

Fisher and Ury recommend continuing to get at the interests behind the attack. Ask why or why not. Remember, the other person is focusing on the ideas, not attacking you personally. Use silence and pauses in your responses to help slow the pace and calm things down. If the negotiation gets too rough, you can always stop the session and request that the meeting be re-scheduled. Restate that you have both parties' interests in mind for a mutually agreeable settlement.

You can find plenty of books and courses on negotiation, including some in this book's Resources appendix. Your business may offer a workshop on the topic. Or you may have a local women's chamber of commerce or women's business association that offers courses to help.

11

Managing the Office Bully

"Charlene, you're being bullied by Fred," says her coworker, Louise.

"No, I'm not," replies Charlene, with a certain amount of indignation. "I ought to know when I'm being bullied. Fred's not so bad. You just have to get used to him."

"But Charlene, he *is* bad. Everyone in the office knows it. We all see the way he treats you. It makes me sick. He picks on you, he calls you names, he yells at you. He never thinks your work is any good. He treats you like dirt. And you don't *do* anything about it. It makes people around here cringe to see the two of you together. You've got to tell him to treat you better and respect you."

Charlene's eyes start to well up. She looks at Louise, then down at the floor. "I don't know what to say," she meekly mumbles. "I just thought he had his own problems or was having a bad day."

"Yes, he has a bad day whenever he works with *you*. Don't you see that? You'd better open your eyes!" exclaims Louise. "What did you do to make him so angry, anyway?"

This conversation is getting a bit much for Charlene. She quickly brushes away a tear. "You know, I don't remember doing anything or saying anything. But you're right, I must have done something to make him not like me. If I could only think of what it is, I could tell him I'm sorry. But I'm sure Fred doesn't mean any of it. It's just his way. I try not to let it bother me."

"Oh, great. Here he comes. You'd better do something, Charlene. He's making a fool out of you. Don't be so spineless. I'll check in with you later, and you'd better tell me you told him off. I'm outta here."

Charlene wipes away another tear as she stands there at her cubicle. She can see Fred approaching her. He doesn't look very happy. She wonders what to do. She feels an awful knot in her stomach.

What should Charlene do? Was Louise helping the situation? Who is the bully? What would you do?

Watch out. There are plenty of bullies out there in the workplace waiting to make their move.

Where Do Bullies Come From?

We don't know why a bully starts bullying, but we know there seems to always be one just around the corner. It's a very lucky woman who has been able to avoid the bullies at work. Usually one person in the work group or department is known as the bully. After all, that's what people are talking about at the water cooler. Did you see that? Did you hear about that? What did she do? Did she start to cry?

We don't know what makes the bully a bully. Maybe he was dropped on his head as a baby. Maybe she never recovered from having her bangs cut way too short. Being a bully involves hostile aggression that certain little boys might have used to get their way on the playground; now in the office, the bullies rely on the same playground aggression to get their way. Or maybe certain little girls used sly, cliquish, and mean remarks to get attention and win their way; those bullies use the same behaviors in their office to make their point and show they're the one in control.

Could low self-esteem be causing bullies to play out their need to look better than others? Could their desire for power make them want to see you squirming and humiliated in front of your coworkers? We're not licensed shrinks, so we can't explain fully what stunted the growth of their social skills and made them a walking mean streak. Let's just say that bullies are people you generally want to run *from* rather than *toward* (unless you're carrying a meat cleaver). You know what? That's not funny.

Bullying is not something to laugh at. And that's the problem. Many people don't see bullying as an issue. If you recount your bullying woes, they'll reply, "What are you, a wimp? Get over it." Until you've been on the receiving end of being bullied, you may not realize how devastating it can truly be.

If you're a supervisor or you manage people in some way and an employee approaches you about a bullying issue, take it seriously. Try to find out what's going on and put a stop to it. Get your boss and human resources department involved to make sure that the behaviors stop and that the bully doesn't continue bullying by retaliating in some way. Too many supervisors label the situation as a personality conflict or think it's simply two jealous employees who don't get along with each other. What if the bully is your top software engineer? You believe you need him, so you don't want to punish him.

Stop right there. Your bullied employee is desperate for help—otherwise, he or she wouldn't have shown up at your office. The behavior has probably been going on for months, and your employee just now got up the guts to knock on your door. The bullying is probably impacting others in your work group, too. Bullying involves more than trying to deal with a difficult coworker or a personality conflict. Maybe the first or second time someone exerts this behavior, he can be considered difficult. If the behavior continues, he's a full-fledged bully.

What's Bullying?

Bullying is behavior that is disrespectful, persistent, negative, destructive, and demoralizing. Its purpose is often to show or gain control and power. Bullies tend to verbally assault others. Imagine bullies wearing a sign that says "I'm everything and you're nothing," and then making you kneel down to them every day as a reminder of who's pulling the strings. Bullying is aimed at humiliating and embarrassing the recipient of the behavior; it emphasizes the bully's one-up position and may serve to protect the bully's territory.

A bully's behaviors can be physical or psychological. Male bullies often use physical and psychological tactics, while female bullies often use a psychological approach. Bully behaviors may include teasing, badgering, poking fun, laughing, screaming, mocking, insulting, isolating, using continuous profanity, withholding job information, giving the silent treatment, shunning, doling out impossible assignments, backstabbing, gossiping, shoving, sending rude e-mails (cyberbullies), spreading rumors, sabotaging, belittling, and controlling.

A man who is loud, forceful, aggressive, pushy, and a take-charge person is generally viewed as a man, not necessarily as a difficult person or a bully. When he uses these types of behaviors, he is living up to male stereotypes. A woman displaying those same behaviors is often considered a difficult person and/or potential bitch or even a bully.

Recipients of bullying often say that the behavior went on for several months, even years, before they were able to tell someone about it, demand that it stop, or quit and find work elsewhere. Over a period of time, bullying can cause recipients to develop physical ailments, such as headaches, stomach and digestion problems, high blood pressure, depression, and other stress-related problems. Recipients take off more sick days than normal. Not focusing on the job and missing work days impacts productivity. Chances are, some co-workers have witnessed the bullying, have spent time talking about it, and may even be participating in the bullying. Therefore, the employer is losing even more work time from its employees. Employers should take bullying seriously.

Bullying is often compared to sexual harassment behaviors. If the bullying has a sexual component, then, as repeated behavior, it may constitute an illegal, hostile work environment.

If the bullying behaviors focus on particular characteristics that federal law, state law, or company policy protect, they could be considered discrimination or harassment; the bully may be violating policy and breaking the law. These characteristics include race, religion, age, gender, disability (real or perceived), skin color, nationality, veteran status, pregnancy, equal pay, sexual orientation, marital status, or other characteristics particular to your state or company policy. In November 2009, a new law preventing discrimination based on genetic information (for instance, information about genes or DNA) will become effective. Exhibiting questionable behaviors based on family medical history or genetic background will be prohibited, too—as an example, this would come into play if you weren't hired because a preemployment medical exam indicated that you could get cancer.

We're not offering legal advice. Always consult the company's attorney or your human resources office for the legal advice you need to do your job. Outside the company, you can check with your local civil rights office to find out how some of these laws may impact you.

Cases that wind up in court can cost the company litigation fees and settlement costs. If the bullying is considered general bullying and isn't focused on one of these characteristics, it may be harder to resolve in court because it may not be legally considered harassment, a hostile work environment, or discrimination. Keep a journal of the bullying incidents. Write down who said what, who was there, and the time, place, and date. Hopefully you won't need it for anything, but if you do, your notes will support your credibility when you talk with management.

If the recipient ends up out of work due to illness—perhaps because of depression or stress—the company still incurs the cost for dealing with the disability and hiring a replacement worker. Unfortunately, many recipients leave their jobs after being bullied. The Workplace Bullying Institute's 2007 survey conducted with Zogby International reported that 77 percent of the recipients left their jobs, 13 percent transferred, 24 percent were terminated, and 40 percent quit. This survey indicates that almost one fourth of the bullies were disciplined for their behaviors. Unstopped bullying behaviors, like unstopped sexual harassment, can cost the company big bucks.

Aaron and Alan, both cooks at a restaurant, were constantly bullied by another cook, Gene. He made fun of them, smacked them with his bandana, and overly criticized them. Management did not handle it right, and the bullying continued to escalate. Finally, a fight broke out. All three of the men were injured and the police got involved. If the restaurant managers had intervened or done something when they saw it—which they had— they would have saved the company a lot of court fees, not to mention three fired employees.

Who's Your Bully?

Some say men do the most bullying; others say women do the most bullying. Men bullies tend to bully other men slightly more than they bully other women; women bullies tend to bully other women much more than they bully men, according to the Workplace Bullying Institute's survey. Our focus is how to talk with men. However, some of our recommendations also apply to female bullies.

This same 2007 survey found that 37 percent of the approximately 7,700 workers said they were recipients of bully behaviors. This survey found that almost three fourths of the bullies were at a higher level than the recipient. The bully could be the recipient's supervisor, the group coordinator, the team leader, or a similar position.

Bullies tend to look for someone they think is vulnerable in some way or someone they think may not complain or stand up to them. If you are a new employee or have been newly promoted, a bully may think you are a threat or see you as competition. As with sexual harassers, bullies come in all sizes. There's no way to predict who will be a bully.

As in sexual harassment cases, some recipients never tell their management about the behaviors. According to the Workplace Bullying Institute survey, 40 percent of the recipients never reported the bullying behaviors; another 38 percent said they filed an informal complaint at their company.

Silence Is Not the Answer

Being bullied is a horrible reality. You find yourself giving up your power unwillingly to someone else who pushes you around looking for your breaking point. The recipient is being humiliated many times in front of colleagues for many weeks, months, or more. Sometimes colleagues join forces with the bully, to keep the recipient down and out. Being bullied can be embarrassing to talk about; it can make you feel foolish or ashamed.

No matter how awful you feel, you must report this behavior. Don't blame yourself for the bully's behavior. A bully's a bully. If he's not picking on you, he'll be picking on the next person who shows up.

Some people try to reason with the bully, but in most cases, the bully isn't interested in reasoning. The bully gets his kicks from seeing you squirm. Talking back to the bully, trying to reason, or responding with anger only fuels the bully's fire and keeps him going. The more you argue or fight back, the louder and more arrogant the bully gets.

You may think that you can handle this on your own and that you don't need to report it. Keep your safety in mind. If the bully has a habit of throwing things—like your stapler—across the room, this guy isn't safe to be around. If he has bullied you more than once or twice, then how you've been trying to handle it isn't working. Seek assistance from your manager or someone in human resources. Young school children are often advised to run away from a bully and get help from a teacher or other adult. This is great advice. Turn and walk away when you see him coming down the hallway.

A woman may pride herself in thinking that she can work with anybody. Once the bully attacks her, she will try harder to work with him. She'll think that if she's only friendlier or nicer, it'll all work out. After all, she has great people skills; she communicates well and has friends in the office. She keeps trying to work with him and gets more frustrated. The more she tries to be friendly and talk with him, the more he rejects her. She starts doubting herself and her skills because this has never happened before. She may think she can work on changing him and his behavior. She may take it on as her pet project to see if she can get him to reform his ways. But a bully isn't interested in changing his ways. She will get frustrated and upset with herself for not getting him to act differently. We're not interested in changing the bully. We are interested in making sure you know your options and how to respond.

It's not your personal responsibility to help or change someone with obvious social problems. You are responsible for yourself and your work. Because women are so relationally focused, sometimes they tend to feel overly responsible for other people's problems, especially if they are relational problems. But this is not your child whom you need to teach. This is not your battle, so remove yourself from it. By trying to invest in changing a bully, you are blurring the boundaries and putting yourself in danger, even if not physically.

Sometimes people being bullied think that if they ignore the behaviors, the bully will stop. This doesn't work, either. Ignoring the behavior allows the bully to think that maybe he didn't come on strong enough to get your attention. So the next time the bully comes by your desk, he's twice as loud and obnoxious. Another thought may be to try to placate the bully by agreeing with him or being extra nice to him, thinking that he will see what a sweet person you are and leave you alone. You may try to do everything the bully wants, hoping he will stop. But chances are, the bully will still come back and pick on you. There's generally no logic to the way the bully acts. If you try to apply logic to the situation, it most likely will not work.

When Your Boss Is a Bully

Confronting your boss about his behavior can be risky business. Most bosses appreciate getting feedback that will ultimately help them and their team succeed. That's the logical approach you'd use with a boss who behaves logically. But bullies don't function on logic.

Stacey found out too late that she worked for a bully. Looking back at her interview, she found she'd missed a clue. Her soon-to-be boss, Leonid, got into a short shouting match with one of the other interviewers. Leonid said that the schedule was incorrect and that she would have to come back the following day. The other interviewer said that the schedule was exactly as Leonid had approved a week earlier.

Stacey got hired and started her programming job at a small branch office Leonid led. Leonid soon started exhibiting his all-out bully behaviors. At a group meeting one day, for no apparent reason he began yelling and cursing at Stacey about her programming project. The rest of the group sat silently watching. When his tirade ended, Stacey took a deep breath and said in her most professional voice, "Leonid, I understand that you have a concern about the report. I do not appreciate your shouting and cursing at me. That behavior has to stop. I will talk with you privately after the meeting about the changes you need." Leonid launched off again about how she was new, didn't know anything, and had no right to tell him what to do. This time Stacey said nothing. Just under 6 feet tall, Stacey was not used to someone trying to make her small and insignificant.

After the meeting, a peer, Mike, told her that Leonid did that to everybody. Every week or so, he'd single out someone and read them the riot act. Mike said it was no big deal and that she'd get used to it.

But it was a big deal to Stacey. Over the next few months, she tried to talk to Leonid about his bullying behavior. When she brought it up, he yelled at her to get out of his office. She started reading self-help books on how to handle bullies, to figure out what to do. She started getting headaches. Nothing she did changed the situation.

A year went by, and Stacey never got used to being demolished by Leonid. Sometimes she'd cry. Sometimes she'd turn and walk away. Stacey had always been a top performer at the past companies where she'd worked. At her performance review, Leonid told her she was ranked the lowest and was now on probation. She protested and said she wanted a meeting with Leonid's boss. That sent Leonid out of control, and he raised his voice louder and louder as he belittled her. It was a small office area, and Stacey knew the others could hear everything.

The next day, Stacey scheduled a phone call with Leonid's boss. Bob listened to her story and said he was very sorry to hear all this and would talk with Leonid. As soon as Leonid got off the phone with Bob, he was in Stacey's office yelling at her again. Stacey called human resources for help. They assured her they would look into it.

Three months went by, and Stacey never heard anything from Bob or human resources. Then one day, Leonid called her into his office. Stacey sat across from him, on the opposite side of his desk. He started yelling at her, telling her she was a loser and an idiot, she was stupid, she dressed like a slob, she'd ruined the project, no one liked her, and on and on. Stacey knew she should leave the room. It was too late. She couldn't take it anymore. She snapped. Within two seconds, she stood up, reached across the desk, grabbed Leonid's shirt on either side of his neck, and started shaking him while yelling back at him. Leonid's eyes got wide as he stared at her, and he finally shut up. For Stacey, it was like an out-of-body experience. Ten seconds probably passed before she realized what she was doing. She let go of him, stepped back, turned, and left his office. He could have claimed assault and called the police, but he didn't. Stacey had gone over the edge. She quit the next day.

This bully was out of control. It was clear his boss and those in human resources were not going to do anything about it. Don't wait until you go over the edge like Stacey; she could have been hurt physically if he had reciprocated. Your physical and mental health are worth more than any job. Leave as quickly as possible. You're worth it! Better to go where they'll appreciate the talent you have to offer.

If your boss is doing the bullying, how can you possibly report the behavior to him? You can't. Report the behavior to the next level of management, go to another supervisor, or go to human resources. It can be difficult to go around your supervisor to the next level to raise the issue. Chances are, though, you are not the first one to complain. His management and the human resources manager will either help you or ignore you. If they help you, you're better off on a daily basis without the bullying. If they ignore you, then they have told you in not so many words that they value the bullying supervisor more than you and your contributions. If that's the case, you'll need to decide whether you like your work more than you like getting bullied. You may need to transfer to another job or decide to update your resumé and start looking elsewhere.

code SWITCH *You have one more option. Be a tough tigress and fight to the finish. If you've accepted that you're leaving and looking for your next job, you could start responding to him in a direct civil manner, telling him that you find his behavior disrespectful and it must stop. Keep pounding that same message at him every time he starts his bully routine. Do it in front of others and do it when you're alone with him. However, remember, your safety is more important than getting in the last word. It's one thing if the bully is basically obnoxious; it's another if he seems unstable or you don't feel safe around him. This is when you pack up, leave, and never look back. Your safety is paramount. Always.*

Nip the Behavior in the Bud

The first couple times your boss or coworker cuts you down are the times you should reply to him and set him straight. This is the pre-bully stage. Right now, he's labeled a difficult person; if he's not set straight, he'll keep at it and become the bully you don't want to be around. At this beginning pre-bully stage, think about how you can best respond rather than how to help him be a nice person.

code **SWITCH** *Take charge of the situation. Use your comments to direct him and the discussion where you want it to go.*

In Audrey's workshop on dealing with difficult people, she suggests the following steps:

1. Evaluate what is going on before you get involved.

2. Label the behaviors so you know exactly what you're dealing with.

3. Stay detached and pay attention to what's going on around you.

4. Identify your feelings.

5. Develop a strategy.

6. Rehearse.

7. Take action and evaluate your response.

When addressing the difficult person, remain positive and respectful. Responding in the same difficult manner yourself won't get you anywhere; it will simply prolong the problem. Likewise, replying spontaneously or emotionally will only make matters worse. Don't get emotionally pulled into remarks—the bullying is not about you.

Let's use Audrey's suggestions and check back in with Charlene, whom we met at the beginning of this chapter. Ideally, Charlene would have addressed Fred's behavior when it had first started. That didn't happen. Based on the information we have, Fred's disrespectful behavior isn't something new. He is well on his way to establishing himself as the resident bully.

A full analysis of the seven steps we discussed earlier would take several pages, but here are a few illustrations. Using these steps will help you handle a situation with a difficult person—and even a bully. In step five, note Charlene's strategy for talking separately with Louise and Fred.

Maggie was an operations manager at a high-tech company in Denver. She was one of a few women at her level in the organization. She was used to being surrounded by men at meetings, during meals, on business trips, and just about everywhere at work. She got along fine with everyone, except George. She and George never clicked the way she did with the other guys. He always seemed distant. A couple of the other women agreed with her. A few weeks of intense work on a critical project were coming to a close. Everyone was on edge trying to meet deadlines. George approached Maggie for current budget numbers, and when she didn't have them done, he exploded. He went ballistic on her in the hallway. He totally lost it, yelling at her about her incompetence. A couple people stopped in their tracks and watched the spectacle. George's face was red. As he screamed, spit flew every which way out of his mouth.

Maggie stayed composed and thought to herself, "I am not playing his game. I don't have time for this." She remained quiet for a moment. He kept goading her with demeaning remarks waiting to see her crack. She took a deep breath, looked into his bulging eyes, and spoke calmly. "George, I see you're upset and you want the numbers. I will get them to you as soon as the report is complete. I don't have time for this discussion right now."

George looked surprised at her calmness. He was still breathing heavily from his yelling and was pumped up to do more. He stammered a bit and then said, "All right." He turned and walked away. Maggie walked back to her office and closed the door. As she sat at her desk, she realized she was shaking a bit. She smiled and thought she had handled George rather well.

code SWITCH *Be direct. Use short responses. Use a calm, even tone when responding to a man's anger. He's used to fighting to survive. Don't fight back in the same manner. Don't play his game. Give him the information he needs and move on.*

1. Evaluate What Is Going On Before You Get Involved

Louise jumps in and gives her evaluation to Charlene: "You're being bullied." Louise blames the victim when she asks Charlene, "What did you do to make him so angry, anyway?" Charlene, not Louise, is the one who needs to define the problem and evaluate what she needs and wants to do. Charlene is unaware that Louise and the group are talking about her. She defends Fred by making excuses for his behavior, such as "He's not so bad."

If Charlene had recognized Fred's behavior as controlling and disrespectful, she could have begun planning earlier an appropriate response that would exhibit her strength and show that she would not tolerate his behavior.

2. Label the Behaviors

Louise has labeled Fred's behavior as bully behavior. Louise is disrespectful and hurtful toward Charlene, calling her a fool and spineless. Louise's behavior is threatening when she tells Charlene that she expects her to tell Fred off. Charlene is in denial. She does not readily admit to recognizing Fred's behavior as inappropriate, disrespectful, or bullying. She feels that she has disappointed Louise and her team members by not standing up to Fred.

If Charlene had recognized and labeled Fred's difficult behavior when it had first happened, she could have responded in a direct style that Fred could hear. That could have limited or stopped his disrespectful behaviors.

3. Stay Detached and Pay Attention to What's Going on Around You

Louise needs to work on being detached. She's gotten herself emotionally involved with Charlene's situation with Fred. Louise is plugged into what she sees happening between Fred and Charlene, but she may not have all the facts. Charlene is working on being detached from Fred's remarks. At first, she won't recognize the behaviors as bullying. Charlene needs to work on being plugged in. She is unaware that the group is concerned about Fred's behavior toward her.

4. Identify Your Feelings

Louise is trying to help Charlene stop a bully and is frustrated that Charlene has let Fred's behavior continue. She thinks she is helping. Charlene is upset that the group has been talking about her. She's hurt because Louise thinks she's a fool and has called her spineless. She feels pressured to confront Fred, and that scares her.

5. Develop a Strategy

Louise plans on inviting Charlene to talk privately at lunch or at break time. Without being critical, she'll use "I" statements to express her concerns to Charlene. Charlene is thinking about Fred's behaviors and how they impact her and her relationship with Louise and the group. Charlene takes ownership of her working relationship with Louise and with Fred. She'll talk with Louise privately and use "I" statements to let Louise know her feelings about Louise's comments.

Charlene thinks about her strategy to approach Fred to resolve the situation. She determines her desired outcome and plans to talk with Fred privately. She'll stand up for herself and her viewpoints, using "I" statements to let Fred know how she feels about his behavior toward her. When listening to Fred, Charlene will keep an open mind and not attack Fred. If Fred gets angry, she plans to stop the meeting and approach him later, when he is calm. During the meeting, she will set limits with Fred, explain her expectations for their working relationship, and thank Fred for talking with her.

Charlene will document her discussion with Fred and note any other disrespectful behaviors that happen (along with the date, time, place, and any witnesses). If Fred's behaviors don't change immediately, Charlene will take further action and notify her supervisor or the human resources manager.

6. Rehearse

Louise and Charlene both write down bullets to remind themselves of what they want to say and accomplish at the discussions. These points include questions and phrases they want to use (especially "I" statements to express their opinions and feelings). They can read over their notes before the meeting, and they can bring those notes with them when they meet with the other person.

7. Do It and Evaluate It

Louise sets up a meeting with Charlene, then uses her notes during the discussion. Afterward she thinks about what statements went well and where a different approach might have been helpful. Then she plans her next steps.

Charlene agrees to meet with Louise and sets up a meeting with Fred. During both meetings, Charlene uses her notes as needed. Afterward, she thinks about what statements went well and where she might have used a different approach. Then she thinks about the next steps, including considering whether her supervisor or the human resources manager needs to be made aware of the discussion (especially if it did not go as well as planned).

Steady As She Goes

Sometimes the only thing that helps is having a thick skin to deflect a bully's comments. However, that does not mean you have to tolerate disrespectful, mean behavior. It does not mean you have to work in an environment where you don't feel safe. Pamela Lutgen-Sandvik, a communication professor at the University of New Mexico, suggests three ways to get management's attention for resolving these situations. These include filing an internal complaint, providing documentation of the bullying behaviors, and providing articles by "experts" that describe bullying behaviors. Following the channels in your organization will help get the behaviors stopped.

code SWITCH *Step out of the shadows and take 100 percent responsibility for your happiness. Do not allow another human being to rob your enjoyment of life for one minute—even one second. Stay out of the bull's-eye.*

12

Workplace Humor

Have you ever heard a woman tell a joke at work and forget the punch line? Why are men often the primary joke tellers? Men and women use humor for different reasons, and that affects their reactions to humor. Women use humor, as they do communication, to build relationships. Men use humor, often as they do communication, as a form of competition, a win-lose, and the process of competition fuels a type of male bonding. At work, humor may be used to break the ice, bond with each other, indicate power, include people, or exclude people. How are male and female differences in the use of humor viewed in the workplace?

Communication research reveals that men tell the majority of jokes, and that men and women's choices for humor differ from knock-knock jokes to dumb blonde jokes, to comic strips like *Garfield* and *Cathy*. Were we born sensitive to humor, or did we learn what makes us laugh? And more important, should we make the boss laugh? For women, learning how to use humor strategically is critical to improving their lot at work, especially in a male-dominated environment. We suggest that if women can get a grip on male workplace humor, they'll have a better chance of getting men to listen to them. Humor and jokes aren't just behaviors that put a smile on your face; they're behaviors that, when used wisely, can put added dollars in your purse.

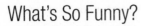

What's So Funny?

Being funny or humorous is having the ability to lead someone down a particular path and then suddenly shift gears. That shift, the incongruity of the
message or behavior, is what's so funny. The ability to see that shift—our
sense of humor—is what stops us in our tracks and makes us laugh at the
joke, and a bit at ourselves for having been led so neatly in the wrong direction. For example, consider this comment by comedienne and Vegas star Rita
Rudner: "Whenever I date a guy, I think, is this the guy I want my children
to spend their weekends with?" Or consider this classic by comedian Henny
Youngman: "I take my wife everywhere, but she keeps finding her way back."

The Three Stooges, Laurel and Hardy, the Marx Brothers, and Abbott and
Costello helped develop many Baby Boomers' sense of humor. Those old TV
shows and movies continue to be shown today as humor classics, and they still
influence what we laugh at.

Only funny men? During that same time, women comediennes were making
the rounds as well. The 1950s and '60s variety hour *The Ed Sullivan Show*
also showcased women like Phyllis Diller, Totie Fields, and Carol Burnett.
Eventually, Carol Burnett got her own show, and if you're lucky, you can
catch reruns of that, too. Men and women were exposed to the slapstick,
aggressive, pointed, put-down humor from the funny men; the self-
deprecating, tongue-in-cheek, make-a-fool-of-myself humor from the funny
women, à la Lucille Ball. Men and women vary in their use of these types of
humor in the workplace.

These different styles of humor hold true today. Look at female pop-culture
funny girls, such as Chelsea Handler and Sarah Silverman. Most of their
humor comes from making fun of themselves.

One female humor columnist, whom we'll call Lizzy, says she receives dramatically different reader feedback from columns when she jokes about
others or herself. In one column, she posted 10 ugly Christmas sweaters and
asked readers to rank them in order of the most "abominable of all snowmen"
to the least offensive. (It was quite a daunting task.) Many readers laughed
and voted, but a handful were irate—especially at the appliqué-loaded sweater
Lizzy called a "traditional school teacher uniform—and the truth behind

snow days: schools had to close down over Christmas because too many students were going home with headaches and stomach aches from the fashion atrocity."

"How dare you make fun of teachers? Not everyone can afford to buy designer clothes," one reader wrote. "That's hardly the holiday spirit," another wrote. Finally, Lizzy responded. All of those ugly sweaters—purchased at various thrift stores for under $5 each—came from her own closet. And as for the teacher mocking—well, Lizzy let readers know that she teaches part-time at a local high school, so she could talk.

And voilà! Suddenly, the column was absolutely hilarious. How you use humor can change a situation from bad to good—or at least better—in the case of Lizzy. While this was a column with readers as her customers, how men and women use humor in other work settings also impacts their customer and coworker relationships. Will men listen more if a woman is making jokes about herself? We're not suggesting that a woman be the office clown or let herself be singled out as the butt of all the office jokes. It's not that simple.

It's a battle: the bad-boy humor of office pranks, drinking, naked women, bodily functions, bathroom talk, and football versus the not-always-good-girl humor of elegance faux pas, sophistication quirks, family mishaps, self-sabotage, verbal barbs, and men-are-pigs.

The men-are-pigs female perspective, and the women-are-complicated and "naked-anything-and-alcohol" male perspective show the contrast in how men and women approach life and work, and what makes them subsequently laugh. Learning about humor and learning from what's around us makes sense. In general, that's how we learn all of our behaviors—from our surroundings: parents, TV shows, movies, classmates, music, magazines, and ministers.

It's a Man's World

Male humor involves more vulgarity, sexual topics, put-downs, physical slapstick, mocking, jokes, pranks, and stories than women's humor, suggests psychologist Dr. Lillian Glass, author of *He Says, She Says: Closing the*

Communication Gap Between the Sexes. Male teasing and derogatory humor or put-downs are their bonding banter.

Women like a sense of humor, tend to play fewer practical jokes, use fewer put-downs, and enjoy more word plays than men, according to Glass.

Pranks and practical jokes reign supreme on NBC's comedy series *The Office.* The "straight guy," Jim Halpert, is usually busy either thinking up pranks or playing them out against his nemesis, Dwight Schrute. Who didn't laugh at Dwight finding his stapler buried in Jell-O or seeing his wallet and name plate in the vending machine? At this office, it's the men playing or receiving the practical jokes and the women watching the joking or sometimes helping with the pranks.

As in the world of *The Office,* the world of humor and what is deemed funny has long been viewed as the male domain. Men's style of humor and joking has set the bar for what's funny and what gets the laughs. It's not that their jokes rate higher than women's on the funny scale; it's that a male-dominated workplace is naturally dominated by male humor. Let's face it, how many women have glued down everything on a colleague's desk?

> Mark was particularly known for his shenanigans, often to the extreme. His coworker John started noticing a plethora of fruit flies around his cubicle. Several months—yes, months—later, he found a banana under his desk. Mark had duct-taped it there. Mark's disclaimer: it had been Vanessa's idea.

Funny Versus the Good Girl Syndrome

"Good girls" and "funny girls" often don't gel. Being funny means a woman speaks her mind, is straightforward, powerful, strong, and even aggressive— all things that usually don't mix with our image of a "good girl," according to Professor Sevda Caliskan. Because humor has been defined as a male domain, women have been viewed as having little or no sense of humor and unable to tell a joke, since "telling a joke" equates to "telling a joke like a man would tell a joke."

And if a girl happens to be funny (read: man-funny), she is probably not pretty, or so goes the stereotype. Pretty girls don't need to be funny. Try telling that to our humor columnist, Lizzy; turns out, she writes a fashion column. A humorous column about beauty? Could it be?

Professor Caliskan mentions Paul McGhee, author of *The Role of Laughter and Humor in Growing Up Female*. He suggests that a woman telling a joke or clowning around violates the pattern of expected behaviors of a woman. Therefore, to get laughs, women must use a different style of humor— self-deprecating humor—by making themselves the butt of the joke.

Does a good girl laugh out loud with a big guffaw, express a small tee hee, or just smile to indicate that she found something funny? Does a woman compromise her virtue by laughing at the visiting salesman's sexual innuendos? Men may be strutting their stuff and joking to determine who's king of the copy room, but women tend to be more cautious about their displays of humor.

The ways women have been socialized apply to their use of humor, too. The good girl is quiet and passive, laughing when expected; the bad girl is loud and abrasive, often initiating the jokes to show that she can be one of the boys. The good girl provides her smile or laugh when she's supposed to— usually in response to any joke or humorous remark he makes. The bad girl laughs loudly when and where she wants; she decides what's funny to her.

But is that really bad? The bad girl's behavior is somehow unexpected, break-ing the female stereotype that a woman doesn't laugh out loud, especially if she's with the guys. It's like when a woman orders the full slab of ribs with three sides—the baked beans, coleslaw, and corn bread—and the waiter brings her meal on three plates. The salesman she's having lunch with goes into shock and comments on her healthy appetite: "It's so nice to see a girl who doesn't eat like a bird." She's breaking the stereotype that all women are on diets and eat salad with low-fat dressing on the side. To carry the bad girl stereotype further, a woman laughing and carrying on with the guys is often viewed as loose, with her morals and virtue in question.

A sense of humor is often defined along the same lines. A man has a great sense of humor when he tells jokes, creates practical jokes, and makes every-one laugh. It used to be that a woman was thought to have a sense of humor when she laughed appropriately at the man's jokes. The assertive woman knows how to use humor to stand on her own and mix it up with the guys. Is she, then, the bad girl? If she's slinging back name-calling and sexual innuendos, then it's the bad girl image.

code **SWITCH** *Use your humor to confirm you're smart and witty. You're showing him your power and willingness to play.*

Author and professor Regina Barreca writes about men's and women's use of humor. She finds that women don't tell jokes or one-liners like men do; women prefer telling stories. Women don't like humor that makes fun of people who are victims or have physical difficulties. Men tend to poke fun and laugh at everything; all are a fair target. And women don't care for humor that is vulgar or physical (think of belching words, making fart sounds, tripping someone, mooning the boss—prime areas for a good laugh for many men). We realize not every man laughs at fart sounds, but let's be real: it's a tempting way to get the guys to bond.

At Claire's old office, there was a conference room with big vinyl leatherette (faux leather) chairs around the conference table. The short, chubby 50ish supervisor had a habit of wearing short skirts and no stockings. She thought the no-stockings look made her look younger, but to others she looked silly, not to mention unprofessional, with varicose veins popping out of her calves and serious spider veins circling her ankles. Everyone dreaded and simultaneously secretly couldn't wait for a meeting to happen in that conference room.

After she'd been sitting in the leatherette chair for about a half-hour, she'd stand up and everyone would hear her skin peeling off the chair. When she'd uncross her legs, they'd hear her skin peeling apart. When she re-crossed them, they could hear a fart sound from some secret air pocket being demolished (at least, they thought the sound was from crossing her legs and not the real thing). She never missed a beat and kept on talking. Claire and her distinguished colleagues would bite their lips, trying not to look at each other, but knowing that they were all convulsing inside trying not to laugh. Men and women alike, laughing at fart sounds. Looking back, they were probably grasping at the only thing that kept them sane with that particular boss: laughter.

Women do joke around with each other. They enjoy laughing just as much as men. They tell their stories and laugh at the punch lines they can't quite remember. They laugh at themselves—their weight, looks, clothing, and appearance. Beware. This self-deprecating style can be a problem at the office, where men or others not used to this style wonder if any of it might be true, as suggested by Barreca. If a woman jokes about her weight—how she manages to eat everything in sight and still can't lose weight—someone may wonder about her lack of self-control or inability to manage her own needs.

If Sheila jokes with Ken on a regular basis about her bad hair days and how she's not going to leave her cubicle or do that presentation, he may begin to wonder about her self-esteem and her ability to get her job done. Mary and Sue can totally empathize with Sheila. They've been there themselves. Mary may offer Sheila the phone number of her stylist, Carlos, and the work day moves on.

Part of what made the TV show *I Love Lucy* so funny is that Lucy was always trying to be good, to do the right thing, and to be a devoted wife and mother. But she couldn't stop herself from trying out her ideas and schemes. We'd always root for Lucy to succeed—be able to bake the bread, stomp the wine, wrap the chocolates, sing and dance with her husband, Ricky, but she never quite made it. She'd look foolish and people would feel sorry for her, but Ricky still loved her.

It's All in Your Head

Women love their cartoons! A 2005 study by the Stanford Medical Center found that male and female brains react differently to cartoons. Researchers showed test subjects 70 cartoons. While the male and female subjects rated them on a funny scale, an MRI (magnetic resonance imaging) machine scanned and measured their brain functions. Pretty high-tech for a couple of laughs! Researchers found that the parts of the brain that address language processes and memory were activated more in women than in men. The funnier the jokes, the greater the activity measured in the women's brains. The brain's reward center, which signals pleasure, was also more active in the women than in men.

It's thought that these findings show that women were analyzing the language more than men, were not expecting a punch line as much, and were more surprised and pleased when the punch line finally happened. "Men seemed to 'expect' the cartoons to be funny from the start," according to the study; their brains showed less activity. The men and women did not show differences in what cartoons they rated as funny, but the women were faster at indicating what they thought was *not* funny.

We mention these findings not to make you laugh, but to let you know that there are physical differences in how men and women respond to funny cartoons—and most likely other forms of humor, too. Strange but true.

Laughing Your Way to the Top

How can you succeed at work? Good managers are described as having excellent communication skills and people skills, in addition to knowing the job. People skills include having a good sense of humor. Think of your favorite boss. Was she or he able to laugh at themselves, tell a joke, and get the group to gel with some humor? A successful manager knows when to laugh, when not to laugh, and who to poke fun at. The good ones choose to laugh at themselves or make a joke at their expense. They don't laugh at someone else's mishaps (unless it's an adversary from another company). Humor consultant Kathy Klotz-Guest noted from a *Harvard Business Review* 2003 article that "managers that laugh more than twice as often as their counterparts make more money (are promoted faster), have more fun, and are seen as more competent." Creativity during a brainstorming session often leads to funny, along with serious, ideas suggested. The funny ideas open the door to more alternative creative ideas that can move the group toward its goal.

Laughter is a great antidote for stressful situations at work, too. Laughter is a healthy step to reducing stress. Have you tried a laughter yoga class? Laughter yoga uses laughter as an exercise that is practically aerobic. Hearty laughing opens the lungs and brings in more oxygen to feed the brain. We don't mean laughing hysterically for no reason in the corner—not psycho laughing. It does help to have a reason to laugh.

Joking around and kidding with your coworkers can actually build trust and forge a stronger relationship. It can help make you seem friendly and approachable (as if you aren't already, right?).

In fact, as we are writing this right now, our friend's editor just received a postcard from a female coworker, Rebecca. The postcard is a random picture of two sock monkeys, and on the back it reads, "I thought you might enjoy this photo recently taken of us. Feel free to frame it and/or use it as your new MySpace pic or driver's license pic." Talk about unexpected. Talk about laughing hysterically for no (logical) reason in the corner. They'd been having a particularly rough month at work, and this is how Rebecca handled it. We insist: women are freaking hilarious.

code SWITCH *Joking and being able to use humor properly can help deflate workplace conflicts. When the tough guy starts up, sometimes a simple humorous remark can put the brakes on the anger and help all take a different perspective. By the way, if you do this successfully, you'll get office bonus points.*

Humor, Territory, and Power

Using humor is risky, and it is a power play. Who will the group laugh *at* or *with?* For a woman working in a male-dominated workplace, the chances are high that there will be some of the frat boy (beer, sports, and naked women—not necessarily in that order, and preferably all at once) humor unless a supervisor runs a strict harassment-free environment. Even with the tight ship approach, some sex-free pranks still may be going on. As the men use these behaviors for bonding, they will approach the new woman employee in the same way, to test her out. Will she walk away embarrassed? Will she start to cry? Will she run to the boss or human resources? Will she get angry and tell them to stuff it? Will she reply in a like manner or from a higher ground?

When testing out a new player, whether a man or a woman, the men in the office may pull out some of their more aggressive, sarcastic remarks to make their point: I'm in charge—this is my sandbox, and you can play here only by my rules. It's the male-to-male aggressive/funny banter that often maintains the office hierarchy and shows new people where they fit in. It's generally not personal, but it's a way to let the new person know and remind the rest of the team that there's a certain pecking order in how their working relationships get played out. It's a way of marking territory; the new woman is tested to see if she's in or out.

Does your work group have the tough guy, the buffoon, the boss's pet, the smart one, the helpless one, and the resourceful one? Aggressive humor and banter are used to cement some of those roles. Men come to the office knowing that it's a game, a competition; that it's not personal; and that they definitely want to win. Women often don't realize that it's a game being played out in front of them and that they are being tested as a potential player. Instead of taking the bait and playing the game, a woman may view the men's joking as a personal attack that's mean or unfair. She may leave the area, or if she decides to stay, she may scold them for their insensitivity. They may be insensitive, but they're looking for a smart and witty comeback to show them that you can take it and give it back. According to Barreca, men don't think they have anything to lose by zinging a woman because they believe she won't reply with anything other than a "hurt look."

code SWITCH *Be ready for his jokes or remarks. Don't take them personally. Separate yourself from the comment. Understand the game.*

It's hard to be smart and witty if you feel you've just been insulted. You may want to keep a few one-liners ready in case that witty reply doesn't come to you. A sarcastic and unamused (offered with a smirk) "Brilliant!" can do the trick. Or you might say, "Stay up all night thinking of that, did you?"

What if the remark or joke demeans someone or is racist, sexist, homophobic, and so on? Joke telling is one of the most common examples of "intent versus impact," as we discuss in Chapter 14. From communication research, we know that most jokes demean, ridicule, or are derogatory toward a person, group of people, or subject. So-called clean jokes are rare. Audiences are always challenged when we say, "Someone quickly tell me a funny, clean joke."

If it's so funny, would you offer it as an anecdote in a religious setting or your child's classroom? Would it embarrass you or your family to see you and your joke in the local newspaper's headlines? Then don't say it. Humor should be fun and raise your likeability factor. Slamming women isn't funny. Neither is slamming men. That type of sexual humor goes beyond aggressive to hostile. Don't make Joe the butt of the joke, either. While it may seem like fun, it's disrespectful—and unless it's done with perfection and a knowing wink, you'll be the one viewed as the aggressor and jerk, not Joe. Men will tend to take note and stay away from you; you could be excluded from work happenings and needed insider info.

Don't laugh—don't even smirk—at any jokes of a sexual nature or those that put down women (or anyone, for that matter, based on their race, color, religion, national origin, sexual orientation, sex, disability, veteran status, and so on). A woman with a good sense of humor knows the difference between what's funny and what's a put-down. Watch your workplace humor.

Also be aware that humor varies by culture. What you grew up thinking was hysterically funny may not translate into funny for someone from another neighborhood, culture, or country. That's something to consider in the diverse workplaces of today.

Humor Hierarchy at Work

Laugh it up! In their book *Sex Differences in Human Communication*, Barbara and Gene Eakins, gender communication pioneers, mentioned a study by sociologist Rose Coser. Coser analyzed three months' worth of staff meeting conversations, recording when and how men and women used humor and what got the laughs. She found that men told most of the jokes and the women laughed the most. She noted a hierarchy in the humor. The senior staff members made the most jokes, then the midlevel staff, and finally the lower, junior-level staff members. Plus, staff members aimed their jokes at people at the same job level or lower, but never at those in a higher job level. Coser equated women's use of humor as that of the low-level junior staff: telling the fewest jokes, laughing the hardest, and not interrupting those (men) in charge.

The Eakinses noted that when a group starts laughing, "control is temporarily taken out of the hands of the chairperson or director who is conducting the meeting." There's a temporary shift in clout. What does this tell us? Don't make your boss the butt of your humor unless you're looking for an immediate job change. When you get the group laughing, you become the center of attention and have control over the group at that moment.

code SWITCH *Being funny or humorous doesn't mean you have to do stand-up routines at group meetings (unless you're a writer at* Saturday Night Live*). Look at yourself and your managers. See what they laugh at and where they use humor. Think about what makes you laugh and how you may apply that to your work setting.*

To Laugh or Not to Laugh

Try *not* smiling at the boss's jokes, and watch the reaction. A fabulous example of power and men and women's differing view of humor comes from a *Friends* episode on NBC. Chandler and Monica are at Chandler's boss's home for dinner. Chandler laughs out loud at every joke the boss makes, whether it's funny or not, and whether it's at the expense of someone else in the office. When the boss leaves the table, Monica tells Chandler that the jokes are terrible and tells him not to laugh. Chandler is concerned that it will impact his job if he doesn't laugh, but with Monica pressuring him, he agrees not to laugh. The boss enters the room telling another joke. Chandler doesn't laugh. The boss asks, "What's wrong? Didn't you hear me, didn't you get the joke?" After some awkward silence, Monica explains the joke to Chandler and then starts laughing, signaling Chandler to laugh. Then the boss smiles, knowing that his jokes are, indeed, hilarious. In this situation, Monica tried to exert her relational concept of humor but gave in when she saw that the only relationship the boss wanted was to maintain his one-up/one-down hierarchical status quo. In other words, Monica learned what Chandler already knew: the boss is always funny.

When a man tells a joke, he may be using humor as another avenue to compete, to outdo others and show his management potential. Chandler laughing at the jokes is showing his managerial potential, too. He's a fun guy, he's easy to be around, and he understands what's comical.

I'm Just Not Funny

You're probably funnier than you think. You *are* funny. When you wake up in the morning and look in the mirror, tell yourself, "I am funny. I have a great sense of humor. I will make someone at work laugh today."

In fact, by very virtue of not being funny, you're funny. You've got great stories to tell, and life is really not *that* serious. Remember that time when you …? Create ha-ha pages in your journal. Write down what makes you laugh. Write down what you say or do that makes a coworker chuckle. Think about where or when you might be able to say that funny line again or tell that story to connect. Remember, men are waiting for the punch line so don't keep them waiting too long for your story's amusing twist.

code SWITCH *Use your relationship skills; add humor to connect with people but not put people down. When you tell someone a funny story, it's an effort to include that person in your circle of trusted colleagues.*

Need more ideas on what's funny? Take an improvisation class; check out your local comedy club, especially when a woman is the headliner. Buy a couple books on humor and learn about timing and writing your own witty stories that you can use in your presentations or lunch meetings. Or stop trying so hard. Simply pay attention to what is going on around you. Amusing twists are one of life's constants. Things rarely turn out the way you expect. The key in turning something average (or even upsetting) into something that can bring a smile to your face is one word: perspective. Shift it constantly.

> Giselle has a twisted ankle. She could wallow around her house, lamenting her hurt ankle and all the things she can't do. Or she could think about how it happened: she was wearing incredibly tall heels, and in her near-hysterical excitement to get to her favorite Mexican restaurant for dinner, she raced out her front door and suffered a face-plant. Sure, her ankle hurts, but that pain is only temporary. The humorous memory of her Mexican-fueled love dive will last forever. (And it can teach her a lesson.)

Using humor means never having to say you're sorry. Stop apologizing before you tell a joke. Get these statements out of your repertoire:

- "I'm not really funny, but I thought I'd tell you this joke anyway."
- "Oh, I can never remember the punch line, but here it goes."
- "You might not think this is funny, but here it is."
- "I'm sorry. You've probably heard this one."

Men don't apologize *before* they tell a joke. If it's off-color, they may end up apologizing to human resources *after* they have told the joke. If you don't remember the punch line, don't tell the joke.

code **SWITCH** *No apologizing before you tell your hilarious story. When he laughs, you've got his attention. He's listening. You're a smart, witty, confident woman!*

Use with Discretion

Comedian and pianist Victor Borge once said, "Laughter is the shortest distance between two people." The type of humor you use can draw people together or push people apart. It can build mountains or cause great divides. It can create confidence or humiliation. Remember, most humor ridicules a person or group of people; you don't want your jokes at work (or anywhere) to fall into this last category. If his work humor is sexual, vulgar, or full of body sounds and functions, don't let your humor sink to his level. Laughter lightens the load, but don't be the office clown with constant jokes or funny pranks: you'll risk not being taken seriously. Think about how you use humor to promote the positive and bring out the best in your men and women colleagues. Sharing humor is like sharing a slice of cherry pie. It can fill you up and make you feel good, or it can be full of pits. He's listening and laughing with you.

13

Don't Wear Your Heart
on Your Sleeve

Pick up the latest issue of *Glamour* or *O* magazine. If you believe what you read (or see on TV), women are emotional, are apt to change their minds without reason or warning, and are most confusing for men. Many men wish for a barcode on women's foreheads so they can decipher what women want and what they are suppose to do about it. In one seminar, one man shouted, "Could someone please do a book *How Women Work?* Just provide an operating manual. I will do whatever it takes to keep the peace. For guys, it is a constant guessing game."

The Danger of Show and Tell

But watch what you ask for. When women let it all hang out, the result can be fireworks. Women will express the entire continuum and range of emotions. Then men are often perplexed and overwhelmed, and don't know what to do—especially at the office.

Women, consider a word of warning concerning what you talk about at work. If you consult the psychic hotline to determine whether you are going to score the big contract, do you really want to share that with your cube-mate? We know you spend more time at work (sorry to remind you) than any other single activity in your life, and your coworkers are the folks you see the most. However, they don't need to know all your personal activities and viewpoints. Whose business is it, anyway? How will that information contribute to your office image? Will it come around and bite you? Ask yourself this before you share your personal opinions or what you do on your own time.

She Is Emotional and Subjective

A 2001 Gallup poll asked American adults whether a series of qualities and characteristics applied more to men or to women. Ninety percent of those surveyed said the characteristics of "emotional" applied more to women. It seems likely from these results that many Americans perceive women as either able or prone to experience a much wider range—and intensity—of emotions than men do.

In the office, women see everything from the budget to the year-end report with an objective eye, but they also use a layer of subjectivity. If it doesn't feel "fair" or something seems "off," a woman often chooses to express this gut feeling. You can almost see men rolling their eyes. Men come from primarily (and almost exclusively) an objective stance.

Evidence over the past four decades indicates that women adapt their style to that of men when they are interacting with men, but women rarely have adopted men's styles completely. So a woman will offer up an objective account of "facts" and "data" (which resonates with him), but she will not completely dismiss her "inner knower." This subjective element has little credibility in the eyes of men. Right or wrong, we have been conditioned to view objectivity as superior to subjectivity. Even though feelings are "facts," you'll hear men say things like, "Why do you feel that way?" or "You shouldn't feel like that; you have no reason to feel that way." For men, credibility is built not on feelings, but on facts. Detective Joe Friday's mantra while interrogating witnesses is most men's mantra: "Just the facts, ma'am, just the facts." Women know that feelings are often the deeper truth, and a man's objective reasons and opinions are a more superficial one.

code SWITCH *Be careful when announcing your concern about a potential vendor and your wish to more fully check out the offer. You don't need to let it all hang out. Don't say that you have a bad vibe or that someone makes you nervous. Men don't need to know your subjective opinion; it is all voodoo to them.*

Your antenna is tuned to both the objectivity and subjectivity of the world. This is a good thing, but one you want to sometimes keep under wraps. Instead, follow your "hunches" to help uncover tangible problems with the situation, issues that both men and women can prove, discuss, and understand.

Remember, men like to solve problems. How can he solve a "bad vibe"? But if your bad vibe causes you to scrutinize the budget more closely, uncovering mismatched numbers, that is something fixable.

Most organizations are structured hierarchically; people are ranked according to position and power. One defining characteristic of workplace relationships is the equality or inequality of relationship partners in organizational power and position.

Another dimension in which relationships vary is the *intimacy* dimension. Cultural rules in some organizations dictate that it is not a good idea to hang out with your employees or become friends with them. The unspoken rule is, don't mingle with the help—maintain a distance to maintain your status. These managers remain strictly professional and restrict communication to work-related concerns.

On the other end of the continuum, some participants in our seminars say that they hug each other when they come into work and that their children play on the same little league teams. They socialize outside work and share family and sport activities. One woman claimed, "We are a small community and everyone knows everyone. We are close knit outside of work and at work." So in this latter, more interpersonal climate, employees may face the temptation to talk about home life and personal issues at work. A word of warning: limit that conversation to outside of work.

We have a mantra in communication: "Communication is context-bound." In other words, the context should dictate the communication. We are successful if we match our communication to the demands of the context (place, people, and occasion). We all know what it's like when someone drops a bomb. They say the wrong thing at the wrong time or to the wrong people or in the wrong place.

Angie used to have a personal policy to not mix her work and personal lives. She worked at her office for two years, keeping to herself. When coworkers invited her out for drinks or dinner after hours, she always said "No, thanks." She felt like this professional boundary made her a more focused worker and kept her workplace drama free.

Then Candace joined the staff. Angie immediately connected with Candace's sense of humor and attitude, and suddenly Angie forgot her policy. She began hanging out with Candace outside of work, and soon they were best friends.

One day, over drinks, Angie mentioned something about how much she earned per hour—something along the lines of, "I don't know how they can expect to keep up with my margarita habit on only $21 an hour!" Candace's face grew red. "Is that how much you make?" she said. She had been offered only $15 an hour, and she had the same amount of experience.

The next day, Candace went to their boss and said that she wanted $21 an hour, too. He said he couldn't afford that, and she said, "But that's what you pay Angie." The boss was furious that Angie had put him in that position—so angry, in fact, that the next time Angie went in for a review, he threatened to drop her salary to $15 an hour. "You should be grateful that I pay you more than I pay everyone else, not pit them against me," he said. It became clear to Angie that if she wanted to stay friends with Candace, she wouldn't be able to tell her everything about work. She had to remember to keep her work and personal lives in balance.

Emotional Talk

Una Stannard, a satirical writer on women's issues, claims, "Men are no more immune from emotions than women; we think women are more emotional because culture lets them give free vent to certain feelings, 'feminine' ones, that is, no anger please, but it is okay to turn on the waterworks."

Women talk freely and openly about problems at home and problems at work. This is an integral part of women's communication. Emotions around these problems are sometimes expressed involuntarily.

We addressed the issue of the crying game in Chapter 9 and its potentially adverse impact on women's credibility. Both welling up and weeping are dangerous territory. Another aspect of crying is the connection between crying and expressing commitment and passion about an issue.

When Hillary Clinton was in New Hampshire during a grueling and rigorous campaign schedule, she was asked a question about the difficulty of campaigning that was a trigger for tears. It was framed compassionately toward her—and she teared up. She did not break down and sob. For a moment, she choked up. A tear never rolled down her cheek. She quickly regained her composure.

But not quickly enough. It was like the shot heard around the world. The press would not let go. Douglas Brown, a writer for *The Denver Post*, said Clinton did not cry—she just "welled up." His distinction was that "though only slight in physiological terms, [it] is in politics like the difference between skiing to the lip of a cliff and stopping, and skiing to the lip of a cliff and ... not stopping." Was Clinton stressed out and worn out? Sure she was, and undoubtedly it contributed to her emotional reaction.

Tears can express compassion and commitment and actually come to a professional woman's service, if kept in control and kept in the proper context. Betty, the founder of a nonprofit organization, was giving a speech to the Rotary club in hopes of acquiring a big grant for her medical work in third-world countries. Midpresentation, she caught a glimpse of a picture of a child in her slide show, and despite her deep breath and a big gulp, a few tears fell from her eyes. She tried to ignore the tears and kept moving forward in the speech.

She was disappointed with herself and was sure she had blown it—until after the presentation. Several Rotary members approached her and said they had been listening to different presentations every week for a year, and hers stood out like no other. The reason: they believed she was sincere, dedicated, and selfless, and that reflected upon her whole organization. Betty's tears—in moderation, and also from a place of honest passion—earned her credibility and trust. But if she had broken down and begun wailing on the spot, it would have made everyone uncomfortable and made her nonprofit appear disorganized and out of control.

If you overheard your teenager setting up a drug deal at home, keep this news at home. What happens at home should stay at home. Share it with your gal pals outside of work. If you have close confidants at work, make sure you trust them not to spread the news. And if you are sharing confidences with them, make sure you have a secure location; the local burger joint near work may have ears.

Martha had the largest portfolio of all the partners in her public account-ing firm. One day out of the blue, her biggest client called to say he was pulling everything from his account with her. She was in shock and un-prepared for this unexpected bad news. She was sobbing when her boss came into her office and said, "Why don't you take it like a man and just go into the bathroom and throw up?" The lesson is this: if you can't con-trol your emotions, leave the office. Take a break. Take the rest of the day off. (Note: we're not encouraging you to act like the man in this case and throw up instead of cry.) And don't think that the ladies' bathroom is a sanctuary. Many women retreat there like it is a safety zone. Other women visiting the ladies' room will feel compelled to ask what you're doing in there. It will get around the office that you are having a crying jag and have lost it.

The Power of Emotional Endurance and Resiliency

Audrey is a long-distance altitude hiker. She has learned that the single most critical skill to her success on the trail is endurance. And so much of physical endurance has to do with emotional endurance: the ability to keep up, hold your own, understand your limits, and keep going—a metaphor for our emo-tional behavior at work.

We all know there are ups and downs in our work life and home life. We all make mistakes at work, lose a client, or screw up an order. Successful women don't let their emotions dictate their behavior. They are pragmatic and think about the big picture, such as "I have to work with this jerk on this project for the next year, so I'd better learn how to get along with him." Successful women keep their emotions in check in order to enhance their career.

Tina is emotionally impulsive and struggles to separate her work and personal lives. Granted, she owns a photography business with her boyfriend, so the separation is harder to make. And being emotionally impulsive, this means their relationship is always on the rocks. Tina can't figure out why her business struggles and why she loses so many clients. Her photo work and editing are far superior to any of her competitors, and her prices are lower. People love her work—until they experience her impulsivity. Every time Tina and her co-owner boyfriend have a small fight, she calls, e-mails, or texts all of her customers, announcing, "I am sorry to announce that the business is closing due to personal problems." Two days later, the fight is over and the couple is happily back together again. She never apologizes for her announcement, but she begins contacting customers again like nothing happened. Needless to say, the customers feel confused and put off, and they rarely come back after that. If Tina could slow down and not be so reactive before crying wolf and shutting down the whole company—on a monthly basis—she would appear more professional and reliable. Who wants to work with someone who throws in the towel publicly at every bump in the road?

Emotional endurance requires resiliency. When the going gets tough, the tough get going. A resilient woman knows that the best antidote to despair is action. She does not retreat in the face of adversity.

Women can rise above the "ain't it awful?" people and the negativity that often arises when an organization is experiencing rough times. See above it and down the road.

Resiliency is most crucial in the face of failure and disappointment. Maintaining a positive attitude and putting a crisis in its place is key. This is a gift that your organization will find priceless and that, incidentally, often impacts the bottom line.

Remember, your ability to do a good job at work comes from inside. Even if the external structure where you express your work ethic and skills is struggling, it does not define you. Think about the sinking *Titanic* and the musicians who played until they literally could not any longer. They refused to be defined by the environment around them, and they even used their personal skills to comfort themselves and others when the environment around them was in chaos. That's valuable. That's resilience.

> ## ➤ SWITCH IT UP! ◀
>
> When you feel strongly about something but are surrounded by negativity toward your ideas, use the technique of *contrasting*. Clearly state what you do want and don't want: "I want us to be on target and not over budget. I cannot accept going over budget." You can cue people to be patient with you by saying, "This is difficult for me because I see the situation differently than you do." Do not give in or acquiesce if a person acts offended and you know you were not offensive. Sometimes people use a crazy-making tactic when women are respectfully assertive and clear. They are simply offended because a woman is being assertive, but they will accuse you of being offensive when you are not. Acknowledge their feelings, but don't give in to them: "I can see you are struggling with my idea."

Emotional Management at Work

You're at work and a coworker unloads about the boss, in front of other colleagues. As you listen, you think to yourself, "He's so right about how unfair the boss can be." He may be right in his assessment of the boss, but his behavior is unprofessional. You are thinking, "Oh no, not here, pal. Not now. You are so wrong to do this. You are screwed if this gets back to the boss."

The idea of professionalism is central to emotional management in the workplace. The workplace requires us to mask our feelings, especially our negative emotions. When we deal with a customer's unending questions that we have answered already, we must mask our frustration and impatience. You may be disappointed or unhappy from a decision that headquarters made, but you'd best slap a smile on your face! Wait until you get home, where it is safe to unload how you really feel. This may seem emotionally limiting, especially for women. But emotional management in the workplace is in everyone's best interest. Now, we don't want to create a robotic image of people acting and talking in a highly prescribed way, but there is a balance between *spontaneously* expressing emotions and *strategically* expressing them. Expressing emotions effectively isn't a simple matter. It doesn't matter whether it is negative emotions, like boredom or anger, or positive emotions, like love or affection. Showing these feelings is not always wise. On the flip side, always withholding emotions can stunt relationships from growing and developing.

Some emotional rules of engagement can help us monitor appropriate displays at work:

- Know thyself. What are you feeling?

- Control your impulse to act. (Don't be reactive. Be proactive.)

- Go to that happy place or somewhere else in your head. This might just mean taking 10 deep breaths, going on a walk, or thinking about things that make you happy.

- Choose your words carefully. Be intentional, not impulsive.

- Sustain and maintain during resistance. Don't give in to pressure.

Alice, an engineer employed by one of the world's largest telecommunication companies, had a problematic and alienating communication style. Many of her female coworkers claimed that every time they were around her, they left the interaction feeling out of sorts. Most could not put their finger on what this woman engineer did or said—they just felt like they had been "slimed" (one person's words). They felt bad. One woman thought about it and said that Alice always had a way of diminishing her, making any contribution she made seem meaningless and unimportant. "I would just like to smack her. She is so insulting," one woman said.

This impulse was a fantasy. All emotions are impulses to act. And this impulse has evolutionary roots. How we choose to act has a lot to do with family history and cultural norms. The root word for emotion is *motere*, the Latin verb "to move." So we know we need to act, but the question becomes "How?" What will we say or do? We have a choice. Making the right choice has a lot to do with our workplace success.

code **SWITCH** *Controlling the impulse to act is huge. Most of us suffer from impoverished emotional vocabularies. But don't let something leap out of your mouth as soon as the other person is done talking. Take a moment or two. Hesitate so you don't come from a reactive place.*

Sometimes you may be so shell-shocked that you are speechless. Try one of the following suggestions to calm down:

➡ **Ask for a break:** "I would like to take a 15-minute break" or "Let's resume this discussion later this afternoon so I have some time to process what you have said." This gives you time to ponder and reflect. It helps eliminate the possibility of a reactive response. If taking a break is not a practical logistical maneuver for your circumstances, go to another place in your head and have a conversation with yourself.

➡ **Practice self-talk:** "Ouch, that was mean. But I have my daughter's graduation to look forward to. My life is full of good things, and this nasty comment isn't going to dictate my behavior or get me down."

➡ **Develop an "emotional reset" button:** When Mandy has something tough happen at work, she has a simple cheer-me-up code with her boyfriend. She sends him a text that says, "Emergency cheer-me-up notification!" He knows that something upsetting happened but that she doesn't have the time (or the desire) to talk about it. He almost always responds with a simple "I love you" or "Think about how funny Fluffy looks in her new pink sweater." Just a tiny connection with something positive is like Mandy's emotional reset button. It puts the issue into perspective. Life does go on.

➡ **Take a bathroom break:** Another way that women can always buy a little time is a bathroom break. The bathroom can become a place to get centered. That doesn't mean wailing in the corner or complaining to the next woman who walks in; women love to get each other's opinions and overanalyze together. But at work, that might be risky and appear gossipy. Instead, take a deep breath, stretch, get some water, and put some space and time between the issue and your reaction.

It's also important to teach people how to treat you. When a coworker lobs an insult at you during the Monday morning staff meeting, you cannot let him get away with it. If you do or say nothing, you send a message that you are a doormat. That concern needs to be balanced with helping him save face while setting boundaries. Everyone in the staff meeting knows that what he said was inappropriate. They also feel uncomfortable with the insult done in such a public way. This difficult situation is an opportunity to shine. Show people what you can do. Show them that you can rise above it and keep the meeting on track. Do this by deescalating and deflecting. Don't address the "name calling." If someone suggests that you are "incompetent," trying to defend yourself will take the conversation nowhere and make you look defensive.

Instead, try a technique called *sorting*. Sometimes you have to choose to sort and ignore the insult, to stay focused on the issue: "John, I know you have a lot invested in this proposal. Sounds like my idea will not work for you. Can you and I meet later today to see how we can accommodate my concerns and yours?" You will be the heroine of the Monday morning staff meeting. Everyone will breathe a collective sigh of relief. You tackled the issue and stayed the course. You did not take things personally. And remember, the pig loves it when you get in the mud and get dirty with it. You know the old saying: don't stoop to their level.

Women also have a tendency to overqualify emotions: "I'm pretty worried" or "I'm sort of upset." Both women and men may experience emotions like happiness or anger in a similar way, but women have been taught that they can strongly express the emotion of happiness, whereas men have been taught to control it. Anger, on the other hand, is taboo for women to express and one of the sanctioned emotions for men to express. The impact of socialization practices accumulates over time, so these stereotypes are likely to apply more strongly to adults.

code **SWITCH** *Try to express a feeling verbally: use a single word, without overqualifying. "I'm upset." "I'm thrilled." Use metaphors: "I'm so angry I can't see straight." "I'm worried I will rock the boat." Use action: "Right now, I want to run away from this project." "This is so overwhelming that I want to give up."*

The differences in the expression of an emotion, not the experience of an emotion, underlie the gender emotion stereotype. Adults can distinguish between men's and women's emotional expressions and emotional experiences, and the documented gender-differentiated perceptions occur for emotional expressions only. Specifically, people perceive *women as expressing their emotions more often than men,* but no differences were found between perceptions of men's and women's emotional experience.

Women struggle with the "heart" and "head," or emotional/rational dichotomy. At work, the scales need to be tipped more to the "head," or rational side. Yes, of course, you can relay your heartfelt concern or passion for an idea, but the *rational* expression of emotions needs to dominate the overall message. You can be your emotional manager.

14

Keep Your Hands to Yourself

What do you need to know about sexual harassment to make you be a successful businesswoman? Although the law requires companies to work to prevent sexual harassment, many companies still don't talk about it or do anything to remind their employees about this despicable workplace behavior. Almost 30 years ago, none of the companies where Claire was an employee or with whom Audrey consulted mentioned or did any training to prevent or respond to sexual harassment.

Have things changed? Oh sure, you may see the policy on your starting day or in the new employee orientation—along with 20 other policies and procedures that you're asked to initial to show you have read them and agree to comply.

Some of the young women Claire teaches at a local college think of sexual harassment as a thing of the past, part of the dinosaur era; it's extinct and just doesn't happen anymore. Others argue that it does happen, but no one makes a big deal about it; it's the expected banter between women and men at work. Some of the older women students talk about it from personal experience, having gone to task to stop it from continuing at their workplace.

Wherever you fall on the opinion spectrum, sexual harassment is against the law. But what does it have to do with how to talk so men will listen? A lot. Making sure the men you work with know you won't tolerate this kind of behavior is imperative. Correcting and stopping inappropriate comments and behaviors targeted at you is a critical skill needed to succeed in the workplace. We mentioned in earlier chapters that if you don't say or do anything to stop a behavior, others may think that you agree with it, it doesn't bother you, or you condone it. What if you do agree with it or think the sexual banter or innuendos are funny? Guess what? The behaviors are still most likely against your company policy. Your professional resumé is on the line here. You don't want to have your career turn into damaged goods because you stood by and let the behaviors continue. You need to know what to say to men (and yes, it is mainly men who sexually harass women) to stop that behavior.

A Look at the Laws

Every woman needs to understand the laws that may affect her in the workplace. These include Title VII of the Civil Rights Act of 1964 that defines sex discrimination; the Pregnancy Discrimination Act included under Title VII; the Equal Pay Act requiring equal pay for essentially the same work done by men and women at a particular company; the Lilly Ledbetter Fair Pay Act of 2009 that looks at unfair pay and the time frame for filing a discrimination charge; and the U.S. Equal Employment Opportunity Commission's (EEOC) Guidelines on Sexual Harassment. Refer to the website www.eeoc.gov to learn about these federal laws and others (discrimination, harassment, related retaliation, and a hostile work environment based on race, sex, age, religion, national origin, disabilities, veteran status, and color) that may impact you or your colleagues. Check your individual state's laws for similar regulations that protect your rights. Some state laws also prevent discrimination based on marital status and sexual orientation.

The EEOC defines sexual harassment as this:

> Unwelcome sexual advances, requests for sexual favors, and other verbal or physical conduct of a sexual nature constitute sexual harassment when this conduct explicitly or implicitly affects an individual's employment, unreasonably interferes with an individual's work performance, or creates an intimidating, hostile, or offensive work environment.

Unwelcome behavior of a sexual nature can be verbal (jokes, innuendos, suggestive comments) or nonverbal (inappropriate touching, ogling, posters, e-mails, stares at body parts, leering, whistles, brushes against another's body, and behaviors up to and including sexual assault or rape).

When talking about sexual harassment, you may hear the Latin words *quid pro quo*, meaning "this for that," or an exchange of sexual favors for some type of employment decision, such as demotion, promotion, financial bonus, transfer, or termination. For example, if you agree to date the boss, you'll get that promotion. To be considered sexual harassment, such a request must be unwelcome (you don't want to date the boss) and/or you may perceive that you have no other choice but to comply, to avoid losing your job, being demoted, or being impacted by some type of work action.

A hostile work environment consists of a pattern of unwelcome sexual behaviors that are persistent or so harsh that they interfere with your ability to do your job. You may feel so overwhelmed by the constant barrage of sexual jokes and innuendos that you find it difficult to even come to work each day, let alone do your job. Be aware that it generally takes more than one sexual joke to establish a legally defined hostile work environment. Our goal is to help you stop the behavior when it first happens so that the behavior is not repeated day after day and there's no chance of creating a hostile environment.

Generally, the courts don't view one inappropriate remark, unless extreme in its vulgarity, as constituting a legally hostile environment. But several inappropriate comments, or name-calling—such as "honey," "sugar," "sweet thing," "love," or "hottie"—that are aimed at the women may indicate in court that the work environment does not value and support women.

Understand that a legally defined hostile environment based on sexual harassment is *not* an environment in which the boss is mad, angry, or mean toward you. We often get questions during training discussions asking, if an employee doesn't get along with the boss or other coworkers, wouldn't that be a hostile environment? Yes, it may be hostile or difficult and unfriendly, but unless the unwelcome behaviors are repeated and of a sexual nature, it is not legally considered a hostile environment based on sexual harassment.

I Think We Have a Policy Somewhere …

Know your company policy in addition to knowing the laws. Now, you don't have to memorize the policy line by line. A company's sexual harassment policy usually defines harassment and provides information on what to do and where to go to get help if and when it happens. Good information. The policy may say to talk to your supervisor. Or if your supervisor is doing the behavior (yikes!), go to another supervisor, your supervisor's supervisor, or the human resources manager. A good policy states that retaliation against someone for seeking help, filing a complaint, or participating in an investigation also violates the policy and the law.

Ideally, your organization promotes a safe and harassment-free work environment for all its employees, both men and women; its leaders are well aware of their legal responsibilities and act as role models to maintain a respectful workplace for everyone.

Some people think that having a policy in place will stop bad-boy behavior. Reality, as witnessed in the press, on TV, and in EEOC-filed cases, continues to prove that there are a lot of men out there testing the workplace waters with their sexual remarks and behaviors.

Does He Harass Her or She Harass Him?

Both women and men can be sexual harassers or recipients of harassment. In 2008, 16 percent of the 13,867 sexual harassment complaints filed with the EEOC were submitted by men. The remaining 84 percent were complaints filed by women. While there are a few cases of men harassing other men, women harassing other women, and women harassing men, the overwhelming majority of the EEOC cases filed involve men harassing women.

Still, the number of sexual harassment cases being filed *by* men has been steadily increasing during the past 16 years. In 1992, 9 percent of the cases reported to the EEOC were filed by men, 7 percentage points lower than five years later. This increase may indicate that as women have started obtaining positions with power, they, too, have fallen into abusing that power by sexually harassing those around them.

But because most sexual harassers are men and most of those harassed are women, we focus on that. It would be great if we could say that all male sexual harassers were 6 feet tall, Caucasian, and muscular, with brown wavy hair and a mustache. Then we'd know what to watch out for. But we can't. Sexual harassers come in all colors, sizes, and shapes. We knew of one man in a wheelchair who had the habit of rolling up behind women and caressing their butts to get their attention.

One characteristic that sexual harassers tend to have in common is power. Either they have assigned power (your boss, director, CEO) or they perceive that they have power over you. Even if you are colleagues at the same work level, they feel that they can exert their views over you. And harassers tend to look for the most vulnerable member in the group. It could be a woman who is a new employee, an isolated employee, someone who goes along with the group or never speaks up, or someone the harasser feels won't stand up for herself.

The harasser could be the vendor who comes into the office once a month and provides an array of sexual jokes to the receptionist, who is always alone in the front office. She doesn't like the jokes and thinks the guy is slimy. It could be the 80-year-old part-time volunteer who likes to tell all the "girls" (the 55- to 65-year-olds) how pretty they are and what he'd do with them if he was 20 years younger. Some of the women ignore him, others shoot down a different hallway when they see him heading their way, some feel sorry for him, and others want the creepy guy to leave them alone. It could be your sales director at the vendor conference in Toledo. After a few drinks, he takes you aside and expresses his deep longings for you. You say you're not interested and head back to your hotel room. A few hours later, at 2 A.M., you hear loud banging at your door. It's him and a buddy, and they want to see how good you look in your nightgown.

Are these situations exaggerations? Hardly. These are situations in which you need to take some action. Don't sit there and let the behavior happen to you.

code SWITCH *Be assertive. Let the harasser know that his behavior is not wanted, is not appropriate for the workplace, and has to stop.*

Christine was new to the office, and Dan sat nearby. He was known for his off-color jokes and uncomfortable comments, but no one stood up to him. It's not that he was particularly powerful. He had a sort of default power by having worked at the office for years longer than most others. He was a hard worker. No one wanted to upset him because he did get a lot done.

Then one day, Christine was eating a peach at her desk when she noticed Dan staring at her. She tried to ignore him, but he continued leering. Then he made a perverted comment about how she was eating the peach. Instead of laughing it off or ignoring him, she stood up and matter-of-factly said in front of everyone, "I do not want you talking to me that way." He was so upset and shocked that he quit one week later. The other women in the office later told Christine thanks and said that they felt so relieved not having to deal with him anymore.

Court Cases and Women Who Speak Up

The October 2007 headlines of New York Knicks' coach Isiah Thomas were sickening reminders that working women have not come as long of a way as you might think. This situation proved how costly a public relations disaster could be for the famed basketball team's owners, Madison Square Garden, and for the coach. As reported in the media, the jury sent an $11.6 million message that there is no excuse for calling an employee a "ho" and "bitch," among a laundry list of other offensive behaviors. Hmmm, guess that's a no-no. Puh-lease! Whenever a man uses these kinds of words to describe a woman, he is talking about someone's mother, sister, daughter, or grandmother. In today's world, one of the best methods of correcting the situation is financial punishment.

Anucha Browne Sanders, a former Madison Square Garden marketing executive, filed her case with the New York federal court in January 2006 after management failed to do anything to stop Isiah Thomas's unwanted behaviors, according to media stories. Browne Sanders had repeatedly complained, and when Madison Square Garden investigated and couldn't support her complaints, they terminated her. After the $11.6 million settlement, the executives might see things a bit differently now. But hey, why not fire her? They're the big boys. What's she going to do? Sue Madison Square Garden and the coach of the New York Knicks? And win? Well, yes.

Browne Sanders had the will, ability, and perseverance to prevail. She endured the three-week trial during which the defendant's profanities and inappropriate behaviors were examined in the light of day from the clear-eyed perspective of third parties. Questionable behaviors included the "no-love hug," as described in an ABC news article. According to reports, one day Thomas approached

Browne Sanders from the back, touched her shoulder, and leaned over to kiss her cheek. She pulled away and Isiah Thomas said, "What, no love today?"

Isiah Thomas agreed that it was wrong for a man to call any woman of any color a bitch. However, a former Knicks executive, Jeffrey Nix, testified that he was in the office many times when Thomas called Browne Sanders a "bitch" or a "ho" and also heard him say to her, "Don't forget, you (explicit) bitch, I'm the president of this (explicit) team," according to the media reports. Throughout the proceedings, Thomas denied any wrongdoing; he was innocent, he said. Jurors saw it differently and awarded Browne Sanders a huge judgment.

This may be considered an extreme case, with the woman losing her job and then at the trial being awarded $11.6 million. But it could have easily been resolved when Browne Sanders first came forward, told management, and asked for help to stop the behaviors. These were the assertive things to do. Unfortunately, according to the media, Madison Square Garden management could not substantiate the complaints and the behaviors, and ultimately fired her. Knowing the laws and understanding that she had certain rights helped Browne Sanders move forward and continue pursuing her complaint through legal avenues.

Are Compliments Harassment?

The Merriam-Webster online dictionary defines a compliment as "an expression of esteem, respect, affection, or admiration," "an admiring remark," or a "formal and respectful recognition." We think most people would enjoy being complimented in the workplace. Some people have even said that they get put off when they have gone out of their way to look good at work and no one seems to notice.

Others suggest that a compliment can easily be misunderstood. Saying to a woman, "You look great in that blouse" (verbal message) while staring at her boobs (nonverbal message) just isn't right. Saying "For a woman, you had a lot of good ideas in the meeting" is a backhanded remark obviously couched as a compliment to hide the insinuation that it is extraordinary for a woman to contribute a good idea. Had she been a he, the compliment would have been simply, "Great idea, Joe! Nice contribution to the discussion."

Any compliment—whether verbal or nonverbal—should always comply with the company's policy about sexual harassment and foster a respectful workplace. Language and expressions used on the street or outside of work often are not okay for the workplace.

> Claire was walking down the hallway when a male employee entered the hallway walking toward her. They nodded hello as he passed her. She then heard him say "Lean and mean" in kind of a sing-song way. For an instant Claire thought, "Oh, do I really have to deal with this?" And then she turned around. He was still leering at her. She said, "Did you just say that to me?" He said he didn't mean anything by it. She introduced herself to him as the Equal Employment Opportunity (EEO) manager, told him it was an inappropriate comment for the workplace, and asked him not to say that again to her. Claire was pretty angry for the rest of the day that he'd felt comfortable enough in the work environment to say that. It showed a total lack of respect for her and her job. Clearly, Claire had her work cut out for her in that office.

When you receive a compliment that makes you feel uncomfortable, let the person know. If someone comes up to you, rubs your back, and says, "I really like your blouse. Was it a gift?" and you're uncomfortable with the compliment and/or don't want to be touched, let the person know.

⇒ "I'm uncomfortable with you touching me. You don't want me to feel uncomfortable, do you?"

⇒ "Don't touch me. That's reserved for my boyfriend/girlfriend/wife/husband/significant other."

⇒ "Don't do that, ever."

⇒ "Listen, I don't like being touched. Thanks for not doing that anymore."

⇒ "Look, you and I have to work together on this project and I want everything to go well. I consider your touching me and rubbing my back to be out of line. Please don't do that again. Let's focus on getting the job done."

Sometimes you need to keep saying the same phrase over and over to get your point across. Using the previous example ...

Him (while rubbing her back): "I really like your blouse. Was it a gift?"

You: "Don't touch me. That's reserved for my boyfriend."

Him: "I didn't mean anything by it."

You: "Don't touch me. That's reserved for my boyfriend."

Him: "You look so nice, I had to touch you."

You: "Don't touch me. That's reserved for my boyfriend."

Him: "I was just trying to help you relax."

You: "Don't touch me. That's reserved for my boyfriend."

Him: "So you don't want me to touch you?"

You: "Don't touch me. That's reserved for my boyfriend."

Him: "Okay, I get it. I won't touch you."

You: "Good. Don't touch me. Let's get back to work."

A nonverbal response such as pulling away may get his hands off you, but not everyone gets the nonverbal message. Men are not mind readers (and they don't pick up nonverbals as clearly as women do). You need to say what you want.

code `SWITCH` *Set your boundaries! You have the right and responsibility to reject unwanted and inappropriate behavior. Be direct. Be specific. How about this? Tell him to keep the compliments work focused!*

One restaurant waitress, Beth, got smacked on her butt by the male cooks and dishwashers every time she walked in back to get her orders. The other waitresses did not mind it and, in fact, had helped contribute to the environment by not drawing a line. When Beth complained to corporate, a half-dozen of the workers lost their jobs. Beth quit, too, because she felt too awkward and demeaned to return. Everyone was mad at her, but she had done nothing wrong. Remember, by tolerating sexual harassment, you are not only violating company policy, but also setting a standard that other women might not be comfortable with. It isn't only about you.

Don't accept being called names or words that have a sexual connotation or a high level of vulgarity, even if you welcome them or say it's okay. These words are most likely a violation of your company's policy. Don't fire back with your own version of sexual names. Don't allow yourself to be brought down to the harasser's level.

When you get that knot in your stomach from a compliment, let that person know that they've crossed the line and that you expect an immediate change in their behavior. Work is work.

Many times even one inappropriate compliment (verbal messages and non-verbal ones such as an admiring or leering stare) is a violation of policy. And don't think that you're all clear to avoid women and compliment only the men. Such a company may be setting itself up for a claim of sex discrimination: treating women and men differently.

Save the Hugs for Your Stuffed Teddy Bear

To hug or not to hug? As trainers brought in to teach a male-dominated company's manufacturing employees about preventing sexual harassment in the workplace, Audrey and Claire talked about touching and hugging in the workplace. Most men say they don't like to be hugged, especially by another man, in the workplace. Women usually say they don't mind a hug, depending on the type of hug (groping versus hugging) and who gives the hug (a strange man or a friend). Men generally say that a hug outside of work is okay if it's from their wives or family members. Some men are still hesitant about getting a hug from a male family member.

Claire worked with a colleague, Joan, in a company in Colorado for many years. There no one hugged as part of the daily greeting. When Joan went to the company's headquarters in northern New Jersey and finally met Bill, a colleague she had been speaking with for several months by phone, he gave her a big hug and a kiss on the cheek. Joan's face immediately turned red; she wondered for days what he had meant by his greeting. Well, he'd meant "Hello!" She thought it was some sicko sexual advance and she'd have to transfer to get away from him. She later saw many in the New Jersey office hugging as they greeted each other, and some even did the kiss-on-the-cheek routine. Claire encouraged Joan to let Bill know that she was not a hugger and preferred a handshake greeting. Joan did this; Bill confirmed that he'd just been saying hello, and it all worked out.

Also consider cultural differences. In some countries, it is standard to kiss on the cheek and hug when you meet someone, whereas in other countries, a touch-free bow with your eyes diverted is expected. Know your environment and group before you jump to conclusions—or overstep your boundaries.

Still, don't let cultural differences be excuses for inappropriate comments or comments that make you feel uncomfortable. The custodian at one large office building is an older man from Korea. The women avoid him because of his comments, but they tolerate them because they consider it "cultural." His comments are gender demeaning and backhanded, such as, "That dress is so tight, I don't know how you got in it or how your husband will get you out of it tonight" or "I like your dress. Your husband must be making a lot of money to buy you such nice clothes." He always follows up with a big burst of laughter (as if that diffuses the inappropriateness) and then walks away, preventing any kind of response from the women, positive or negative.

Tell Him You're Not Interested

Your coworker, Bob, thinks you're special. However, being asked out on a date by Bob should happen only once if your initial answer is "No." If you're on the receiving end of Bob's unwanted dating requests, be direct and tell him that your answer is no and that you don't want to be asked again. Take notes on what happened and what you said, in case you need to talk with human resources if the behavior continues. If you find that Bob keeps asking you out or giving you unwanted gifts or compliments, it will start looking like a repeated pattern of unwanted behavior of a sexual nature. In other words, it could build a hostile work environment for you. No is no. He needs to stop and look elsewhere for that special someone. You've made it clear: it ain't you. If Bob doesn't take "No" for an answer, get your supervisor or human resources manager involved.

Whether in the public arena, government, the military, private industry, or just about any business in the United States, when a sexual behavior is unwelcome, it can easily be labeled as sexual harassment. Even when a seemingly consensual relationship turns sour, there can be sexual harassment repercussions in the workplace. What started as "he loves me" after the breakup may turn into "he forced me to have the relationship in order to keep my job." Poor judgment and inappropriate behaviors are usually warning signs that more may be happening at work than appears on the surface.

> ### SWITCH IT UP! <

Even Dear Abby, Jeanne Phillips, gave advice in a December 8, 2008, column on what to do each time a certain trade representative visited the office and repeatedly flirted with a particular woman. He moved in close to her, lowered his normal speaking voice, and whispered that she has a nice smell. The woman didn't like it and didn't know how to make him stop. Abby told "Had it in Beaufort, S.C." to be direct. "[Say to him] clearly (and loudly) that he is making you uncomfortable and if he doesn't stop immediately, you will report him to your boss. And if he tries anything again, follow through." Abby suggested writing down what he did and how the woman responded for each of his visits. Don't put up with this kind of behavior. You have a right to be harassment-free on the job.

Watch Out for Blaming the Victim

Is it the woman's fault that a man sexually harasses her? Does she encourage him in some way to harass her? Blaming the victim is a sociological concept that has been around since the 1960s, when minority groups were blamed for the cause of their own social problems, such as low income and poor housing. It has been broadened and used to describe battered women or victims of crimes such as rape. "Surely, the victim did something to deserve her or his fate."

Consider the following examples of blaming the victim. Former Gov. Eliot Spitzer of New York resigned from office over his relationship with a call girl, according to the media. The headlines in the 2008 Spitzer scandal revealed the inclination to blame the victim. Meredith Vieira, from the NBC *Today* show, interviewed Dr. Laura Schlessinger, a radio host, on this topic in March 2008.

"Are you saying the women should feel guilty, like they somehow drove the man to cheat?" Vieira inquired.

Schlessinger replied, "Yes, I hold women accountable for tossing out perfectly good men by not treating them with the love and kindness and respect and attention they need."

His wife was being blamed for not being able to keep her husband away from a prostitute. Forget self-control and responsibility!

A discussion with Anne, a manager, also illustrates the tendency to blame the victim in sexual harassment cases. Anne was 35, a single woman; worked for a Virginia tech company; and was the only female in a sales and marketing team. Among many examples of the sex-charged culture of this team was a business card with a salesman's name and contact information, as well as the fake title "traveling gynecologist."

The male team members carried the card to give to vendors, customers, and colleagues. While the team was in Palm Springs for a conference, Anne decided to hit the hot tub (she mentioned she was careful in the selection of her bathing suit—it was a modest one-piece) after a long day. She went alone, but some of the men from the team showed up. The men had been drinking. What happened next caught Anne off guard. One of the men put his hand between her legs and said, "We should get it on." Anne was quick. She pushed him away and said, "Never." She left immediately and retreated to her room.

When Anne returned to the office, she met with her boss to report the incident. After she shared her account of the event, he replied, "Why did you go to the hot tub?" He went on to interrogate her about her behavior: "Were you drinking?" She'd had water.

Anne said, "From that day on, things were never the same." She was scolded by her boss and told to be nice to the men in her group. She was excluded from social activities and separated from her peers. Using exclusionary tactics and ignoring the individual are common retaliation behaviors aimed at the recipient. Retaliation behaviors should be stopped and reported, too.

Why is it that if a woman is attractive or single or wearing a tight skirt, some men conclude that they may make lewd and suggestive comments or fondle her, as long as "it's all in fun" or it's "to be expected?" Remember power plays and socialization that we talked about earlier? Generally whether or not a man has an assigned power position like supervisor, just by socialization as a man in the U.S. culture, he may see himself as having power over others, especially women. So he may make comments about her tight skirt or visible cleavage; he may even make comments about her turtleneck and pants suit. He sees himself having power and no one's there to stop him. However, there's no excuse for inappropriate comments in the workplace. Men and women both have responsibilities to look and act professionally at work. (See Chapter 8 for reminders on appropriate work wear.)

I Didn't Mean Anything by It

Intent versus impact is a basic concept in discussions of preventing sexual harassment. With sexual harassment, the focus is on the impact of the behavior on you, personally. The person who did the inappropriate behavior often says he didn't mean anything negative, he was joking, he was trying to be nice, or we can't have any fun around here—anything to indicate it was not his intention to make you feel uncomfortable. But the impact is just that— you're uncomfortable, embarrassed, or hurt by the remark.

Audrey is reminded of an event in which she served on a board for a women's shelter. The guild (the fundraising arm) decided to put on a fashion show. The fashion show opened with women models coming out in revealing lingerie. There was a collective gasp from the coed audience. The board knew the women on the guild had intended to raise money, but did not consider the impact of parading models in lingerie for a benefit for abused women and children. Here it was good intention, but a bad impact.

The "go along to get along" principle happens with sexual harassment behaviors, too. We have both been involved in investigations of sexual harassment situations. Invariably, we discover that the recipient goes along with the harassing behavior so as not to make a mess of the situation. It's easier to laugh at the dirty joke or accept the long, tight hug just to fit into the crowd and go with the flow. Most people want to be a part of the group and conform to the work culture. They don't want to stick out, or be too different, or be the one who stands up and says that sexual remark just isn't funny. Unfortunately, the behavior doesn't stop, and at some point, someone needs to speak up or find help to get the behavior stopped.

code `SWITCH` *Say to him, "I know you didn't mean anything by it and you were just trying to get a laugh, but your comment was offensive and made many people feel uncomfortable."*

Sometimes the harassment can be subtle, which makes it easy to choose to not rock the boat. Angie had been working in her office under the same male boss for five years before he began getting extra friendly. It started as compliments about how she looked. This didn't bother her. Then he began asking her to get a drink after work. She was married and always said "No," but he wasn't pushy, and she couldn't prove he wasn't just being nice.

Then one day they were talking about good movies, and he brought up a few she had not seen. He offered to bring her his copies so she could watch them over the weekend. Sounded great—until the next day, when he handed her a stack of movies. Wedged in between the flicks they had talked about were two extremely vulgar pornos. Angie did not know what to do. Had it been intentional? Was it an honest mistake? She kept quiet and gave him back the movies on Monday. She said she hadn't had a chance to even look through them because she was so busy, but thanks anyway. She felt like she should have said something, but she didn't know how—or what. "Um, I think you left your pornos in the stack"? "There were some movies from you I didn't want, and I'm giving them back"? She chose the quiet route, even though it made her feel worse.

Audrey was conducting prevention of sexual harassment training for a large U.S. company. A few days before the training, a manager passed around a postcard (he said, in preparation for her training) that read, "I thought 'Dictaphone' was a form of sexual harassment." He thought it was funny and would "ease the tension people were feeling" about the upcoming training. Of course, it simply tried to use humor to discredit and undermine the training. There's nothing funny about sexual harassment.

A different firm asked Audrey to assess an incident for liability concerns. When she first walked into the office, she noted a male employee in flip-flops and shorts. His cubicle was adorned with travel posters featuring thong-clad women. She got this entire visual from the receptionist's desk. Five minutes later, during her first interview with the CEO, she learned that some of the men acted like they worked at Animal House. Yup, a bunch of frat boys just having a little fun. One of the daily rituals in this office was for one of the male employees to emulate the sex act in the break room while holding on to the water cooler. Never mind who was present. The intent was to have a little male bonding banter. In their minds, the intent was just being funny. The impact was creating a sexually charged, hostile environment.

Would any reasonable person want their daughter, wife, or mother subjected to such behavior?

The impact of the behavior, not the intent of the person who did the behavior, determines whether sexual harassment has occurred. Courts have found that a hostile environment exists if the recipient believes the environment to be abusive and if a reasonable person would find it to be an abusive environment. Would a reasonable man or woman find these types of behaviors offensive in the workplace? Yes. These types of behaviors do not contribute to a safe and harassment-free workplace.

Your Liability as the Supervisor

Lucky you! You've been promoted to supervisor. You now have additional responsibilities you didn't have before. You're considered an agent of the company, and all you do—or don't do—represents the company. If an employee approaches you with a sexual harassment issue, take it seriously. Take notes and let the person know that although you'll keep the situation as confidential as possible, you'll need to alert the human resources manager or other designated official at your company. A supervisor must show that she has taken immediate action to stop the behavior. We have worked with too many supervisors who acquiesced when their employee asked them to please not tell anyone. Because you are a woman, a woman employee may play on your sympathies and ask you to not do anything. Or she may say she just needs someone to listen and not do anything. You're in trouble if you agree to that. Remember, you are liable and you are placing your company in a position of liability if you don't take immediate action to correct the situation. The action may be as simple as calling the human resources (HR) director and telling her there's a situation that needs to be looked at. By alerting HR or your boss, you've taken action to get the behavior stopped.

Taking Care of Numero Uno

Take care of yourself at work. Speak up when someone hurls a sexually charged remark at you. Here are some basic rules of engagement when sexual harassment is lurking:

- Know your company's policy and what steps are recommended if sexual harassment happens to you.

- Think of your safety at all times.

- If someone's behavior makes you feel uncomfortable or is unwanted, tell the person you're uncomfortable. Ask the person to stop the behavior and not do it again.

- Be direct. Be specific. You don't have to explain yourself. "I need you to stop telling sexual jokes. That behavior is against our policy. Don't do it again or I will have to alert HR about the inappropriate behavior."

- No requirement says that you must tell the person to stop before you go to a supervisor or human resources and ask for help to stop the behavior. Check your policy. Depending on the severity of the situation, you may feel safer going to HR for help than trying to address the situation yourself.

code SWITCH *Have a meeting with your boss and HR. Let them know you have concerns about the office culture and how sexually charged it feels. Give examples. Let them know that a client remarked it was a sexual environment.*

➡ Take notes. Write down who said what, whether anybody else heard the remarks, your actions (you asked the person to stop), and whether the person agreed to stop. Hopefully that will end the issue. If it happens again, you'll have notes of what happened the last time that you can share with HR or a supervisor.

➡ If you hear or observe inappropriate behavior such as sexual jokes, innuendos, or suggestive remarks that are not directed at you but still make you feel uncomfortable, you have the right to have those behaviors stopped. Tell the person the conversation is inappropriate for work and/or talk with a supervisor or HR to help stop the situation.

code SWITCH *Tell him you are concerned about his "professional health" and how his sexual bantering may be the demise of his career.*

➡ If you're not sure what to do about a particular situation or if your company is slow to correct these types of issues, seek help and advice from your local EEOC or civil rights office.

Take charge of the situation and get the questionable behaviors stopped.

15

Cupid at the Office

Overall, dating at work is a bad idea and should be discouraged. However, the reality is that people flirt, sweet talk, date, and catch a kiss in the hallway when no one is looking. For women, this can jeopardize credibility with men (and other women) at work. Simply, women sacrifice their ability to influence men and get them to listen. She will be viewed as unprofessional. A sex object for sure, but not a business partner.

Helen Gurley Brown gave birth to the movement of flaunting women's sexuality everywhere, including in the workplace. Her book *Sex and the Single Girl* was an immediate best-seller, and she went on to become editor of *Cosmopolitan* magazine.

At a time when *Reader's Digest* and *The Ladies Home Journal* still insisted that a "nice" girl had only two choices—"she can marry him or she can say no"—Gurley Brown openly proclaimed that sex was an important part of a single woman's lifestyle. According to Brown, "The single girl is the new glamour girl."

Helen Gurley Brown rejected the rule to "forget about sex when there is work to be done." Brown maintained that the days when management "preferred a little brown wren at every desk" were long gone. In fact, one of her office rules for women was to hold out "the carrot of romantic perks" to men.

Brown became famous for her take on the business lunch: "Lunch with men is a chance to have dates in the daytime on the pretext of business. … Lunch dates with men are sex at high noon." For Brown, sex and work success go together. This was the 1960s and the sexual revolution. Brown epitomized this newfound freedom and power for women.

Fast-forward to today. Once sex and the office were out of the closet, they stayed out. To this day, Brown's *Cosmopolitan* magazine is the most-purchased women's magazine in the country. We have *Sex and the City* as our media role model for Gen X women on dating and working. What's a woman to do? This historical review reveals that we have come a long way, baby, but with it comes a big responsibility to yourself, your organization, and your career.

When Cupid Strikes: 9 A.M. to 5 P.M.

Many of us would like to think that our personal and professional lives are separate. Our personal life consists of friendships, relationships with romantic partners, and family. Our work life seems to be a parallel universe filled with coworkers and casual relationships with acquaintances.

However, this division is a pretense. As far as the dating pool goes, there is no more fertile ground to meet a potential romantic partner than in your workplace. You spend more time at work than any other place, and the number of people you interact with is greater than in any other context. An office romance survey conducted by Vault Inc., a New York–based media company focused on careers, found that 58 percent of employees have been involved in an office romance. More striking, the results show that people are more comfortable admitting to workplace romance than a decade ago. The 610 responses to the survey came from a variety of industries across the United States. The findings show many couples tried to hide their relationship with varying degrees of success.

code SWITCH *If you have a work lover, talk with him or her about the pros and cons of trying to keep it a secret. What do you have to gain or lose? Most important, get familiar with the company policy on dating. Yes, many organizations have dating policies in place and what employees should do if they become romantically involved.*

Cubicle Action

For some people, the office has a sort of aphrodisiac impact. Urban Dictionary (www.urbandictionary.com) calls it "work hot": you feel attracted to someone at work, but if you met that person outside the office, you might not be attracted to him. Valerie jokes that the work hot phenomenon is a by-product of being bored at work or just being around the same limited number of people all day. "Call it survival," she jokes.

There's also the allure of the forbidden and the allure of power. Given how closely people work together, it is natural that people can develop close relationships. Why are we surprised that people develop romantic feelings? The issue becomes what we do with the romance at the office.

Workplace romances are *mutually* desired relationships between two people that have an element of intimacy and/or sexuality. Employees need to understand that it may be okay to ask a coworker out on a date. However, they need to also understand that harassment occurs when the person indicates no interest and the unwanted attention continues. All employees need to understand where the line is. Many organizations ask employees to sign a document indicating that they understand and will abide by the sexual harassment policy, which includes a dating policy.

Workplace romances represent a unique kind of relationship. At work, approved relationships arise between employees for work-related reasons. Office romances are not officially sanctioned and are pursued for reasons that have nothing to do with the organization's business goals. They are extraneous and have nothing to do with getting work done.

Coworkers usually perceive most romantically involved workers in their organization as friendly and approachable. Also, many coworkers don't feel that most romantically involved people are any less productive because of their relationships. However, the perceptions of workplace romances are not always positive. Here are some concerns:

- People will gossip more about the romantic couple.

- People will think they are paying more attention to their romantic partner than their work.

➡ People believe the relationship will impact work decisions such as delegations, project approvals, and team composition.

When Love Goes Bad, Look Out!

If the United States has an almost 50 percent divorce rate, what is the success rate of dating? Even lower. Everyone at the office is holding their breath for the inevitability of the big breakup. When the breakup happens, people may take sides. Coalitions may form. Who's the bad one who caused the breakup? This makes for high drama at the office.

The same Vault Inc. survey found that only 22 percent of office romances led to marriage or a long-lasting relationship. When the love is good, everyone is happy—but when the love goes sour, watch for the fall out. Many people feel office dating is not a good idea because if the happy couple breaks up, they still have to see and work with each other on a daily basis. Your coworkers— the audience—watches and waits for the broken couple's drama to unfold. This is not conducive to a productive work setting for anyone.

Sam was an operations manager for a security organization. He became romantically involved with a direct report, Ginny, who was married—a major no-no for two reasons. First, he was her boss, which set himself up for a potential sexual harassment claim later down the road. Second, she was married, which set up office workers to make moral judgments.

The organization's policy prohibited romantic relationships between supervisors and subordinates. Of course, everyone at the office found out, and it almost brought the house down. Everyone felt uncomfortable and conflicted. Sam's relationship with Ginny impacted his credibility. His department was not functioning, and the problem of morale went all the way to the top. By the time the two were called into a disciplinary meeting, the relationship was over. But the damage had been done to their respective careers. Sam stayed, but Ginny left the organization. For two years, Ginny's friends at work held on to hostility toward Sam, and the atmosphere at work was tense and uncomfortable until her friends eventually left.

Today Sam is militant about not allowing workplace romance. The organization has taken extreme measures, such as no holiday luncheons, company barbeques, staff birthday parties, drinks with coworkers after hours, or offsite dinner award banquets.

Does Cupid Have a Place in the Office?

Workplace romances sometimes present a threat to organizational effectiveness through their negative effects on participants and coworkers. Other times, workplace romances can enhance workplace effectiveness through their positive effects on participants and their coworkers. Everyone enjoys being around people who are happy and walking that high of a new relationship. But remember the danger and potential landmines lurking in the hallways.

One of the major red flags of an office romance landmine is hierarchy, when one person reports to another (as with Sam and Ginny). Another kind of office romance is utilitarian, in which one participant satisfies personal/sexual needs in exchange for satisfying the other participant's task/career needs. Yes, it is often called sleeping your way to the top. Sex is provided as a utilitarian vehicle to get that promotion. It's not a behavior we advise.

Get your organization to provide training for supervisors and managers about how to discreetly address overt sexual behavior in the workplace. Also encourage them to make the supervisors comfortable in coaching the dating couple if the relationship results in lowered morale and productivity for themselves or coworkers. Few organizations take this kind of proactive measure. Save your organization a lawsuit and enhance productivity by making the supervisory staff as comfortable as possible with managing inevitable workplace romances.

Also know that women may pay a higher price for office romances. The negative outcomes are more pronounced for women, especially if a woman is under direct supervision of the man. It's the "she-slept-her-way-to-the-top" syndrome. Coworkers may not say it, but they can't help but think it, right?

Women can't win in this dating game, regardless of their status. If a woman is a subordinate, she gets special favors; if she is the boss, she is perceived as overstepping her boundaries more than a male supervisor. No getting around it—the double standard exists.

Let's reverse the status. Janet was a supervisor in a city government agency. Her employee, Jim, was attracted to her. Eventually, they began a romantic relationship. It was good for about nine months, and then it was over. Jim knew part of the thrill and adventures of a forbidden romance was breaking the rules. He decided to take advantage of the newfound power that he held over her when they broke up. Janet became a hostage to the fear that he would tell her supervisor. So he began coming to work late and not attending required meetings in the county. Those were just a few of the offenses. Janet turned a blind eye but was well aware that he was neglecting his job duties. The longer Janet was paralyzed with fear, the more outrageous his behavior violations became. At one point, she walked into his office and he had a woman sitting on his lap. If that wasn't enough, the woman made no effort to get off his lap when Janet walked in. Janet lost credibility with her staff. She felt trapped, and Jim knew it.

So Janet made a bold move that could have cost her a 20-year career with the county. She had no choice. Coworkers were lined up at her office door reporting one frustration after another with Jim's poor performance (or no performance, in some cases). Janet went to her boss and admitted her mistake dating Jim. They got the county attorney involved, and disciplining Jim became a long and difficult process. Eventually, Jim left the county and went to work for another city government.

We can all learn from Janet's story.

code SWITCH *If you are a supervisor thinking about becoming romantically involved, you have options. Your employee can move to another department. Remember the double standard; women pay a higher price.*

Where Do We Draw the Line?

Many organizations ask themselves where the line is between "none of our business" and "hurts our business." Recent cases in any newspaper make it all too clear that there's no precise way to predict what may happen when office romance doesn't blossom. If the two employees involved are in a supervisor/subordinate position, there is no way to predict whether the subordinate will later feel obligated to continue the relationship to keep his or her job or to climb the corporate ladder. What if feelings are not returned and, in extreme cases, a restraining order becomes necessary? How do the two work together then?

From a legal liability standpoint, these issues may be easy to disregard as mere feelings, but these feelings may later become the basis of an adverse employment action, a hostile work environment claim, or even a criminal matter. Any of these could cost the company a large settlement.

How can a woman successfully maintain a workplace romance? Consider these guidelines:

- Leave your love at home. Communicate in a strictly professional manner at work.

- Use e-mail and texting judiciously. Work e-mails should never contain romantic or intimate messages.

- Be familiar with your organization's written and unwritten policies about romantic, extramarital, or dating relationships.

- Avoid public displays of intimacy in the office, including the company parking lot. No flirting with your partner.

- Do your best to keep the relationship private until you are ready to go public with it.

- If you and your partner are attending the same conference off-site, remember that you are still at work.

- Don't hesitate to express different opinions and conduct yourself in the same way you did before the relationship. If you always challenged your partner's ideas, continue to do so.

➡ Don't date up. Don't date the boss.

➡ Don't date down. Don't date your employee.

All Eyes Are on You

Now that you have an office romance, everyone is watching. Your coworkers will stop what they are doing to study how you walk by your partner's office when you come to work in the morning. You are on stage.

code SWITCH *People are curious and are on the hunt to see displays of affection. Disappoint them. Be professional and leave the touches, love cards, and winks at home.*

Many employees use e-mail for personal reasons. However, when you are involved in a romantic relationship, it is wise to write e-mails that comply with company policy. Remember, there is no such thing as "delete." Forensic computer experts have been able to dig up all kinds of forbidden e-mails and Internet use. Anyone with any kind of know-how can access your e-mail messages. Just ask yourself, "Would I be okay with this message posted on the company billboard in the hallway?"

Don't hesitate to go to human resources and discuss the organization's policy on dating. You can ask for the conversation to be confidential. You can indicate that you and a coworker have a mutual attraction and are considering pursuing it. This kind of meeting not only informs you, but can also offer some protection. You are attempting to follow company policy.

The office includes the company parking lot and the hotel for the retreat. You are still at work, so don't forget it. No holding hands on your way to your car. No love cards left on your partner's desk. None of these behaviors go unnoticed. Remember, most organizations have security that includes surveillance cameras in the parking lot and stairwells. Don't even think about grabbing a smooch in the utility closet. And no shoulder massage while he is sitting at his desk.

Flirting is also inappropriate workplace etiquette. Flirting is socially acceptable in the right contexts, like at parties and in clubs. There may be no universal law because each workplace has its own unwritten rules governing flirtatious behavior. There may even be *zones* at work where flirting can take place, like in the cafeteria. But be careful and make sure you have a handle on these unspoken codes of conduct. We ask, why even go there, especially consider the higher price women pay for any kind of "intimate" display? He is a stud, and she is a slut.

Have a plan for going public. Think it through. How and who will you tell? Do you want it to spread through the rumor mill or make an announcement at the Monday morning staff meeting? You can also combine this public announcement with your commitment to remaining professional and serving your organization's best interest. This is one of the best proactive measures a couple can take.

Make sure both parties are on the same page before you decide to go public, too. Otherwise, you may have a whole different set of rumors to burden. We know one man, Jonathan, who had gone on several dates with Cindy. He told one coworker, and soon people were talking. So at the next meeting, he decided to do what he thought was the mature thing and tell the group that, yes, he had been dating Cindy. Well, as it turned out, Cindy had also gone on several dates with Robert—who was sitting in the meeting for the announcement. For Cindy, it was just casual dating, nothing to announce to the staff. Jonathan looked like a fool rushing in, Cindy looked like a player, and Robert looked oblivious. Needless to say, this hurt the professional relationship among all three of them—and no legitimate relationships blossomed at all. This could have been avoided if Cindy had told the men her intentions and they had asked her before making assumptions.

At the annual conference, don't think about bunking with your partner. Stay in your separate hotel rooms. You know that as you attempt to sneak out of his room at 6 A.M., a coworker will also be exiting his or her room. Embarrassing. It's the stuff of soap operas. At social occasions, don't hang on to each other. Make sure you mingle with everyone, and don't spend most your time with your partner. Again, you may be off-site, but you are still at work.

Your coworkers will expect you and your partner to be joined at the hip. They will anticipate that the both of you are a coalition and will voice similar opinions about company plans and decisions. Surprise them. Don't be afraid to be your vocal self. Go ahead: play devil's advocate and take on his input. Most of all, be yourself.

And remember, you are in control. From the moment you sense that magnetism with either your boss and/or a subordinate, the decision is yours. You have a choice. Are you going to date up and/or down? A romantic relationship with a subordinate could expose your company to a claim of sexual harassment, especially if the subordinate says it was not mutual or welcome. You also may be accused of playing favorites. If your supervisor asks you out, ask him if he has checked with human resources to get their opinion and policy about extending such invitations to subordinates.

If Cupid strikes and you find yourself attracted to a coworker, these guidelines will minimize any possible damage to your career.

16

Leading the Way Up the Corporate Ladder

"You have a woman boss? Oh no, I feel for you. I had a woman boss once, and it was terrible." Heard those words before? Why would someone feel that way about having a woman boss? Who would you rather work for, a man or a woman? Most men say they'd rather work for a man. And most women say the same thing. How can that be? Why wouldn't you want to work for a woman? Is there a difference? What's the big deal?

The Woman Boss: She's a Keeper—or Is She?

Here are some of the reasons we hear in our training classes from men and women about why someone may not want to work for a woman:

- She has no real power to make decisions.
- She's not a problem solver.
- She doesn't think up anything new.
- She is always hormonally driven (that time of the month, PMS, menopausal).
- She doesn't support other women.
- She's focused on her family (if she has one).
- She's focused on getting a man (if she's single).
- She plays favorites.
- She cries a lot.

She doesn't have the experience.

She has no sense of humor.

She's not direct. It's always a guessing game with her.

She's like a queen bee. There's no room for anyone else in the game.

She got the supervisor job because of affirmative action.

She's a bitch.

She has no spine. She's too soft.

She can't make decisions.

She's afraid to make decisions.

She makes wrong decisions.

She's not connected to inside information or the powers-that-be.

She doesn't see the big picture.

She's focused on making everyone feel good instead of getting the job done.

She's not tough enough.

She's afraid to tell it like it is.

She's too nice.

She's too aggressive.

She acts like a man.

She cares only about herself and what you can do to make her look good.

She's a perfectionist.

She sets unrealistic goals.

She acts more like a mom than a boss. (I already have a mom.)

You won't get the good, challenging assignments in her group.

No one gets promoted from her group.

She doesn't take a stand against management.

This list tells us that there are a lot of thoughts and assumptions out there about working for a woman. There's not as much talk about why people don't want to work for a man, simply because people figure they will have to work for a man; most bosses are male.

Some people tell us their best bosses were women. Some say their worst bosses were women. Just about everyone has a story, good or bad, about who they'd prefer as their boss. Let's take the first half of this list and switch the *she* to a *he:*

⟹ He has no real power to make decisions.

⟹ He's not a problem solver.

⟹ He doesn't think up anything new.

⟹ He is always hormonally driven (that time of the month, PMS, menopausal).

⟹ He doesn't support other men.

⟹ He's focused on his family (if he has one).

⟹ He's focused on getting a woman (if he's single).

⟹ He plays favorites.

⟹ He cries a lot.

⟹ He doesn't have the experience.

⟹ He has no sense of humor.

⟹ He's not direct. It's always a guessing game with him.

⟹ He's like a queen bee. There's no room for anyone else in the game.

⟹ He got the supervisor job because of affirmative action.

⟹ He's a bitch.

Some of the items don't make sense when we use the *he* instead of the *she:*

⟹ *He is always hormonally driven (that time of the month, PMS, menopausal).* Men don't menstruate, so they don't have a particular time of the month when they act differently (although some may say that men have hormone cycles to a much lesser degree than women and that older men go through a male menopause). If someone says to a man "It's that time of the month," it's usually said with sarcasm or in a joking manner, as a putdown for his femininelike behavior or complaints.

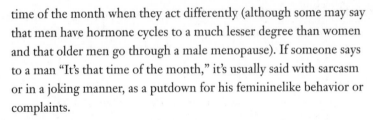

- *He cries a lot.* Nope, haven't heard that one about a man. We have heard "He sweats a lot," for instance, when stressed. You don't want people to see him sweat; that could give away his position.

- *He's like a queen bee.* People don't call a man a queen bee. Instead, when acting like a woman queen bee, they might just call him a conceited jerk who hogs all the glory.

- *He got the supervisor job because of affirmative action.* Assumptions are that the supervisor is a white man, so unless he's an ethnic minority, people wouldn't accuse him of being an affirmative action hire— which, by the way, is meant as an insult, implying lack of skills and experience to do the job.

- *He's a bitch.* At the office people usually have plenty of names for a man they don't like working with, but it usually isn't "bitch." Perhaps they'd call him a bastard.

Well, you get the idea. The ways we describe an unwanted female boss differ from how we talk about an unwanted male boss. Labels, stereotypes, and assumptions influence how we perceive the boss—whether male or female— and potentially our expectations of our relationship with that person. Some of the other descriptors could apply to either a male or female boss. When you close your eyes, who do you think of when you think of the best boss ever? Is it a gender thing or a personality thing? Is it about skills and knowledge? Is it charisma?

Women and men have different leadership behaviors and communication styles. This doesn't mean that one style is necessarily better than the other or that one style is right and the other is wrong. They're just different styles, and an excellent leader is familiar with both. It's not only men who use a masculine leadership style or only women who use a feminine leadership style.

code **SWITCH** *Use leadership behaviors that are viewed as masculine or feminine to best meet your needs and help you make the impact you want.*

It's a Man's World—or Is It?

The problem in the United States—and, to a great extent, around the globe—is the socialized belief that being a boss, being in charge, or being the leader means being a man and using a masculine leadership style. Perhaps in a matriarchal society we'd see the boss character as a woman with a more feminine approach.

In fact, it's a joke at one Colorado office that in order to be a boss, you have to have a mustache. All the members of upper management are portly white men with the same thick, dark mustache. One day, one of the female employees, Anne, went to get her eyebrows waxed. The woman waxing her brows asked if Anne wanted the hair on her upper lip waxed, too.

"I don't have any hair up there," Anne responded, shocked.

"You do. You have a mustache," the woman said back.

"No, I have no hair there," Anne insisted.

The woman shrugged and applied the wax to Anne's brow. As she leaned in, her face just inches from Anne's, she mumbled angrily, "Mustache."

Anne came to work the next day, and upper management pulled her aside. They offered her a promotion and a salary increase.

As Anne was sharing the good news with her coworkers, she couldn't help but wonder—facetiously, of course—would she have received that great promotion if she had waxed her upper lip?

Of course, it's not that simple. But it's true that the skills and behaviors we associate with being a boss or manager are those that we have been socialized to think of as male behaviors. These include perceived behaviors such as being able to make tough decisions, craving more responsibility, not wimping out, taking things at face value, having a sense of humor, knowing how to play the game, being willing to move or relocate, being a problem solver, being aggressive, engaging in competition, displaying knowledge, being powerful, showing motivation, acting logically, thinking analytically, having physical strength, exhibiting ambition, being dominant, staying focused on the job, being well connected, acting like a winner, and seeming controlling, political, and confident.

The male leader's communication skills follow suit. Men tend to be direct, forceful, and assertive. Male leaders don't whine—they have a strong, deep voice and speak loudly when needed. The masculine leadership style is authoritative, hierarchical, and structured.

Much research and many articles written during the past 40 years have looked at male and female leaders' behaviors and management styles. When people describe a successful leader, they often use the same adjectives used to describe a man. Virginia Schein, professor at Gettysburg College, looked at these issues in the mid-1970s. She and her colleagues continued similar research in the mid-1990s and early 2000s, looking from a global perspective at perceptions of men, women, and successful managers in the workplace. In the countries studied, most men viewed men and successful managers as similar. However, women's results varied by country. Some women viewed men, women, and managers as similar. Women in other countries still viewed men and successful managers as more similar. This is significant for women seeking to add an international assignment to their resumé.

Because the business world was generally established by men, the concepts that describe a successful manager are those that describe men and men's interactions. Women entered the work-world picture late in the game and came into a world already established by men with men's rules of engagement. For women to succeed, they essentially had to play by the existing rules—the men's rules, also referred to as the "old boy network."

Over the years women have introduced their own style of management. Yet they are often still compared to and judged by the masculine leadership style, which many consider to be the "right style," the style of a "true" leader. Even as organizations create programs to support and develop women leaders, the stereotypes, expectations, and socialization often get in the way of a woman's success.

Women's Leadership Style

Various research and books during the past 15 to 20 years have begun look-ing at the distinct behaviors and skills that women bring to the workplace as a different kind of leadership.

Books like Sally Helgesen's *The Female Advantage* (1990) and *The Web of Inclu-sion* (1995) started describing a different yet still successful style of leadership that women use. The way women are perceived in society influences how we view a female leader's behaviors.

Perceived traits of a female manager include being thoughtful, people focused, relationship focused, considerate, quiet, nice, helpful, pleasant, understanding, intuitive, emotional, creative, caring, empathetic, knowledgeable, cheerful, warm, empowering, patient, collaborative, and participative. Female leaders tend to go for a win/win, have a sense of humor, want consensus, and share the power. There are also negative perceptions, such as that women leaders are poor problem solvers, are not willing to move or relocate, are too family focused, and will periodically opt out of the system due to pregnancy, child care, or elder care.

For a female leader's communication skills, descriptors often include the fol-lowing: acts spontaneous, asks questions, coaches, teaches, and is assertive. Their voices are soft to midrange in loudness, and they speak with compassion.

The feminine leadership style is interpersonal, nurturing, flexible, and inter-connected, meaning that it networks in all directions with others to achieve the company's goals. These lists of adjectives describing male and female per-ceived behaviors provide the basis for how men and women often interact in the workplace.

Helgesen refers to interconnectedness as a web and contrasts it with a mascu-line style of hierarchy that focuses only on the vertical ranks in the organiza-tion. The web is created in such a way that all employees may contribute and discuss ideas, and it takes advantage of the talents each person brings. Creat-ing and using a web style of management builds on a woman leader's flexibil-ity and personal interaction skills.

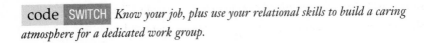

code SWITCH *Know your job, plus use your relational skills to build a caring atmosphere for a dedicated work group.*

SWITCH IT UP!

A male colleague, Larry, said that, if given a choice, he'd prefer a woman boss. He said a woman leader is a *Boss Plus*. Leaders, whether men or women, need to know their business, be excellent at what they do, and communicate well with their management. Using that as a baseline, Larry said that a woman adds a personal approach to managing her employees. She's more flexible and understands the issues better than most men when a family crisis or sick child impacts a deadline. So a woman is a boss, doing the usual job activities just as a competent male boss would do, *plus* she has a genuine concern for her employees' well-being inside and outside of work. Are you a Boss Plus?

If You're Different, You're Different

If you are a woman entering the executive suite, you'll probably be seen as something a bit out of the ordinary. Especially in an organization made up of mostly men, you'll be outside the norm. Women must use a balancing act to align their femininity with the masculine leadership style. If a woman acts aggressive or pounds the table with her fist, it sometimes backfires and she's viewed negatively for acting against the stereotypes of how a woman should act. However, in 1991, Claire's doctoral research found inklings of the opposite. Her research indicated that women managers who used an aggressive communication style were actually viewed as having more managerial potential than men who used the same style in high-tech and health-care settings. By not following the expected behaviors, the women possibly provided new information about themselves that was used to evaluate their potential.

Even though it's 2009 and women make up more than 50 percent of the management and professional workforce, they are still impacted by gender stereotypes. Underneath many of the proactive company programs and efforts, women are still expected to act a certain way and comply with perceptions of appropriate male and female behaviors. The masculine leadership style is still viewed as the traditional management style. The feminine leadership style is viewed as the nontraditional management style.

If Mary Ann and Allison are directors or department heads leading organizations, they may be considered nontraditional leaders. Their bosses, colleagues, and employees are likely evaluating their actions and successes against the norm of traditional masculine leadership style.

Catalyst, an advocacy group for women, published a 2007 report that looked at the impact of stereotypes on women leaders. The report, "The Double-Bind Dilemma for Women in Leadership: Damned If You Do, Doomed If You Don't," looked at how gender stereotypes can still undermine a woman's leadership and workplace impact. The report talks about three no-win or double-bind situations women leaders often find themselves in. These are situations in which women basically can't win. Due to existing gender stereotypes, biases, and perceptions, no matter what they do, they are viewed questionably, most often negatively.

According to the report, the first situation talks about women's behaviors in accordance with stereotypes. If women act according to female stereotypes, they are perceived as "less competent leaders." If women act outside female stereotypes, they are perceived as not feminine. In the second situation, women leaders were evaluated by stricter competency standards and received "lower rewards than men," including financial gain. In this situation, women leaders felt that they had to continually prove themselves, their leadership ability, and their work, in addition to continually staving off gender stereotypes and biases.

The third situation this Catalyst report describes relates to a female leader's likeability and competence. If a woman leader used male leader behaviors, she wasn't viewed as likeable, but she was viewed as competent. A woman leader using a more feminine style interpersonally was viewed as more likeable. So here is the double-bind: if she is perceived as competent, no one likes her. It's a loss either way.

According to Catalyst, the findings "strongly suggest that, on account of stereotypes, women's leadership talent is routinely underestimated and underutilized in organizations—and organizations need women's talent in order to succeed." To counteract these double-bind situations, Catalyst recommends communicating effectively. Ask questions, be diplomatic, and learn the jargon, Catalyst says. If you perceive bias or stereotypes, be direct and discuss the situation; don't ignore it. Keeping you and your assignments visible is another way of counteracting stereotypes, according to Catalyst. Keep demonstrating and revealing your competence, achievements, and expertise, and share your views with team members and the boss, in private and during meetings.

When you have accomplishments, take credit for them. Don't assume that someone will notice that the project came in under budget and one week early. A woman sometimes hides in the shadows and won't mention her success, or she'll give the credit to someone else.

code SWITCH *Take credit for your work. After all, it's your work. Really.*

Stereotypes about women's appropriate leadership behaviors interfere with how a woman may perceive herself and her leadership abilities and how others evaluate her abilities. Social psychologist Crystal Hoyt has determined that the more self-confidence a female leader has, the better able she is to increase her perception of her leadership actions, lower her anxiety or stress, and disregard others' negative stereotypes about her leadership ability.

code SWITCH *Develop your self-confidence and inner strength. It will help you fight off any lingering negative stereotypes in your workplace.*

One way to build confidence is to start taking a few risks. Start small, like meeting new people, attending a networking meeting, or taking a coworker to lunch. Positive interactions will boost your confidence. Keep a journal of your accomplishments and review it periodically as a reminder of your skills.

Breaking the Glass Ceiling to Find the Glass Cliff

Watch out for being hired or promoted into situations in which it's impossible to look good. Two researchers in England, Michelle Ryan and Alex Haslam, from the University of Exeter, looked at situations in which women were offered positions when there was a good chance of failing. They found that men were brought into new positions or given takeover opportunities when the company was already quite successful. The men continued to look good as they took the helm. Women, on the other hand, were given the chance to lead when the organizations already had an indication that it was in trouble and could easily fail. Ryan and Haslam called this the "glass cliff." If the woman succeeded, she looked great. If she failed, this just confirmed that she couldn't handle the job. Some women leaders may actually like this type of challenge, thinking their success will propel their careers even further.

> ## SWITCH IT UP!

One Midwest university had no women professors in its communication department. The college deans exerted pressure to add a woman to the staff. The department's 11 male professors finally decided to hire a woman for the open-tenure-track position. The graduate students, who were women, hoped she would make it easier for them to work with this difficult group of men. However, she faced difficulties, too, in trying to work with them. Her scholarly efforts declined, and she left the department after a year. She never had the other professors' support that she needed to succeed. Now the men were able to say, "See? We gave one a chance, and she couldn't handle it." She was doomed from the start. This is an example of the glass cliff. A woman is brought into a position where she will most likely fail. And when she does fail, it confirms that women can't do the job. Women, beware of the opportunities for success and failure before you accept that new position.

Stay alert. Sometimes a woman is so flattered that she was asked to lead a particular organization that she may not fully evaluate the situation before accepting the job. It's the promotion you've been waiting for or the extra money you really need. Sometimes the person offering the job makes you feel like he's gone totally out of his way to make sure you were offered the position. Then later you find out that you were the fourth person down the list and the others had all refused. Yes, it could be the challenge you've been dreaming of to go into that fire, be their savior, and turn the company around. It could happen.

code SWITCH *Before you accept that job, investigate the company or the depart-ment. Find out what's going on underneath that offer. Look for your support for that transition; who at the new company will be your mentor and support your decisions and success? If it makes sense, take the job. If it doesn't make sense, wait for a better offer.*

The Power Crunch

Given the differences in leadership styles, it's no surprise that women and men view and use their leadership power differently. Male leaders look at their power as authoritative and controlling. Their power is based on position or job level; there's only a certain amount of power out there in the organization, and men are jockeying to get it. The higher up a man is in the organization, the more power and status he has. Men tend to use their power to put down people in front of others or correct people if they're not performing properly. Power can be used to withhold rewards or other forms of recognition.

Women leaders use their power in a sharing mode and tend to empower others or create a climate in which all employees feel they are contributing as a group to the organization's success. Women leaders' power is viewed as personal power. A woman has her own power and inner strength, which she shares with the people around her. She does not have to earn a promotion or get a particular job to have power. Since power comes from her own inner strength, there's basically an unlimited amount of power; as she shares and empowers others, the amount of power in the organization grows.

Unlike men's view of power, women tend not to get caught up in the status games, such as who earns more and who has the biggest and best job with the most power. Women leaders are focused and learn to grow their personal strength and use it to benefit their employees. Many women use their power to change the workplace climate to be more relational, rewarding people for their actions and creating a space where employees feel that they share power and work responsibilities. Shared power develops from coaching and guiding others to find and use their inner strengths and outer skills as they contribute to the company's bottom line.

Men and women benefit from having a woman leader who shares her power in a more interpersonal atmosphere. It enables each employee to work in a respectful zone, knowing they have their manager's support to take risks and get the job done. The energy that was focused on how to get and take power is now focused on building relationships, sharing skills, and developing self-confidence—behaviors that continue to grow and enable others.

code `SWITCH` *Develop your personal power and let him see you use it. Show him how to share power and coach and develop others to create a power network where all can succeed.*

Leader Behaviors That Work for You

Develop your leadership style. Communicate with panache. A 2003 report from the research and consulting company the Hay Group showed that successful women leaders used masculine and feminine leader behaviors that create "better, performance-driving climates than their male counterparts." The men and women leaders reviewed came from Fortune 500 companies. The successful male leaders used both leadership styles, but not as much of the feminine style as the women. One group of women leaders who were less successful used mainly masculine behaviors.

Pete, a consultant and colleague, told us of his experiences as an employee in a large high-tech company. He thought the key to his success over the years was to figure out his boss's agenda. Once he knew that, he'd have a better picture of his future in the group. Pete gave examples of different bosses. Using the perspective of limited power, his boss Will had focused on moving up in the organization. Everything he did or asked Pete to do was blatantly geared toward establishing his own success. Will was out for himself, excluding the employees and their successes. Another boss, Martin, held grudges. Pete's focus was to make sure he didn't do something that would put him on Martin's bad list. Once on the list, an employee was shunned and ignored; Martin took back and absorbed any power that the employee might have had.

Pete's boss Ed was a sniveling, whiny, wimp—not a stereotypical male leader. He refused to take a stand and never disagreed with his boss. Unfortunately,

Ed expected his employees to act the same way. Ed had basically given up his power, so there was none to support his team.

Pete described his supervisor Erica as terrible; she regurgitated everything from upper management, had no technical knowledge, and showed no initiative to do something different. Her power was status quo and so was the work group. Nothing changed, and she would not make waves. So the work group remained afloat but was going nowhere.

Pete said he'd had two good bosses, Bill and Sally. Each was knowledgeable, stayed open to new ideas, and expressed a personal interest in employees. Bill was a technical expert who readily used his technical knowledge and people skills to coach his employees. Sally used her technical skills, assertiveness, and relational skills to understand and support her employees and their needs. Pete thought both these bosses gave him the best opportunity to get his work done efficiently and grow his technical skills.

Knowing your boss's agenda will help you understand the level of support and empowerment you can expect. Like Pete, chances are, you'll find greater success and satisfaction working for a boss who readily uses both masculine and feminine leadership styles.

code SWITCH *Be flexible in how you use your leadership skills. Use masculine and feminine leadership behaviors that best suit you and the situation. Know your environment. Be direct and he'll hear you. Be short and to the point. He'll get it. Show some personal concern, coaching with care and support for personal development, and he'll be on your side (and so will your women employees and colleagues).*

Some of your best supporters, mentors, and friends in the workplace are men. Respect them and they will respect you. You can learn a lot by watching the men and women leaders around you to see how they interact. You don't have to act the same way they do, but you can learn about how they communicate and balance that with how you want to interact. The fabulous thing about code switching is that once you have the skills, you can maneuver from one situation to the next, alternating feminine and masculine skills to show your personal power and make an impact. Workplaces are changing and looking for the best skills that people have to create the best workplaces. Over the years, many work environments have been moving from an authoritative management style to a more collaborative management style. This is creating opportunities for women to step in and use their relational and interpersonal skills to demonstrate a new style. Remember to be yourself. Let your own strengths shine.

17

Stand Up and Deliver

Historically, being at the front and center of the room has been men's domain. One of the constraints on women's efforts to gain legal rights in the 1800s was the proscription of women speaking in public. Traditionally, women were socialized to be nurturing, sensitive, and emotional, so appeals to the domestic sphere—home and family—usually were more effective with traditional women.

Traditionally, men were socialized to be aggressive, ambitious, and unemotional. Consequently, a presentation to a predominantly traditional male group employed appeals of power, competition, and logic.

The ABCs of Preparation

In the 1970s and '80s, it could be argued that the prescription for successful public speaking was a confident, assertive, masculine style. Take command and take charge. Talk like you know everything and have no doubts. This generic standard does devalue women public speakers. Women have not been conditioned to present themselves this way. But this should not hold women back. See a presentation in front of the board as an opportunity. You have the floor and are on stage. All eyes are on you. This is your chance—go for it. Prove yourself competent and bright.

Only during the last two decades have we finally arrived at a new consciousness of the way sex-role socialization has limited our style of expression in public speaking. Now the lines of the public sphere and private sphere are more blurred; both men and women can relate to the pressure of getting a child to school and arriving to work on time, as well as closing the multimillion-dollar deal. In fact, audiences bristle with a speaker's suggestions that women are primarily still concerned with the domestic sphere, and men are offended at the suggestion that they don't know how to read their daughters a bedtime story. Speakers would be well advised to understand that it is a new world with shared roles, and they can avoid offending a large segment of their audience by staying away from "traditional" notions of women's and men's "work." Stereotypes, in general, can put off listeners and get in the way of them hearing anything else you say.

code SWITCH *Turn a historical disadvantage into an opportunity. The ability to make successful presentations is one of the most important assets in the business world.*

Since many people shy away from making presentations, the woman who is comfortable delivering them has an advantage over others. It is common knowledge, and many of us are familiar with decades of research that reveals public speaking is the number one ranked fear. People fear public speaking more than dying. Yes, people say they would rather die than give a speech.

Do Your Homework

People are very astute observers when you are making a presentation. They sense when you are going by the seat of your pants. Preparing increases your self-confidence, and that will ooze out of every pore in your body. Your goal is to have them saying, "Wow! You really know your stuff."

We have approximately 60 combined years of conducting seminars and keynotes across the United States. Of course, we always review our evaluations, and it is common to receive comments like "Audrey was well prepared and organized" and "Claire really had it together for this seminar." Our audiences are a testimony to the credibility of simply doing your homework and showing up prepared.

We have all been victims of presentations that left us thinking, "Geez, did this person just throw this together last night?" I'll bet you can remember feeling a warm handout that was just "hot" off the press (that is, the copy machine) and a speaker arriving late and looking frazzled. Both are dead giveaways that this presentation was a last-minute deal. Now you're already in a negative state of mind, and that's one strike against the speaker. The speaker must now climb out of the hole and try to prove he's worthy. So if you show up appearing to be "together," you're halfway home to a dynamite presentation.

Before you go live, consider these tips, to save you embarrassment and contribute to a dynamic presentation:

- Analyze your audience. Who are you talking to?

- Start with a warm-up question on the topic.

- Put your presentation in "talking points": bullet words that cue ideas.

- Design a PowerPoint slide presentation that not only helps the audience, but also helps you present a clear message and keep organized.

- Design an attention grabber. Say something dramatic.

- Balance content intensity with your time frame. Delivering too much information in too little time can be overwhelming and can turn off an audience. They can't keep up.

- Provide a clear, easy-to-follow handout that flows with the PowerPoint slides.

- Consider employing a multimedia component (movie clips, music, pictures, and so on). People want to be entertained.

- Have a three-part presentation, just as in writing: introduction, body, and conclusion.

A big part of doing your homework is knowing who will be sitting in your audience. If the audience was originally going to be team members only, but now you find out that three senior-level people are attending, you will need to tweak the message to address concerns they might have, like the budget for your plan.

SWITCH IT UP!

Never, ever bring a script to read. You are allowed only one page, with bullet points, which serve as a trigger so that you can glance at them and already know what you want to say about each. Extemporaneous speaking is a hundred times better than script reading. Talk to the audience like you would have a conversation with a coworker. Be natural and conversational. Acting with some degree of spontaneity also builds trust and believability, two important variables for credibility. Digress. Say something like, "You know, on my way to work, I was thinking about this proposal and … " or "As I walked in the door to work today, someone stopped me and asked …."

The basics to any audience analysis are demographic: age, sex composition (very important for how you will pitch your message), race, ethnicity, and geographic. What part of the country is your audience from? A metropolitan city or rural farming town?

Also know your audience's predisposition toward the topic. Are they neutral, favorable, or hostile? Audrey consulted with a major law firm concerning the retention and recruitment of women. This was a sensitive topic for the firm because of their poor track record. When the day came for Audrey to present her "cultural snapshot" of the firm and recommendations, she knew she had a defensive and somewhat hostile audience. At one point, a lawyer in the firm suggested that Audrey had made up the data (she was quoting directly from interviews she had conducted with employees, partners, and associates in the firm). The truth was, he and other members of the firm had difficulty hearing the "truth" about everyday life for women at the firm. Audrey had anticipated that this would be a difficult audience.

Walk in knowing how you are likely to be received. Know who your challenging people are. How do you get your arms around this? Ask. We always ask ourselves, "Who is going to push back?" or "Has anyone been directly impacted by your topic?" Rehearse what you will say. Have a prepared response. Most important, stay in charge. If someone gets out of hand, ask him to see you during break or after the presentation to continue the discussion and address his concerns. Use peer pressure, and refer to your time constraints and your need to get everyone out by the designated time. Everyone will give him the evil eye.

code SWITCH *Men appreciate a bullet style or concise points and some data-, logic-, or fact-based information. Use statements like, "There are three ways this is going to impact the bottom line." Then list them. They are not interested in a lot of "touchy feely" examples—they just tune these out.*

Grab Their Attention

Start your speech with a startling statistic, question or headline, or statement that a competitor said about your organization. A short story also works well.

For a dramatic impact, a speaker arrived 15 minutes late for his keynote address to a major airline conference and walked brazenly down the center aisle to the stage. The audience was already agitated by his tardiness. There were audible sounds of disgust. He proceeded onto the stage, walked slowly to the podium, faced the audience, and said, "Well, how does it feel to have someone arrive late?" This called attention to the airline's poor performance and high number of late arrivals. His speech was about excellence and performance. It got everyone's attention, and he made his point.

Men listen to facts. They like convincing arguments built around data and research. However, too much concentration on statistics and facts will make any audience's head spin. Yes, use your data. But don't bombard the audience. In your handout and PowerPoint slides, put no more than three facts on a page or slide. Ease the burden of numbers with a story. For example, tell the history or background of the statistic, or compare it with another competitor's. It might sound like this: "This is an interesting number. If you compare it to where we were a year ago ...."

code SWITCH *Presentations to audiences that are primarily male should include quotes from established public figures in the business world. No touchy feely quotes about the philosophy of life.*

One of our secrets to warming up not only the audience but also ourselves is to have the audience answer a simple question. If you were presenting on the topic of improved team performance, you might have them answer the questions, "How do we excel as a team? What do we do right?" Then you'd bring everyone back as a group and solicit the group to share what they just said to their partner. When the audience remains silent (we always allow a good 15 to 20 seconds, which can feel like an eternity but can force audience members to speak up to break the painful silence), we say, "Oh, come on now, don't make me pick somebody." A hand almost always shoots up. This is a guarantee for warming up the audience and easing the comfort level.

Use handouts and PowerPoint slides to help yourself without the audience knowing. This is a secret technique many professional speakers use. Handouts and slides keep you on track and organized, like a security blanket. You can take a quick scan and see how many pages of the workbook you have remaining. This can cue you to speed things up or slow down to meet time limits. You also stay on target for talking points. These aids are supposed to help the audience, but they're also valuable to the speaker. PowerPoint slides also take the attention off you so you can take a "break." Keep slides simple but inviting. We've seen our fair share of boring slides with dull or minimal colors that lack graphic design and pictures. Incorporate quotes and anecdotes.

code SWITCH *When your audience composition is an equal mix of women and men, use the combo approach. Include facts, figures, and maybe a pertinent quote. If you lean to one side or the other too much, you risk losing part of the audience.*

For example, we present the statistical composition of a message (derived from research conducted at UCLA): 38 percent vocal cues (pitch, rate of speech, quality of voice, inflection, pauses, and so on), 55 percent body movement (facial expressions, gestures, posture, position), and 7 percent words. This data supports the point of the power of nonverbal cues. Then later in the presentation, to make the point that the focus of communication is not *intent*, but *impact*, we incorporate a quote from Maya Angelou: "I've learned that people will forget what you said, people will forget what you did, but people will never forget how you made them feel." This quote supports how little words contribute to the overall message and the importance of the final "residue" or impact.

Practice Makes Perfect

Every time you are in front of an audience, your reputation is at stake. People are judging you. There's no dress rehearsal—you can't take back something you said.

Many people approach us and ask how they can present with the ease that we do. They think we must have been born with some innate ability to get up and speak. Not true. Public speaking is an acquired skill. Our number one recommendation is practice makes perfect. You cannot learn to be a good speaker by reading or going to therapy (although both these avenues can help with some aspects of public speaking, like fear). Find any opportunity to present. Volunteer at work to make that presentation to the board. It will also wow your team, because no one else wants to do it. Start out small. Practice by giving a report to a coworker. Then present to your boss. Then go before larger groups. Speak to groups that have no consequence in your work life, like the PTA or a nonprofit board.

One of the venues we suggest is Toastmasters International. Every city has a Toastmasters group. Your local paper or Toastmasters website (www.toastmasters.org) will have the contact information for your city. Some cities have several groups that meet at different times of the day (usually early for breakfast or in the evening, to accommodate work schedules). Toastmasters began in 1924 at the YMCA in Santa Ana, California, to help people improve their public-speaking skills. Today there are nearly 235,000 members in 106 countries. The average Toastmasters group has 20 people. The format of Toastmasters is really the only place to practice in a safe environment with no consequences (except for an occasional bruised ego). Members provide feedback and are very candid. Some of the alumni include Peter Coors of Coors Brewing Company and Debbi Fields, founder of Mrs. Fields Cookies.

Cool, Calm, and Collected

Remember, the moment you walk into the room, people are judging you. Is she nervous? Does she have the jitters? Does she look cool, calm, and collected? Let's go over some rules for women (men have another set of rules) to follow on how *not* to give a presentation.

How Not to Talk

The first set of rules concerns how you should *not* talk:

- Avoid using fillers: "um," "you know," "ah," "like," and the occasional drawn-out "soooo ..." in between thoughts.
- Don't punctuate sentences with a giggle.
- Avoid wishy-washy words: "just," "sort of," "you know."
- Steer clear of words that reflect stereotypical female culture: shopping, housekeeping, makeup.
- Don't apologize unnecessarily.
- Don't tell the audience you're not experienced in the topic.
- Avoid poor grammar, slang, or curse words.

As "nonfluencies" (ums, ers, you knows, ahs) or fillers increase, your credibility decreases. Just listen to a radio or TV interview when interviewees employ excessive fillers. They sound dumb. Using a strong, assertive vocabulary, especially when speaking to men, is imperative. Word choice is magnified in public-speaking situations. Sure, you can get away with slang and wishy-washy language in hallway conversations and one-on-one, but if you do this in front of an audience, you will lose credibility. Your whole presentation can rest on word choice, not just the merits of your points.

Check out our list of the women's top 10 list of wishy-washy words:

- Just
- Kind of
- Sort of
- Well
- Gee
- Maybe
- Yeah
- Oops
- Ish (as in 50ish)
- Little bit

A woman speaker for a human resources conference made three references to her "boutique." She was referring to her books and CDs for sale at the conclusion of her presentation. How do you think the men in the audience resonated with the word *boutique?* When was the last time you heard a man say he was in a boutique? And anyway, what HR conference has a boutique set up outside the meeting room? It was a booth.

You can go one step further and amp up your presentation by bringing several strong metaphors or sayings with you—for example, "train wreck," "top of the class," "get on board or be left behind," and "watch your back." Men hear powerful metaphors, clichés, and sayings. They don't hear "boutique," and, more important, they discount the woman who uses fluffy words and her presentation.

code `SWITCH` *Avoid "feminine" words, metaphors, and clichés for audiences that are mostly men. It's a real turn-off for men.*

Women tend to apologize more than men. You have nothing to be sorry for. If the copy place did not collate your handout correctly, it is their fault, not yours. Never begin a presentation with "I'm sorry." Never. And if something is your fault, proceed. Go forward; don't dwell on the fact that you never secured the quarterly numbers. Simply say, "The quarterly numbers will be e-mailed to everyone by tomorrow at noon." Everyone makes mistakes. Why would you want to advertise them? Let them fade from view rather than bring them forward. Done.

After a senior female manager apologized three times during her presentation, a male supervisor turned to his coworker and said, "Boy, she sure is a sorry person." An important part of the formula is looking competent and helping your audience forget your mistakes.

Also, beware of repeating certain phrases or words too much, or they become their own kind of fillers. The president of one school board, Randy, sure did love the phrase "in terms of." Presumably, he thought it made him sound smart, even though most of the time it served no purpose in his communication. At one school board meeting, an audience member noticed one of the journalists covering the meeting counting on paper. She was up to 56. The audience member asked her what she was doing. She was counting the number of times Randy said "in terms of." She didn't care what he was talking about. All she heard was the dreaded phrase—56 times and counting.

We have both worked extensively with women engineers in high-tech companies. Engineers have a knack for sharing details. Add the gender component, and women engineers will add *even more* details. One woman engineer shared, "I think I talk way too much and slam people with way too many details. But it's hard for me to let go of the details. I feel like everyone needs to know everything." She is wrong. Not everyone needs to know everything. If you think it is important, put it in an appendix to the handout. Tell your audience they can refer to it. People in general want points to be made bluntly, with no excess. Add men to the equation, and they will tell you themselves, "Please don't beat around the bush." Just say it.

code SWITCH *Men will listen more to your presentation if you don't go on and on. At the conclusion during the question/answer part, you can cue your audience: "I did not address the supplier needs, but if anyone is interested, I can answer questions on that now." If he wants to know, he will ask.*

No one knows everything about their subject. We all have areas of expertise and areas of inexperience or little knowledge. Listen to men sometimes. For years we hear women say men talk with such certainty, like they know everything and they have all the confidence in the world. Well, we think this is an opportunity to borrow from men. Fake it until you make it. We're not saying you should fabricate or exaggerate; we're saying that you can reveal what you do know in no uncertain terms, and minimize and not draw attention to the areas of weakness. Women must learn how to act competent. Women should never say, "I have never done that before" or "I have no idea how that works." Trust that you know enough to figure it out. Exude a can-do attitude.

How Not to Act

The second set of rules concerns appearance and movements. These female traps erode credibility instantly and are distracting to a powerful presentation:

➤ Do not touch your hair or flip it to get it out of your face. Pull it back
if you have a tendency to play with it.

➤ Leave off any jewelry that makes noise, such as jangly earrings or
charm bracelets.

➤ Avoid adjusting your clothes: pulling your top down, pulling your
pants up, fishing for your bra strap, adjusting your belt, or fixing your
collar.

➤ Beware of nervous gestures, such as tugging at your earring, jiggling
your leg (yes, the audience can see it behind a podium), or twisting
your bracelet.

➤ Don't wear uncomfortable shoes you have trouble walking in.

➤ Don't adjust your glasses.

End on a Powerful Note

Almost all presentations that run one hour or longer should include a wrap-
up (minimum 15 minutes) that solicits questions from the audience. Everyone
likes the opportunity to ask questions.

Set yourself up for a win. Before your speech, solicit a coworker to ask a
strategic question that you formulated. Here you are putting a *plant* in the
audience. Most people don't object and are happy to accommodate you. Of
course, this provides a chance for you to show how much you know. Strut
your stuff.

code SWITCH *Get a male coworker to act as your plant and ask a question. It
will have more credibility with the men in the audience. In male culture, asking and
even challenging the speaker or "authority" is a way of honoring them.*

There's no getting around it. Women face unique challenges at the podium,
especially with predominantly male audiences. The truth is, a man arrives
at a woman's presentation with the bar lowered. Both men and women perceive women speakers as less credible. But if women get stuck in that unfair
perception, they can't concentrate on how to turn that disadvantage into an

advantage. Men will sit up and take notice if a woman follows the tips offered in this chapter. Such a large part of the challenge of public speaking is how you feel about yourself. Confidence equals credibility. Credibility is the ticket to move audiences and persuade them not only to "buy" your ideas, but to be sold on you. People will begin quoting you around the office. People will come up to you and ask you more questions about your presentation. These are all indications that you made an impact.

18

Power Networking and Mentoring

Women are a long way from reaching parity with men in the executive suites and boardrooms of Fortune 500 companies. But the path to the corner office and out of the pink ghetto seems clearer, and we now know some of the tricks men have used to get to the top. One of the well-known tricks of the trade is "It's who you know." That can make it or break it in the business world. No one gets to the top alone. And women cannot do it without networking with men and seeking men as mentors. Male mentors can help her understand the critical world of how men do business, and how to talk so men will listen and help her make it to the top. Women need both male and female mentors. Having both will ensure that she learns the tricks of the trade.

Why the Good Ol' Boy Club Works

Growing up, Audrey remembers that her father, who was an accountant, was a member of the Optimist Club (similar to the Kiwanis, Rotary, Lions, and other "men's" organizations). She also remembers that the membership was all white males—no women or diverse races.

That was in the 1950s and '60s. Things have changed—sort of. When her father purchased the family car, he went to a member of the Optimist Club who owned a car dealership. When he needed car insurance, he went to a member of the Optimist Club. That's one testimony of how the good ol' boy club works.

The "old boy network" refers to an informal system of friendships and connections through which men use their positions of influence by providing favors and information to help other men. Often men are connected because they belong to the same country club, fraternity, college, or share a similar social background. Many people believe it had its origins in the South, but these networks can be found all over the United States and internationally. Most important, many good ol' boy networks within companies are *informal*. They exist in any setting, from corporate to religious, to social and political associations among white males. Connections and concessions are made at power lunches, at the sports bar, at the country club, or on the golf course.

These good ol' boys have a range of consequences in the business world. Although membership has grown to include more women (and minorities), the white men's club still wrongfully excludes most women. These clubs yield power through their connections. True, it is *who you know*. When introduced to the right person, someone can make important business transactions or close a deal through these networks. These networks function like any other informal social network: to establish connections through mutual friendships. "You scratch my back and I scratch your back" is the mantra of the good ol' boys. And it works.

Is it right? Is it fair? Of course not, but it exists.

code SWITCH *Do not become the constant whiner when you are left out or notice network favoritism. The good ol' boys club needs to know when it crosses the line. Set boundaries and address issues from a position of strength, not weakness. Don't say what they did wrong (whining and negative); say what you want them to do (positive).*

Many women don't want to pay the metaphoric dues for membership in the good ol' boys club, so there has been a movement during the last three decades toward women establishing their own networks, formal and informal. Some women don't want to play golf. Consider Jean, a 15-year partner member of one of the top 10 public accounting firms in the country. She hated the game played by her predominantly male partnership at the firm. When her boss sent an e-mail saying there was going to be a "mandatory golf game," she tried to keep her sense of humor. The e-mail asked partners to submit their shoe size and say whether they were right- or left-handed, to fit them for the appropriate golf equipment and shoes. She responded, "I am right-handed, a size 9, and don't play golf. You will find me in the bar."

Cynthia was the crème de la crème catch for a high-tech firm. She'd graduated from Stanford with a Ph.D. in a select area of engineering. One member of the management team claimed she was a "real find." Cynthia was not only a woman, but also Chinese. Still, her double whammy status as a minority and a woman put her outside the realm of the good ol' boys and their most coveted game—golf—where deals are made, resumés swapped, and decisions established before the Monday morning staff meeting. Cynthia thought maybe it was true. If she learned to play golf, she could advance faster within the organization. Cynthia proceeded to take golf lessons and then entered the annual company golf tournament. To the shock of the good ol' boys, she placed third! Even better, she had a 2-foot-high trophy she proudly displayed in her office as a reminder that she had penetrated the male bastion. That's when a curious thing happened. The good ol' boys began inviting her to play. She now had the inside scoop on this informal network. She was in on critical information. In her own way, she had gained membership into the club.

Jean resented the "required" ritual of golf. Golf has become a metaphor for membership dues, and some women simply don't want to pay the dues. Maybe Master's degree programs need to start including golf lessons. The bottom line is that a lot of business is done on the golf course. It was this way 40 years ago, and it remains the same today.

code SWITCH *Your coworkers and boss don't often miss what they don't see—until someone points it out. You can be that someone.*

Here are some possible signs of a thriving good ol' boy club:

➡ A technical convention features 100 percent male speakers, even though 40 percent of the membership is female.

➡ A company public relations activity for clients solicits only male managers to attend a baseball game.

➡ A female project manager had a meeting with a male vendor who had misrepresented their products. When she pointed this out, the male procurement rep and a male manager backed the male vendor. She then later saw them having lunch together.

➡ You attend a meeting for a decision on a contract and have a strong sense from the conversations with the men in the group that the decision had already been made and the deal closed before the meeting.

➡ You observe groups of men going to lunch together.

code `SWITCH` *Ask the male ring leader if you can forward the e-mail invitation to the baseball game with clients to all managers, including the women. Tell him baseball is the favorite spectator sport among several women in the office.*

Think about starting a good ol' girls club. Get a group of like-minded women with similar goals together and meet monthly. These networks can grow into whatever you like. This could be a handful of women or hundreds of women. These networks can host speaker series and career-building activities. Formally, there has been a strong movement among Fortune 500 companies to incorporate women's professional groups within the organization; Hewlett-Packard, Cargill, Ford, IBM, Xerox, 3M, Texas Instruments, McDonald's, Kraft, and BP are examples. Many of these women's organizations hold regional and national conventions. They have made it their mission to institute best practices that include women to benefit their organizations, help their organizations mentor women, and further women's advancement. Because there are more women in senior-level positions and a general increase in women in the workplace, women no longer fear reprisals for organizing women's networks.

From a historical standpoint, when women were first organizing women's networks, we remember men making comments like "What are you doing at these meetings? Plotting to take over?" or "What do all you women talk about?" One of the best ideas generated to model inclusion was the implementation of Take Your Boss to Lunch and Bring a Coworker to Lunch events. Women used these events as a platform to have a speaker or panel address how women's networking and career enhancement impact the bottom line. That's something every boss or coworker is concerned about.

The No. 1 Success Strategy: Networking

Amanda did not meet the requirements for the job, but she applied anyway. The job required a five-year experience minimum, and she had two. At the interview, things weren't going well and she was not connecting—until one of the interviewers, Samantha, saw on Amanda's resumé her sorority. Samantha had been in the same sorority. The two began talking about the local alum clubs and Amanda's leadership and philanthropic experience in college, and Amanda said she was trying to get involved with the local branch. As it turned out, Samantha was highly involved and invited Amanda to the next meeting.

Amanda got the job—not simply because she had been in the "right" club. Her sorority membership also indicated to Samantha a shared understanding of the importance of networking, the common values the sorority was based on, leadership and volunteer experience, and a respect for tradition and history.

Women are learning today what men have known for the last hundred years: you can use alliances to get things done. You cannot get there alone. Sure, you have strong credentials and solid work experience, but that's not enough. You have to build your lifelong contact base. There's an old saying concerning networking: "It's not what you do 9-to-5 that counts; but what you do 5-to-9!"

A direct correlation exists between how wide of a networking net you cast and your success. Establish connections with all levels, from the administrative assistant to the CEO, to senior-level managers and in organizations outside your company. It is important to develop meaningful relationships with others who may not be in your department. They can often provide an inside scoop about larger strategic issues, such as "right-sizing," budget cuts, and who's in and who's out. Remember, information is power.

Some people think women are strong at building relationships internally within their organizations, but not as effective at building relationships *outside* their organization. You can expand your networking circle in several ways:

> Join nonprofits, like United Way, to meet people in other industries and businesses.

➤ Join the Chamber of Commerce. (Pick the largest membership, to maximize your exposure.)

➤ Join women's formal networking groups. (Business and Professional Women has chapters all over the country, and there are growing number of Women's Chambers in the country.)

➤ Many professions have an organization and conferences dedicated to networking and professional development. You should be a member.

Carly Fiorina, former chair and CEO of Hewlett-Packard, offers this advice: "Networking is not a club, not about seeking out people like you, or about people who agree with you. Find people who disagree with you strenuously. That helps you have the right perspective."

Networks can serve as your insurance for professional longevity. Contacts are like an insurance policy. The more you have, the more security you can have in your career. Many women have cashed in on these networks during career transitions. Take inventory of your current network and consciously start to work it:

➤ Who do you know and what do they do?

➤ How are people you know connected?

➤ Weed your garden of networking organizations. Which ones have been fruitful for connections and which ones have been dead ends?

➤ Think globally. Who do you know on the other side of the country and the globe?

➤ How are your former college buddies connected?

code SWITCH *Ask the men as they are leaving for lunch if you can join them. Plan it ahead, but make it look spontaneous. Wait for them to walk down the aisle and then ask. Now you will hear about the business leads, office issues, and job opportunities. And now you have set a precedent.*

Eva is very outgoing and knows "everyone." She is well versed in networking and nourishes her relationships by staying in touch with clients and business contacts, making referrals, attending business association meetings, and spreading around business and goodwill. She belongs to several networking organizations and holds an office in one strategic and powerful group. She also has formed a mastermind group of professionals outside of work with varied expertise to support each other. Her group was featured in the local newspaper, and they refer business to her. Eva's boss considers her affiliation with networking groups and her constant effort to reach out as a bonus to the business, and he has published his praise in the weekly company newsletter.

Membership continues to grow in Eva's mastermind group. Now her boss wants her to begin a similar group within their organization.

Sheila Wellington, past president of Catalyst, a nonprofit research and advisory organization that works to advance women in business, summarized her findings on the impact of mentoring and networking on women in *Be Your Own Mentor.* She cites an example of a female executive at a Fortune 500 company who was involved in a fundraiser for a local hospital. This woman ran the fundraising event, which exceeded all past records for money raised. The morning after the event, her outstanding success was shared with her company's CEO by a hospital board member while playing golf. As a result, she received a promotion not long afterward and was identified as a "comer with high potential." That's a perfect case in point for how networking can work for you. And you can't network sitting in your office.

Remember, networking is like anything else: you get out what you put into it. Networking assumes a *quid pro quo:* something for something. And if you're not getting anything, move on. Personally, we give an organization a year of our membership. If we get nothing in return, we do not renew our membership. Identify the successful networking groups by asking around. Ask people what kind of connections they have made. Some women go for companionship and to make friends, which is fine but may not be your goal.

Mentor Your Way to the Top

So much evidence indicates that no one gets to the top without a little help. And very successful people often receive help from several mentors, not just one. Especially in human resources literature, the word *mentor,* which is a noun, has become a verb. Many perspectives exist on what exactly a mentor is. Mentoring means different things to different people. A mentor can be a casual relationship or a long-term friendship. Traditionally, some of us may recall the experienced businessperson who took us under a wing and taught us the "ropes" and what "strings" to pull. We wouldn't think about making a major decision without consulting this person.

One of the critical things mentors can do is teach us the unwritten rules in the business world. What works and what will sink your ship? They know. They have made those mistakes. Why not learn from their mistakes rather than make them again yourself? A mentor can help you strategize and take an honest look at yourself.

Some people think mentoring is a womanly task. Just the origin of the word *mentor* reveals a feminine origin and emphasis. We owe this word to the age of Homer. In the *Odyssey,* Mentor is the trusted friend of Odysseus who is left in charge of the household during Odysseus's absence. The goddess Athena, disguised as Mentor, guides Odysseus's son, Telemachus, in his search for his father. The mentor who was so nurturing wasn't really an old man; "he" was really a "she." The "she" was Athena, who took the form of an old man to help the young and vulnerable.

Go a step further. One can argue that the archetype of a successful mentor is the mother. Mothers praise their children's accomplishments and offer criticism for bad choices. The job of a good mother is to teach their young as much as they know and as much as the young can absorb. Finally, as with all good and healthy mothering and mentoring relationships, it is important to know when to let go and push the young out of the nest.

Sheila Wellington of Catalyst makes a powerful claim regarding the fundamental importance of mentoring: "In my experience, the single most important reason why—among the equally talented—men tend to rise higher than a woman is that most men have mentors and most women do not." Her opinion is substantiated by 30 years of research on women conducted by Catalyst, the preeminent source of information and research on women and the workplace. Mentors may be more important than hard work and talent. Simply, mentors help you understand how to operate in the work world.

code **SWITCH** *Go to your boss and produce some data and statistics of how mentoring can benefit the organization. Explain how mentoring figures into the equation of attracting top talent and aids in retention, especially for women. Remind your boss that mentoring programs are often the deciding factor in whether a candidate takes a job. See if your boss can help you engage a mentor, or even take on a mentoring role yourself.*

You want these characteristics in a mentor:

⟹ Has considerably more experience and connections than you have

⟹ Isn't working with you to make money or to boost her ego

⟹ Wants to help you succeed

⟹ Offers a fresh perspective on problems or challenges because she's not personally involved with your business, like other advisors (including attorneys, accountants, and friends)

⟹ Truly cares for you, and vice versa

⟹ Has been where you are going, business-wise

⟹ Serves as an advocate, promoting your strengths

⟹ Fosters intellectual excitement

⟹ Works with you because she is interested in helping people

⟹ Promotes integrity and values of the profession

⟹ Can facilitate networking within the professional community for you

⟹ Is highly respected and well thought of in the business world or within your profession

Mentors can be valuable sources of information at any stage of your career and company's growth. Mentors can often give you the advantage of behind-the-scene operations and decisions in the making. A mentor is a go-to person when times are difficult. For these reasons, it's important to find not only a mentor who has experience and knowledge, but also someone you can trust and feel at ease with.

Can a Man Be My Mentor?

As you advance in the business world, the likelihood of your boss being a man increases. One of the best people to mentor you is your own boss. Of course, a woman can have a man as a mentor. He may be your boss or a senior-level executive.

SWITCH IT UP!

Men, who are more likely to have participated in competitive team sports and dealt with coaches early in their lives, generally have a higher comfort level establishing relationships with mentors. Women just don't have the history or experience of participating in the coach-student dynamics. Gen X and Y women have more experience in team sports and with coaches who took them under their wing. This generation of women is more confident in seeking out advice and counsel. This is viewed as strength, not weakness. One of Audrey's clients, the Women's Food Service Forum, is a model of encouraging mentoring programs within the industry. One of the operational variables: the establishment of internal mentoring programs within food, beverage, and hotel companies. Women's Food Service Forum has also launched a mentoring program for its *own* members.

According to Catalyst, "Male mentors can be very effective in giving advice on career strategies and office politics, especially from their typical position as 'insiders' to the majority culture. Male mentors also often have established networks and credibility and can be very effective advocates at the senior management level." Remember, there are more men in the top ranks to serve as mentors.

Given the demographic composition of today's managerial workforce, most white women involved in mentor relationships will have male mentors. The same is true for minority women. Catalyst's 1999 survey found that 37 percent of minority women were mentored by white men and 26 percent were mentored by minority men. This presents some potential problems of cross-gender mentoring. People will talk and wrong assumptions will be made. She is "kissing up" or "he likes being with younger women." And the most common: "She is sleeping her way to the top." People assume there is some sexual element to the mentoring relationship. The sexual innuendoes will be made.

code SWITCH *Take an inventory of the successful men in your organization. Initiate the possibility of a mentoring relationship with your number one pick. Have lunch and ask him straight out, "Would you mentor me? I could learn a lot from you."*

Can a Woman Be My Mentor?

Of course, women can also be mentors. Although there may not be as many women in senior-level positions, female mentors can give advancement advice and discuss gender issues from a woman's point of view. Sometimes it is hard for male mentors to empathize with "women's work," like getting yourself and the kids ready in the morning and out the door to be on time, or the challenge of making that 7 A.M. staff meeting when the kids don't start school until 8:15 A.M. Female mentors serve as readily applicable and valuable role models who help mentees avoid the same mistakes they may have made and candidly share issues related to gender at work. Some gender issues are easier to discuss with a female mentor than a male mentor. Women can also help with work-life balance challenges.

Unfortunately, there are not enough senior-level women to go around for all the possible mentoring relationships. Women at the top, especially admirable and approachable women, are usually inundated with requests to be a mentor. A senior-level mentor will often pick only the most promising to mentor. Convince her you are one of those women.

Another concern of women mentoring women is the appearance of showing favoritism toward women. Your mentor can handle the criticism because you are the pick of the litter.

Finally, your mentor could be a coworker in the next cube. Don't limit yourself to just women or men in upper-level positions. If your coworker has been with the company for 15 years, she is familiar with the unspoken rules and the history of where the organization has been and what has failed. All are valuable lessons for any newbie. Hierarchical mentoring should not be your sole focus.

Formal or Informal Mentoring Relationships

Many mentoring relationships happen "naturally." They evolve from two people, the mentor and mentee, finding each other because they have an affinity for each other. They have mutual respect. Potential mentors recognize talent when they see it, and they also look to receive some reward and payoff from the mentoring relationship. Many mentors will say their mentee energizes them or brings a fresh perspective. Mentors gravitate toward *winners;* no one wants to mentor a *loser.*

It's possible to have a mentor and never formally call him that; you and your mentor may later recognize the relationship. Your mentor may be the go-to person when you are in crisis and the person you want to consult before taking the plunge on a contract.

Many Fortune 500 companies now have formal mentoring programs and recognize the value of mentoring for retention, for recruitment, to improve productivity, to break down the "silo" mentality that often prevents full cooperation among company departments or divisions, and to enhance professional development at no real extra cost to the company. Mentoring helps organizations use "internal experts" for professional development. Mentoring for diversity is another added value to the organization. Pairing across gender and race creates relationships among diverse employees.

Moving On from Your Mentor

Just as you don't stay under your parents' protection, all good mentoring relationships come to an end. Remember, most successful women have three or four mentors in their career. If you think the beginning of a mentoring relationship can be awkward, so can the end. A good mentor often initiates the break: they have taught you all you need to know at this stage of your career. But this doesn't mean you don't stay in touch.

Organizations that have formal mentoring programs almost always have a rotation, which eases the potential for an uncomfortable break.

Mentoring is a conduit to the top. These relationships are mutually satisfying and really are one of the more pleasant and rewarding parts of work life. They make our work experience not only more successful, but also interpersonally richer. After all, the relationships we form keep us going.

19

Making Career Conquests

You are the one who makes your career happen—not your mom, not your husband, not your boss, and not your mentor. You. Once you learn and accept that, your head will be in a much better place for selecting a direction, setting goals, and going for it. You may say, "I don't know where I want to go" or as some still say to themselves, sometimes facetiously, "I don't know what I want to be when I grow up," and that's okay. The main thing to learn is that you are the one controlling the strings; you are the one deciding how your career will unfold.

How can that be? "I'm not in charge of promotions around here," you might tell yourself. That may be true—literally. But not figuratively. You are in charge of what you do, what you say, who you interact with, and how you present yourself: all these behaviors factor into your career. When you're confident and in charge of your career, it becomes easier to communicate more authoritatively with your male coworkers.

Conquest or Community?

Men and women have different approaches to work. Men tend to come to the workplace looking to win, to make that conquest. It's a competition. It's a contest. If you're not helping him win, then you are the enemy or an unimportant underling.

Men learn quickly that they are the breadwinners. They are expected to work. They have to support themselves and probably a significant other and children. Granted, some men in Generation X and Y have moved back home with the folks and somewhere missed the concept that they actually have to work and earn money. In a 2004 *CBS News* online report by correspondent Richard Schlesinger, an estimated two thirds of college graduates have returned home to live with their parents, some for longer periods of time than others. They even have a name: boomerang kids.

Still, most Gen Xers and Yers are out there working, earning money, and supporting themselves. Most men have gotten the message, and they know that they alone are responsible for their career, for getting ahead and for making the bucks. Men tend to be constantly seeking a more impressive job title, prestige, and professional achievement. After all, that's what marks a real man (or so we've been taught).

Preventing women from achieving their career goals is the fact that women tend *not* to think of themselves as the breadwinner, as someone who has to work and support their significant other and children. Many women have been raised to believe that when they grow up, they'll be part of a family. They may not have to work, and if they do work, their income will be secondary to that of their significant other. If they do work, they will enter and leave the workforce periodically when they give birth and/or raise their children, or they may stop working altogether when they have kids.

For many women, work is a place to build friendships, relationships, and community. Now, that's not the reason behind women working. We don't say, "I need a new friend. I think I'll work." It's one approach to work. It's, "Well if I have to work, I might as well make the best of it and enjoy the people I work with—maybe even meet a new friend." Most women are looking for enough cash to pay the bills, do a good job, meet new people, and make a contribution with their lives.

In a chapter called "Gendered Stories of Career: Unfolding Discourses of Time, Space, and Identity" in *The Sage Handbook of Gender and Communication*, communication professor Patrice Buzzanell and doctoral student Kristen Lucas write about how men and women come to careers differently. There's a masculine approach that is similar to a quest. It's a straight path that starts when the man is young and creates his vision for the future. It's considered the traditional path, with the focus on external material rewards. He must be the perfect worker, always working overtime without any complaints, dedicated, loyal, reflect an image of management, and prefer work over personal and family time. According to Buzzanell and Lucas, this traditional path includes having a spouse and kids, which usually goes hand-in-hand with a higher salary and career advancement. The female career revolves around relationships. It's a career staged in phases that includes a significant other, employment, being a mom, and caring for others, say Buzzanell and Lucas. The typical female career includes a focus on the community and service organizations, and incorporates time away from the job raising children or caring for sick parents. It's not a linear progression, as seen in the masculine career approach. Buzzanell and Lucas suggest the feminine career approach includes full- and part-time jobs, jobs that may better accommodate her family responsibilities, owning her own business, and jobs that empower herself and others.

Men or women may play out either role when seeking their careers. A few men may prefer the feminine approach to careers, and a few women may prefer the masculine approach to careers, according to Buzzanell and Lucas. These two different approaches yield different results: ultimately, more men (many more—97.6 percent) than women (2.4 percent) are CEOs of Fortune 500 companies, according to 2008 Catalyst statistics. The number of women of color in executive positions in Fortune 500 companies is minimal. These numbers illustrate how differently men's and women's careers take shape.

Two Roads at an Intersection

Wait a minute, this sounds like we're in the 1950s or '60s. It's sad but true. Changes in the areas of socialization for men and women happen very slowly. Many of the people in the workplace who are making decisions about who gets promoted, who gets the fat bonus check, and who gets the cushy international assignment are Baby Boomers who grew up in the 1950s and '60s watching TV's *Leave It to Beaver*, with Ward Cleaver on his way to work each day while his wife, June, stayed at home in her apron and pearls taking care of the Beave and Wally. The 1970s brought Mary Richards of the *Mary Tyler Moore Show* into living rooms, and many saw for the first time on TV a single woman, not necessarily man hunting, earning her living in a Minneapolis newsroom.

Today's influential TV programs show us several career women in comedies and dramas. They all seem to have something in common. Whether an attorney, doctor, TV writer, politician, or corporate head, these women are still seen as stereotypical "woman." She must play dumb to get ahead; not embarrass or act smarter than her male co-star, manage her family perfectly in addition to being the star performer at work, and so on. Few programs try to frame women as men's equals. To a large extent TV programs reflect our culture and how we are socialized to view men and women at work. But these TV career women continue to be placed in situations of overcoming gender socialization and stereotypes.

Breaking the Barriers

Oh, please! People don't stereotype working women anymore, do they? There were many media reports about the remarks in 2005 made by Lawrence Summers, then the president of Harvard University. *The Boston Globe* reported that at a conference about women in the science and engineering fields, then-president Summers commented that "innate differences between men and women might be one reason fewer women succeed in science and math careers." He asserted that, in high school, more boys have high math and science grades. This ultimately creates a small pool of women entering college programs in these areas and leads to a small number of women at high levels in science and math jobs, Summers said in the article.

Another reason Summers mentioned was "the reluctance or inability of women who have children to work 80-hour weeks." Summers denied that socialization and discrimination were issues that kept women out of these fields; rather, he insisted it was innate differences and personal family choices.

Along with stereotypes, there continue to be court cases and settlements at companies where women have alleged unequal treatment. Career opportunities, pay, promotions, mentoring, and receiving training continue to be areas where women may find themselves treated differently—less than—their male counterparts. Stay aware of major court cases that impact working women like the 2002 $31 million settlement by American Express Financial Advisors, Inc., or the 2007 Morgan Stanley class action settlement of $46 million— both cases that alleged gender discrimination and unequal treatment of women in career growth and job responsibilities. (See Chapter 14's discussion on some of the laws impacting working women, including the 2009 Lilly Ledbetter Fair Pay Act.)

This stuff still happens. It's important to be aware that stereotypes and unequal treatment may be impacting your career and how you are seen and heard on the job. What barriers are keeping women from achieving their career goals? If the workplace treats everyone fairly, why aren't more women holding higher-level positions? We still hear about the glass ceiling that often seems impenetrable to women, an ultimate barrier that keeps women away from the executive club. Although there's increasingly less talk about the glass ceiling, barriers still seem to be keeping women from climbing the corporate ladder.

We tend to minimize the roles that gender differences, socialization, and discrimination play in maintaining the status quo in the workplace. There's a feeling that, after all, in this day and age workplace gender stereotypes and pay inequities just don't happen anymore. Wrong! If a woman wanted to be president or vice president or lead a country, she could, right? Well, maybe if she lived in Ireland, Great Britain, Israel, Argentina, Finland, India, Chile, or New Zealand, to name a few countries that have or have had a woman national leader.

In our workshops, we hear and talk about the barriers that are keeping many women from promotions, challenging assignments, or the jobs they truly want. These include procedures and policies that are not family-friendly or working-mother-friendly, the ol' boy network still in place, lack of training and specific development goals, unequal pay, differing communication styles, lack of power, and stereotypes and bias. Other barriers women talk about include working in inflexible workplaces, perceiving that you're put on the slow track for promotions, not being part of the network and insider information, continually having to work harder than male coworkers, having decisions constantly questioned, being viewed as a joke, being ignored, being harassed, having no meaningful mentoring, and being isolated as the sole woman in a group or department. These are also perceptions of why some women choose to leave a company and start their own business.

Companies invest lots of dollars into their employees through training, time, and work experience. The last thing a company should want is to lose valued employees.

code SWITCH *Stop these behaviors and comments when you see them. Do everything you can to support and encourage other women in your workplace.*

Understanding that these barriers are out there will help you make the right moves to go around and beyond them. Granted, several companies are doing the right things to support women and position them for career success. However, given that court cases still occur and that many of these barriers are deeply ingrained stereotypes and cultural views, it pays to be aware and take your career into your own hands. Talk with the men you work with when you see possible inequities or stereotyping. Let them know you need their support, too, to create an inclusive welcoming work setting for everyone. Most people want to know when their behavior isn't appropriate or offends someone. Talk with your supervisor or human resources manager, especially when you perceive inequities that seem to be built into existing company policies or company culture, to get them investigated and resolved.

▶ SWITCH IT UP! ◀

Stop the revolving door syndrome. That's when people get hired and then, after a short time, leave the company. It often applies to women and minorities. The recruiters complain that they worked very hard to get her hired. The company invests lots of dollars to train her to think and act like one of them. And then she leaves. So they hire another woman—and then she leaves, creating the revolving door. Her coworkers generally blame her. "She couldn't take it here." "She never was a good match." If asked why she left, she may respond that there is a buildup of microinequities that have let her know on a daily basis that she's not good enough and that the others won't let her into the club.

Be Your Own Career Guru

You get to choose what you will do with your life. Will you have a career or a job? A job is something you do to make some money. You show up, do the work, and get paid. If it's not there tomorrow, you find another place to work and get paid. A career is different. It requires some planning, preparation, probably some type of education, and possible professional certification, and you think of it as your life's calling. Your career is what you want to do with your life and where you want to spend your time. Selecting a job versus a career is neither right nor wrong. Each of us at some point has had a job we didn't really care about but needed for certain reasons (such as paying the bills, sometimes to set us up for our future career). You decide which works best for you at certain points in your life. Jobs may come and go, but your career, your profession, will probably stay with you as long as you see it as your passion, as what makes you happy, or as what gives you the most satisfaction.

Our desire is to help you achieve your career goals. You're encouraged to be proactive and manage your career. You make it happen rather than waiting for it to happen to you. Be your own career coach or guru. Take charge of the direction you're heading and map your course. Become the expert on your own skills and how to market them. Don't sit and wait for someone else to make a decision that impacts your career. Think of your work as something you want to do, not something you're required to do. It may take some getting used to, but once you learn how to promote your skills and abilities, you'll be one step closer to achieving your goals. A woman who shows confidence, stays focused, and knows her goals and the direction she's heading is more likely to grab a man's ear, support, and even admiration as a colleague.

code **SWITCH** *Set up a career plan with completion dates along the way. Stay focused. Tell your supervisor about your career goals. That advice may be just what you need.*

Making the Most of Your Opportunities

Don't get caught up in the stereotypes going on around you. We know, that's easier said than done. While we hope you're working at an enlightened company that treats both women and men employees with dignity and respect, we realize that's not always the case. When looking for work, research companies that have a record of supporting women. Check their male/female ratio. Look at who's on their board and who holds executive offices. Check their benefits. Do they have support groups or offer mentoring programs for women?

Look at your potential work situation before you get hired. If you're working for a man who's basically backward in his thinking about women in the workplace, you may need to change work groups. And by the way, there may be a few basically backward women bosses out there, too, who just will not support a bright, up-and-coming woman. If you think people will hear your message about your career goals and your needing their support, talk with them. Realize that life's too short to spend too much time working for a boss who doesn't support you as a person and a woman. You're not the only one who's noticed that boss is a jerk. Learn what you can from the person and be ready to move on.

Create opportunities to meet people at your work, in your community, or in your profession. Are you a member of your parent–teacher association? Look at the groups where you have membership and think about talking with some of those folks about your career ideas and goals. Are you a soccer mom? While you're waiting for your daughter to score a goal, make connections. Talk with the other moms and dads about where they work, your interests, their advice, and your aspirations. Do it in a social way. Use your relationship skills. Don't cling to people and have them dread seeing you at the next game. Offer your advice and be willing to listen, too, to their story. It's mutual. Refer to Chapter 18 for more networking guidelines.

code **SWITCH** *Be proactive. Think of your values, interests, skills, and needs, and where you can best use them. Being consistent with your goals will help the men in your workplace (specifically, your male boss) understand that you're serious about the job.*

A colleague of ours e-mails authors of books she has read, asking questions or commenting on certain passages. Some authors reply, and she has developed valuable relationships with people in her field. Another colleague looks for opportunities to meet people of interest by checking their online calendars, learning when they'll be in town, and arranging a meeting for coffee or lunch. Now, it doesn't always get arranged, but she has met several influential people in her career area. Like to blog? A woman we work with has started a couple of blogs of her own, creating opportunities to meet likeminded people that exchange information and help each other move forward. Use your online connections to create or add to your work identity and meet and network with new business colleagues who may help move along your career. Step away from your cubicle and go talk with people.

And always be ready to grab an opportunity when it pops up. One writer, Anne, dreamed of being an international journalist. She wrote as many international-themed stories as her hometown newspaper would allow. She networked with humanitarians, travelers, immigrants, and international businesspeople wherever possible. Her dream was always on her horizon, although she did not know how to reach it.

One day, she was driving home and listening to the local radio station. She heard a man talking about his nonprofit in Africa. She jotted down the nonprofit's name and contacted him the next day. She wrote a small story and kept in touch. More than a year later, he called her. He was going to Africa in just two weeks and wondered if she would like to come to write a story. She did not hesitate. Yes. She would go. The networking, coupled with ever-readiness to jump at her dream, ended up changing her career path—and her life.

code SWITCH *Step out of the box. Better yet, get rid of the box and connect with people who may help you with your career journey. It might be a club, a radio station, an overheard conversation, or a flier on the wall at the coffee shop. Your drive will win over your male boss or mentor and he will open opportunity doors. Men tend to like action; they like to make things happen. Get him to make them happen for you.*

Talk It Up!

If you're waiting for a promotion that still hasn't come through, you may need to reevaluate your position and goals. If you love your work, you may decide to stay. If you decide you're ready for a move, start looking at opportunities around you.

Realize that promotions are not always the answer and the path that you need to grow. Be willing to look at lateral moves within the company or moves to other companies that will keep you learning and developing your expertise. Think about what else may work for you instead of a promotion: representing the company at a conference, attending a seminar, taking a more prestigious assignment, meeting with the new client in Paris, learning additional software, taking executive training, or getting a new laptop. Other activities besides the promotion can keep you growing and meeting new people. Talk to the male and female leaders and executives you work with. Ask for recommendations on how you can meet your career goals and learn how they achieved theirs.

Talk about your goals and what you want. Tell your boss. Tell your boss's boss. Tell the department head in the next division. The more people know about your goals and what you'd like to accomplish, the better. People who may be able to help you will be out there with an eye and ear, watching and listening to your needs. This doesn't necessarily mean stopping people in the hallways and telling them you want to move into marketing—although, with job searches, people have taken some extreme steps. One man in NYC wore a sandwich board stating that he was looking for work while he handed out his resumé to interested parties.

When Claire was ready to move into a different division, she pulled out her list of influential women and met separately with a director and a few department heads for career advice and to let them know her job interests. A couple of months went by and then she got a call from a director about a possible job match. She interviewed and got the position (also a promotion). This would not have happened unless she had initiated the phone call to talk with this person about job possibilities. Remember the saying: "Success comes from faith plus action." You can't just sit around believing that something good will fall into your lap. But you need enough faith, or hope, the motivation for change and improvement. Without hope, we stop trying (or taking action). Faith plus action is having that hope and belief that you will find something better, and then doing everything in your power to make that happen. Make a phone call. Meet for career advice. Talk about your goals. Send thank-you notes. Wait for good things to happen!

Male bosses sometimes don't know what to do with ambitious, goal-oriented women. These women are acting outside the stereotypes that the men may be comfortable with. Sometimes you can show the men where to help. We don't mean baby-sit them, but some are open to learning how to be the best boss, regardless of who their employee might be.

Is there a tough assignment in your work group? Don't wait for him to approach you. Convince your boss that you're the one for the job. Then work your butt off to do an outstanding job on time and to make you and your boss look good. An assignment no one wants? Go after it and, again, do your best. Soon your boss and his boss will get the picture that you're the one who can get the job done. Learn as much as you can. Become the expert on a particular topic. Be a problem solver. Other colleagues and managers will begin to see you as the expert, too. Always perform better than expected. Get those visible assignments, and when you handle great accomplishments, e-mail a summary to your boss and his boss to make sure they know about it. Copy or e-mail them the thank-you notes or words of congratulations that you receive from clients or the end users of your project. It's not bragging—remember, it's a game, and you're reminding them that you play the game well.

code `SWITCH` *Your boss will listen if he knows you're an outstanding worker, an expert, someone he can count on, and someone who makes him and his department look good. Don't sit and wait for the boss to notice that you're a good worker. Be proactive.*

Preparation Pays

Did you know you're in the right place at the right time all the time? You're just not taking advantage of it. Every day you meet people who may be able to help you achieve your career goals. Everyone you meet, everywhere you go, there's an opportunity to talk with someone and do some self-marketing. When you meet people, ask about their interests and tell them yours. What are you marketing? You could be interested in moving into a new position, changing companies, looking for information to help you with a career change, getting the name of the hiring manager at their company, gathering information on a particular position, or understanding someone's perspectives on career support. If you know ahead of time that you'll be meeting a particular supervisor or client at work, do some research beforehand and see what you can learn. Then when you meet this person, you'll have some reference points to discuss. If it's a prospective client, you'll be researching this person and company to learn how you can best meet their needs.

A coworker of ours used to keep a file with a note about each client: family members and names, children's ages, pets, hobbies, and birthdays. When she knew she'd be meeting with that person, she'd pull out her notes and help build her relationship with that particular client. That extra information about the client often made the difference in getting a sale or future work.

Have a performance review coming up? Don't walk in and sit down and wait for your boss's evaluation. Prepare by reviewing your accomplishments, looking at issues that may have impacted you throughout the year, understanding what your needs are to improve your performance, looking at areas for training or conferences you'd like to attend, thinking of additional responsibilities you'd like, and thinking of questions you want to ask about upcoming assignments and what's needed to grow to the next job level. Ask to sit in on meetings with your boss or in your boss's place when he or she's unavailable.

On Claire's first annual performance review at a large technical company, her supervisor noted she did an excellent job and recited to her his high praise for outstanding work. Then he showed Claire her rating on the scale (they had a rating scale or continuum). There was a big X marked right in the middle of the performance scale.

"I thought you said I was excellent and outstanding. Why is the X in the middle?" she asked.

"You are excellent," replied her boss. "I hired you because you are excellent. Everyone here is hired because they are excellent. Therefore, you're average, as indicated by the X midscale."

He explained that, to be better than excellent, an employee had to do something fantastic and different, and have a great impact to the organization. He added that very few people get that rating. So Claire learned that she was an average excellent employee. Her shock at understanding this evaluation system could have been alleviated if she had asked this supervisor when she was first hired to explain the evaluation system, his rating scale, and how he made decisions on performance. Lesson learned.

Get the performance feedback you need. Unless you're a clown, don't settle for the "needs to smile more" written on your performance feedback form (yes, it *has* happened) or other comments that don't pertain to your ability to do your job. Ask what the comment means and request that it gets changed, or write an appeal or rebuttal, if needed.

code SWITCH *Don't be quiet and expect your boss to look out for your best interests. Be direct. Ask questions. Show that you genuinely want to learn about this process. Understand your performance evaluation system and how decisions are made for dollars (raises and bonuses) based on performance.*

Beg Forgiveness and Do It Anyway

Be a risk taker. That's what we often hear about men and the winners at work: they take risks. If you have a question or a new approach, sometimes it's best to go for it instead of waiting for the hoped-for answer or stamp of approval. As the Nike ads said, "Just do it." Stay away from the indecisive woman stereotype. Sometimes the woman who stands out in a crowd is the one who makes the decision and goes for it. She can always beg forgiveness later if it's needed.

If an issue is raised about your action, you can apologize. We always tell women that even if the risk fails, people will admire them for taking one! So it is a win-win.

Shanna had always been a risk taker. She had an idea for a new product, but she was new at the company and didn't have the clout to initiate it yet. She mentioned it in passing to her boss, but it didn't stick. She mentioned it a few more times, but it got nowhere. So she did it anyway. In her spare time, she put the entire project together. Then she presented it to her boss. He was still skeptical and said he'd sit on it. She made improvements and brought it back to him continuously for six months. Finally, he agreed—reluctantly—to give it a chance.

Instantly, the consumers went crazy for it. They loved it, and it became one of the strongest products of the company. Shanna was beaming, but she kept humble and happy in the knowledge that she has followed her intuition and pursued her dream tenaciously—and that she and her boss both knew it. Needless to say, after that, Shanna had all the clout she needed.

Look at the big picture. Where does your decision fit? If you have sound reasoning for doing something that makes sense to you, do it. In some decisions, you have to rely on your own knowledge of the job and your good judgment. Generally, if you make a decision using that approach, the fact you made a decision will be respected even if it turns out to be the wrong decision.

code SWITCH *Take well-thought-out risks. Making tough choices on your own will gain you respect from coworkers and management.*

You'll get even more notice and respect if it was the right decision. Men will listen and support you. You're the one who's making all the career moves.

20

Cracking the Gender Communication Code

Congratulations! The easy part, reading this book, is just about done. The challenge is to put the code switching tips into action. In many cases, this requires courage to do things you have never done. Some will be easier than others. You need some spunk and passion to step up and make these tips work for you. Getting men to listen is no easy feat—any woman in any profession can testify to that!

Making Progress While Making a Difference

Working women are here to stay. They are making their mark in companies—their own and others'—across the country and the globe. They are steadily increasing their ranks in management and professional fields. Women and men continue to work together. We don't see that ending anytime soon. It doesn't matter whether your workplace is female or male dominated. Likewise, at the executive level, men tend to fill the top jobs. Women in the pink ghetto—which includes librarians, human resources staffers, elementary education teachers, and nurses—are dominated by women who are usually paid less than their male counterparts. Even in the pink ghetto, we're not surprised to see men at the upper levels. Looking at who's holding what jobs in your company's upper stratosphere often provides clues to your future opportunities.

Most workplaces currently favor a masculine style of leadership and a masculine approach to managing a business. That generally means that they also value a masculine style of communication. Slowly, we are seeing changes in workplaces as they become more receptive to different approaches and ways of doing business. In other words, they are becoming more receptive to a nonmasculine style. When changes impact the bottom line in a positive direction, the executives start paying attention and nosing around to see what's happening.

Yet movement forward and changes in the workplace are painfully slow, as illustrated by the true stories provided in this book. Our goals include having Audrey's daughter and Claire's nieces employed in a world where they are recognized and respected for the gifts and talents they bring to the workplace. We're excited for them to enter new jobs and have new adventures and careers ahead. We feel the same desires for other women just entering the workforce. However, we're also dismayed—or perhaps frustrated—that they may face some of the same conundrums that have faced working women for decades.

Don't get us wrong: women are moving forward a few inches at a time, bringing their collaborative, empowering skills and communication styles to the workforce. But as we wish a son and nephews career success, the thought of them being sexually harassed, bullied, ignored, given unequal pay, not listened to, not mentored, or passed over for promotion—all because of their biological sex—doesn't even enter our minds. We don't send off a son to his first job with a lesson plan on what to do if he's sexually harassed, experiences sex discrimination, or is interrupted or ignored at group meetings.

Understand that we're not male bashing here. We've each learned a lot from male coworkers. We've had valuable collegial relationships with male bosses, peers, consultants, mentors, friends, and significant others. We've learned much from these men that has helped us in our careers.

Some Things Change While Others Stay the Same

As much as some things have changed, others have stayed the same. Claire recalls her mom commenting in the early 1980s that she felt the men in the office never treated her right; they looked down on her and never invited her to lunch with them. She ate lunch by herself striking up a friendship with her waitress in a nearby diner. We're all for women's independence and having a meal alone occasionally, but not every day for a few years because the men don't see you as a colleague. The men instead saw Claire's mom as a worker bee who was there to do a job—not someone who could be part of their club. She gave up trying to invite herself along, and they made it clear she wouldn't enjoy it.

Flash-forward to now.

There are more women CEOs in Fortune 500 companies and pretty much at all levels in corporations. However, court cases abound. Women argue that they are not being treated respectfully and equitably in the workplace, for the many reasons our book has reviewed. A major holdup has been women entering the historically male business world and trying to play in an environment built by men, for men, and with men's rules.

What woman can sort her way through these workplaces and win? How can you survive without feeling torn, spindled, and mutilated? Some women do survive. Some women achieve their career goals. Some women make it to the top, to CEO, as they planned. And some bare the scars and know the costs of making it.

These women pioneers have succeeded by valuing communication, listening, understanding, networking, and collaborating. They know when to take risks, be assertive, be direct, and make those tough decisions. They know their strengths and how to use them. They know their values and how to work ethically to complement them. They're compassionate when compassion is needed. They make the tough decisions their companies require. They know how to play the male game of business. More important, they know how to make new rules for a new game in which they and other women can succeed. These women know how to code-switch. They readily use feminine and masculine communication styles that best suit themselves and the situation. They are self-aware and know their communication choices. They make it happen.

Flash-forward to the year 2020.

Code Switching Solves Workplace Communication in 2020

Hold onto your hat! Here's our best estimate on future changes in 2020. Now there are more women CEOs: 15.6 percent of the Fortune 500 CEOs are women (up from 2.4 percent in 2008). They have cracked the gender communication codes. Collaboration is the key for successful workplace managers. Fewer workplace-related ailments arise because work stresses are a thing of the past. Most people are working in careers—not just jobs—where they feel encouraged and welcomed; they learn, produce, and contribute more than years ago. In 2020 men and women work side by side, mentoring each other so they and their company succeed. Businesses regularly offer workshops on how to listen. Women and men are more self-aware of their choices in how they communicate with each other.

How is this all possible? Code switching is the answer. It became the rage 10 years ago. Women wanted to better themselves and their communication in the workplace. They used their code switching skills to improve communication with their male colleagues. Women were code switching and men were listening. They still are, to this day. Women know how to value their own communication style and when to use it to get across a message and achieve their goals. They know how and when to use different communication styles to suit their needs.

In 2020 we see the feminine and masculine styles of leadership have become more blended. Men and women alike have learned to draw from a vast pool of communication skills to successfully lead in different situations. The popular code switching behaviors have given birth to the code switching communication style. This new way of communicating encourages women to select a communication style they are comfortable with that gets their messages accurately to their coworkers. In the past, the male and female communication and leadership styles were fairly distinct. The new code switching leadership style blends the two styles into a more synergistic approach to leadership and communication. It's dynamic and ever-changing, based on its code switching roots. Men listen to this style. Women listen, too. This style has cracked the past gender communication codes wide open. The code switching communication and leadership style is strong and soft, aggressive and straight-forward, compassionate and not afraid of emotions. Flash back to the present.

We know that women and men bring different leadership approaches and communication styles to the office. Different is good. We don't all want to be the same—that would be boring. One is not better than the other—they're just different. Psychologists, sociologists, and other scientists have recognized this fact for centuries. But these differences contribute to the "potholes" in which we often find ourselves when trying to talk to male peers and bosses. Despite these distinctions, however, working relationships between men and women do thrive. They become rocky only when both genders fail to hear the differences for what they are—behaviors—and have certain rigid expectations of how the two sexes should communicate. How do we move forward and create a new future of gender communication?

Stop the Blame Game

Our natural tendency is to believe that men are the ones who need to change. We think they are the ones with the problem. But we must start with ourselves. We each have a responsibility in the communication process. We may not be able to control the other person's communication style, but we can manage our own. Blaming men gets us nowhere. Although we sometimes enjoy a good pity party, using a few salty words to describe the boss and his ineptness doesn't get us anywhere. In fact, it seems to move us further from our goals. A short venting—keep it to 10 minutes—may alleviate the knot in your stomach, but keep your focus on moving forward. Take responsibility for your own communication. It may not completely prevent communication misunderstandings, but it can help prevent breakdowns and minimize out-of-control situations. Make the choice to stop the blaming and move forward to your fabulous future.

Self-Awareness and Self-Consciousness

Communication self-awareness is the first step toward enhancing effective communication. That may appear difficult, since communication often operates at a stealth level of existence—we leave an interaction feeling that something happened, but we're not exactly sure what. One of the reasons we are so bad at this critical skill is simply that most of us do not know about these sex differences and how they operate. To narrow the chasm between the sexes, we need to turn our attention to this decisive part of gender interactions.

Why be self-aware and understand communication components? Because in the workplace, as well as during the countless errands that consume our day, we continually experience communication minidisasters, often unintended. At work, subtle *microinequities* and disrespectful behaviors that support the business infrastructure occur every day between men and women. The consequences of these behaviors maintain the glass ceiling or sticky floor and ultimately result in less earning potential for women. We are still falling off the glass cliff (see Chapter 16).

In our work, we've seen smart, hard-working, well-intentioned women self-destruct because they are just plain unaware of what they and others are communicating. Although we may not always get the results we want in an encounter, knowing how gender communication works will increase women's effectiveness and enhance all our interactions between men and women.

Question the Status Quo

Our focus has been on you and how you communicate with men in the organization. There's more that can help you move forward and create that code switching future. Your company plays a role in how it supports women in the workplace. We've talked about how, as an individual woman employee, you should understand gender communication concepts and use code switching skills to help men listen to your views. At an organizational level, you can do certain things to support other women and bring about change in the workplace:

> Gain a manager's ear and talk about supporting women in the workplace. The boss—male or female—may not want to hear about this. Do your research. Bring in articles that explain the impact of stereotypes and the loss of productivity due to sex discrimination

(see Chapter 14). Offer to do a presentation on this topic at the next executive staff meeting.

➡ Look for things you can do on your own to support women that won't cost the company money. We've mentioned the women's groups that exist at many large companies (see Chapter 18). Contact one of those companies and talk with one of the women in charge of such a group. You'll learn a lot about how to set up such a group and can apply this to your work setting.

➡ Look for a supportive male or female boss or higher-up who might be sympathetic to your cause. Get recommendations from this person on how to gain more support for women in your workplace. A woman advisor may better relate to your cause, but don't rule out asking a man. Gaining a male advisor could lend credibility to your cause— remember all those stereotypes we've been talking about. A man may have more access to the power network (see Chapter 18).

➡ Remember, even if your company does not have a formal mentoring program, you can still go out and get a mentor (see Chapter 18).

➡ If your community has chapters of various women's associations, check them out. As mentioned earlier, some larger towns even have a women's chamber of commerce. See if your company has a membership in that particular group. If so, find your company contact and see how you can represent the company at association meetings. If not, do your research and put together a proposal explaining how membership would benefit the organization and its women employees. Would the male employees benefit, too? If women are improving their business skills, the whole workplace benefits.

➡ Consider whether training classes would help your organization. Training women and men to understand gender communication skills, workplace dynamics, laws that impact the workplace, diversity, cultural competence, and inclusiveness benefits the company by increasing employees' awareness and skills. Retention increases when employees feel that they are in a welcoming environment where they can fully contribute and thrive. Add code switching as a workshop for your women employees to enhance their communication skills and make sure the men are listening.

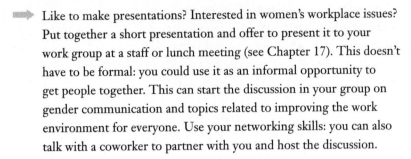

Like to make presentations? Interested in women's workplace issues? Put together a short presentation and offer to present it to your work group at a staff or lunch meeting (see Chapter 17). This doesn't have to be formal: you could use it as an informal opportunity to get people together. This can start the discussion in your group on gender communication and topics related to improving the work environment for everyone. Use your networking skills: you can also talk with a coworker to partner with you and host the discussion.

Like to write? Select a topic related to women's workplace goals, statistics, or communication, and write a short article for your community newspaper. Bring the article to work and use it as a tool to start discussions on the topic. It will also serve as visibility for a great accomplishment: being in the town's paper.

Don't like to write? When you see articles in magazines or newspapers related to women's workplace issues, bring them to work and circulate them FYI (for your information) to your work group. You may also offer to talk about them at your staff meeting; think about the implications that article has for your work group. What would your group do if the illustrated scenario happened to someone in your office? Do the actions suggested in the article make sense? These discussions can heighten the group's awareness of women's workplace dilemmas.

You and your organization may already be doing some of these items. If so, that's fantastic! They are definite steps to creating a new welcoming workplace for the future. Make sure you are taking advantage now of the resources your company offers.

An organization that wants to demonstrate support for working women also has many avenues. Does your company offer executive training or some type of leadership training? If so make sure women are aware of the program and what they must do to participate. Encourage women to take advantage of this program.

Does your company offer tuition reimbursement? If so, make sure women are aware of the program and what they must do to participate. Support women who take advantage of this program. Remember our socialization. Some women may have more family and home responsibilities than other women or other men. Talk with women interested in furthering their educations, and look at campus or other resources that may help women in going back to school. This is the future of your business; make it the best it can be for you and your company.

Consider a few other ideas that companies can do to help women advance in the workplace:

- Review statistics on a quarterly basis for men and women in terms of hirings, transfers, promotions, demotions, firings, and people choosing to leave the company. This includes reviewing salary levels for men and women in similar and different job levels in the organization.

- Conduct exit interviews when someone leaves the company, to become aware of any issues related to women's treatment or workplace flexibility in response to their needs.

- Create a mentoring program that provides mentors to everyone who is interested. Include training for mentors to better understand their roles.

- Broaden the search for new employees to include campuses with more women graduating in the degree areas you need. Think of different settings. For instance, host a networking gathering that might attract more women from the fields from which you hire.

Women and companies partnering together can help women move further and accomplish more in their work environment. The key to those accomplishments is always communication skills. Your self-awareness and code switching skills will make a positive difference in your workplace. You can contribute to setting goals and partnering with your company to meet and move beyond our 2020 vision!

Leading the Code Switching Path

Code switching implies movement and action. *Code Switching: How to Talk So Men Will Listen* is about change. This book has brought up unsettling questions that go to the core of how we define ourselves and relate to others as businesswomen. It is meant to stimulate you to question your behavior, examine yourself, and even feel a little uncomfortable at times. It's always helpful to understand your communication and leadership styles and how others see you. We must consider new ideas of what it means to be male and female. When women and men embrace the journey by observing gender communication at the office and questioning the traditional conventions that our culture and society have accepted, we will be better able to reach out to, respect, and understand each other.

The corporate world is a more enjoyable and fulfilling place when you have the right toolkit. And that toolkit—your toolkit—is full of code switches lining your path to career success.

We want you to be reflective. We want you to become more self-aware about how you interact with men. Self-knowledge is critical to your success. Communication is key. Knowing men's receptivity to certain communication patterns can make or break a deal or career.

The time is right to crack that gender communication code and use your code switching communication skills. Men and women will continue to work side by side. And the times are changing. More women are entering senior-level positions and need to know how to bring men over to their side.

It's official: we deputize you as certified code switchers. Go out into the business world and into your workplace, and enforce the opportunity and success you deserve. It's your future.

Resources

Books

Babcock, Linda, and Sara Laschever. *Women Don't Ask: Negotiation and the Gender Divide.* Princeton, NJ: Princeton University Press, 2003.

Barash, David P., and Judith E. Lipton. *Making Sense of Sex: How Genes and Gender Influence our Relationships.* Washington: Island Press, 1997.

Barreca, Regina. *They Used to Call Me Snow White ... But I Drifted: Women's Strategic Use of Humor.* New York: Penguin Books, 1991.

Blum, Deborah. *Sex on the Brain: The Biological Differences Between Men and Women.* New York: Penguin Group, 1997.

Borisoff, Deborah, and Lisa Merrill. *The Power to Communicate, Gender Differences as Barriers,* Second Edition. Prospect Heights, IL: Waveland Press, 1992.

Brizendine, Louann. *The Female Brain.* New York: Morgan Road Books, 2006.

Brown, Claire Damken, Charlotte Snedeker, and Beate Sykes, Editors. *Conflict and Diversity.* Cresskill, NJ: Hampton Press, 1997.

Coates, Jennifer, Editor. *Language and Gender: A Reader.* Malden, MA: Blackwell, 1998.

Dow, Bonnie, and Julia Wood, Editors. *Sage Handbook of Gender and Communication.* Thousand Oaks, CA: Sage Publications, 2006.

Dowd, Maureen. *Are Men Necessary? When the Sexes Collide.* New York: G.P. Putnam's Sons, 2005.

Doyle, J. *The Male Experience*. Madison: Brown & Benchmark, 1995.

Eakins, Barbara, and R. Gene Eakins. *Sex Differences in Human Communication*. Boston: Houghton Mifflin, 1978.

Evans, Sybil, and Sherry Suib Cohen. *Hot Buttons: How to Resolve Conflict and Cool Everyone Down*. New York: Cliff Street Books HarperCollins, 2000.

Fisher, Roger, and William Ury. *Getting to Yes: Negotiating Agreement without Giving In*. New York: Penguin Books, 1987 reprint. Original copyright 1981 by Houghton Mifflin: Boston.

Flett, Christopher. *What Men Don't Tell Women About Business*. Hoboken, NJ: John Wiley & Sons, 2008.

Friedan, Betty. *The Feminine Mystique*. New York: Dell, 1963.

Gallagher, Carol. *Going to the Top*. New York: Penguin, 2001.

Gamble, Teri K., and Michael Gamble. *The Gender Communication Connection*. Boston: Houghton Mifflin, 2003.

Gilbert, Susan. *A Field Guide to Boys and Girls: Differences, Similarities: Cutting-Edge Information Every Parent Needs to Know*. New York: HarperCollins, 2000.

Gladwell, Malcolm. *Blink: The Power of Thinking without Thinking*. New York: Little, Brown and Company, 2005.

Glass, Lillian. *He Says, She Says: Closing the Communication Gap Between the Sexes*. New York: G.P. Putnam's Sons, 1992.

Goleman, Daniel. *Emotional Intelligence: Why it Can Matter More than IQ*. New York: Bantam Books, 1995.

———. *Social Intelligence; The New Science of Human Relationships*. New York: Bantam Books, 2006.

Gurian, Michael, and Barbara Annis. *Leadership and the Sexes: Using Gender Science to Create Success in Business*. San Francisco: Jossey-Bass, 2008.

Harvey, Carol, and M. June Allard, Editors. *Understanding and Managing Diversity*, Third Edition. Upper Saddle River, NJ: Pearson Prentice-Hall, 2004.

Helgesen, Sally. *The Female Advantage: Women's Ways of Leadership*. New York: Currency/Doubleday, 1990.

———. *The Web of Inclusion*. New York: Currency/Doubleday, 1995.

Holmes, Janet and Miriam Meyerhof, Editors. *The Handbook of Language and Gender*. Oxford: Blackwell Publishers, 2003.

Ivy, Diana, and Phil Backlund. *GenderSpeak: Personal Effectiveness in Gender Communication*, Third Edition. New York: McGraw-Hill, 2004.

Mehrabian, Albert. *Silent Messages: Implicit Communication of Emotion and Attitudes*, Second Edition. Belmont, CA: Wadsworth, 1981.

Nelson, Audrey, and Susan Golant. *You Don't Say: Navigating Nonverbal Communication Between the Sexes*. New York: Prentice Hall, 2004.

Payne, Kay. *Different But Equal*. Westport, CT: Praeger, 2001.

Pearson, Judy. *Gender and Communication*. Dubuque, IA: William Brown Company, 1985.

Pease, Barbara, and Allan Pease. *Why Men Don't Listen and Women Can't Read Maps*. New York: Broadway Books, 2000.

Sherman, Ruth. *Get Them to See It Your Way, Right Away*. New York: McGraw-Hill, 2003.

Tannen, Deborah. *The Argument Culture: Moving From Debate to Dialogue*. New York: Random House, 1998.

———. *You Just Don't Understand: Women and Men in Conversation*. New York: William Morrow, 1990.

Tingley, Judith. *Genderflex: Men and Women Speaking Each Other's Language at Work*. New York: AMACOM, 1994.

Ury, William. *The Power of a Positive No: How to Say NO and Still Get to YES*. New York: Bantam Books, 2007.

Wellington, Sheila. *Be Your Own Mentor: Strategies from Top Women on the Secrets of Success*. New York: Random House, 2001.

Wilmot, William W., and Joyce L. Hocker. *Interpersonal Conflict*, Fifth Edition. Boston: McGraw Hill, 1998.

Wood, Julia. *Gendered Lives*, Sixth Edition. Belmont, CA: Wadsworth/ Thomson Learning, 2005.

Magazine, Newspaper, and Journal Articles

Anderson, Kristin, and Campbell Leaper. "Meta-analysis of Gender Effects on Conversational Interruptions: who, what, when, where, and how." *Sex Roles: A Journal of Research*. 39, 3-4: 225-52, 1998.

Baram, Marcus. "Jury Finds Thomas Sexually Harassed Team Executive." Oct 3, 2007 ABC News. Ret Oct 12, 2007. http://abcnews.go.com/Sports/ Story?id=3656074&page=1.

Berkowitz, Lana. "Hand-wringing Over Hand-holding: Saudi Official Says Bush, Prince Showed Respect." *Houston Chronicle*, Apr 27, 2005.

Bogaers, Iris. "Gender in Job Interviews: Implications of Verbal Interactions of Women and Men." *International Journal of the Sociology of Language*. 129: 35-58, 1998.

Bohnet, Iris, and Greig, Fiona. "Gender Matters in Workplace Decisions." *Negotiation*. April 2007, p. 4-6.

Bombardieri, Marcella. "Summers' Remarks on Women Draw Fire." Jan 17, 2005, *The Boston Globe*. Ret Jan 3, 2009. www.boston.com/news/local/ articles/2005/01/17/summers_remarks_on_women_draw_fire/.

Brandt, Michelle. "Gender Differences are a Laughing Matter, Stanford Brain Study Shows." *Stanford School of Medicine Office of Communication and Public Affairs*. Nov 7, 2005. Ret Jan 13, 2006. http://mednews.stanford. edu/releases/2005/november/humor.html.

Caliskan, Sevda. "Is There Such a Thing as Women's Humor?" *American Studies International* 33.2: 49-60, 1995. Ret Nov 14, 2005. http:// weblinks1.epnet.com/DeliveryPrintSave.asp?tb=0&_ug=sid+6E3E45B8- 4B039.

Catalyst Report. "The Catalyst Pyramid: U.S. Women in Business." November 2008. www.catalyst.org.

Catalyst Report. "The Double-Bind Dilemma for Women in Leadership: Damned if You Do, Doomed if You Don't." October 2007. www.catalyst. org.

Chen, Jessica. "Psychology study changes perceptions on gazes." TheDartmouth.com News. July 26, 2005 Ret Nov, 17, 2008. http://thedartmouth.com/2005/07/26/news/psychology/.

Giles, Jessica W., and Gail D. Heyman. "Young Children's Beliefs about the Relationship between Gender and Aggressive Behavior." *Child Development* 76 (2005): 107-15.

Gyimesi, Karen, and Matt Tatham. "Nielsen Reports Americans Watch TV at Record Levels." www.NielsenMedia.com. Sep 29, 2005. Nielsen Media. Nov 19, 2005. www.nielsenmedia.com/newsreleases/2005/AvgHoursMinutes92905.pdf.

Hargittai, Estzer, and Steven Shafer. "Differences in Actual and Perceived Online: The Role of Gender." *Social Science Quarterly*, 2006.

Hay Group. "Style Matters: Why Women Executives shouldn't Ignore their 'Feminine Side.'" Boston, MA: The McClelland Center. 2003. Ret Jan 7, 2009. www.haygroup.com/downloads/sg/rb-Women_Executives_Brief.pdf.

Holmes, Anna. "It's A Girl Thing." *Cosmopolitan*, Oct. 2002: 246-50.

Holmes, Janet. "Women, Men, and Politeness: Agreeable and Disagreeable Responses." *Disourse Analysis*. Eds. A. Jaworski and N. Coupland. London: Routledge, 1999, cited in Reznik, Deidre. "Gender in Interruptive Turns at Talk-In-Interaction." *TESOL & Applied Linguistics* 4.Spec: 1-12, 2004.

Hoyt, Crystal. "Women Leaders: The Role of Stereotype Activation and Leadership Self-Efficacy." *Kravis Leadership Institute Leadership Review*. Fall, 2002. Ret Jan 7, 2009. www.leadershipreview.org/ 2002fall/article2_fall_2002.asp.

Klotz-Guest, Kathy. "Make Humor Work for You - Not Against You." Jan 2006. *Bay Area Business Women*. Ret Jan 7, 2006. www.babwnews.com/articlePrinterFormat.php?id= 480&PHPSESSID= 9ea16fc2593ee9becf555108ac66e854.

Lagace, Martha. "Negotiating Challenges for Women." *Harvard Business School Working Knowledge*. October 13, 2003. Ret Dec 12, 2008. http://hbswk.hbs.edu/item/3711.html.

Lutgen-Sandvik, Pamela. "How Employees Fight Back Against Workplace Bullying." February, 2007. *Communication Currents*. Ret Jan 9, 2009. www.communicationcurrents.com/index.asp?sid=1&issuepage=8.

Ryan, M. K., and S. A. Haslam. "The Glass Cliff: Evidence that Women are Over-represented in Precarious Leadership Positions." *British Journal of Management*. 16 No.2: 81-90, 2005.

Sandomir, Richard. "Jury Finds Knicks and Coach Harassed a Former Executive." Oct 3, 2007. Ret Oct 12, 2007. www.nytimes.com/2007/10/03/sports/basketball/03garden.html?_r=1&oref=slogin.

Schein, Virginia. "The relationship between sex role stereotypes and requisite management characteristics." *Journal of Applied Psychology*. 57: 95-100, 1973.

———. "Relationships between sex role stereotypes and requisite management characteristics among female managers." *Journal of Applied Psychology*. 60: 340-344, 1975.

Schlesinger, Richard. "Boomerang Kids Keep Coming Home." Jan 8, 2004. CBS News. Ret Jan 8, 2009. www.cbsnews.com/stories/2004/01/08/eveningnews/main/592186.shtml.

Stanley, Alessandra. "Mars and Venus Dissect the Spitzer Scandal on the TV Talk Shows." Mar 12, 2008. Ret Dec 27, 2008. www.nytimes.com/2008/03/12/arts/television/12watc.html?_r=1.

Stross, Randall. "What has Driven Women out of Computer Science?" *The New York Times*, November 16, 2008. www.nytimes.com/2008/11/16/business/16digi.html?_r=3.

Willis, Janine, and Alexander Todorov. "First Impressions: Making Up Your Mind After a 100-Ms Exposure to a Face." *Psychological Science*. 17 No.7: 592-598, 2006.

Websites

Equal Employment Opportunities Commission. www.eeoc.gov. This website provides information on laws and resources related to workplace discrimination.

Catalyst. www.catalyst.org. Catalyst is a nonprofit research and advisory organization that works to expand opportunities and advance women in business.

Toastmasters International. www.toastmasters.org. Find resources and Toastmasters chapter locations at this website to help develop your public-speaking skills.

Workplace Bullying Institute. www.bullyinginstitute.org. Understand how bullying impacts you and learn the statistics describing the number of bullies.

Other

NBC *Today* show. Dr. Laura: Women Share Blame for Cheating Men: Syndicated Radio Talk Show Host Stirs Controversy with Remarks about Wives. March 11, 2008. Today Show.com report by Mike Celizic. www.msnbc.msn.com/id/23575221/.

Index

T

X–Y–Z

A Letter to Our Readers

Code Switching: How to Talk So Men Will Listen

Invite us to talk with your Book Club!

Dear Readers:

Are you a member of a Book Club in the United States or Canada? If so, invite us to join your Book Club by phone for a 30-minute discussion.

We'd love to talk with you and your Book Club and hear your thoughts about our book. All you need is a speaker phone and at least 10 members. A phone meeting can be arranged any time Monday through Friday, from 5:00 P.M. to 11:00 P.M. EST. Please e-mail or phone us with your interest, suggested dates and times, club size, location, and dial-in number. Either Audrey or Claire will confirm the call and personally talk with your Club about *Code Switching: How to Talk So Men Will Listen.*

If you're located in the Boulder, Denver Metro, or Front Range areas in Colorado, we may even be able to join your Club in person!

E-mail us at:

AudreyandClaire@CodeSwitchingHowToTalkSoMenWillListen.com

Or phone:

303-448-1800

We love Book Clubs!

We look forward to talking with you.

Our Best,

Claire and Audrey

www.CodeSwitchingHowToTalkSoMenWillListen.com